Children in Changing Families

Understanding Children's Worlds

General Editor Judy Dunn

The study of children's development can have a profound influence on how children are brought up, cared for and educated. Many psychologists argue that even if our knowledge is incomplete, we have a responsibility to attempt to help those concerned with the care, education, and study of children by making what we know available to them. The central aim of this series is to encourage developmental psychologists to set out the findings and the implications of their research for others – teachers, doctors, social workers, students, and fellow researchers – whose work involves the care, education, and study of young children and their families. The information and the ideas that have grown from recent research form an important resource which should be available to them. This series provides an oppportunity for psychologists to present their work in a way that is interesting, intelligible, and substantial, and to discuss what its consequences may be for those who care for and teach children: not to offer simple prescriptive advice to other professionals, but to make important and innovative research accessible to them.

Children doing Mathematics
Terezhina Nunes and Peter Bryant

Children and Emotion
Paul L. Harris

Bullying at School
Dan Olweus

How Children Think and Learn, 2nd edn.
David Wood

Making Decisions about Children, 2nd edn.
H. Rudolph Schaffer

Children's Talk in Communities and Classrooms
Lynne Vernon-Feagans

Children and Political Violence
Ed Cairns

The Work of the Imagination
Paul Harris

Children in Changing Families
Jan Pryor and Bryan Rodgers

Children in Changing Families

Life After Parental Separation

Jan Pryor and Bryan Rodgers

BLACKWELL
Publishers

The right of Jan Pryor and Bryan Rodgers to be identified as authors of this work
has been asserted in accordance with the Copyright, Designs and Patents Act 1988.

First published 2001

2 4 6 8 10 9 7 5 3 1

Blackwell Publishers Ltd
108 Cowley Road
Oxford OX4 1 JF
UK

Blackwell Publishers Inc
350 Main Street
Malden, Massachusetts 02148
USA

British Library Cataloguing in Publication Data

A CIP catalogue record for this book is available from the British Library.

Library of Congress Cataloging-in-Publication Data

LOC data applied for

ISBN 0 631 21575 1 (hbk)
ISBN 0 631 21576 X (pbk)

Typeset in 10 on 12.5 pt Sabon
by Ace Filmsetting Ltd, Frome, Somerset
Printed in Great Britain by MPG Books Ltd, Bodmin, Cornwall

This book is printed on acid-free paper.

This book is dedicated to the memory of
Kate Funder (1941–98)

Contents

Figures and Tables

Figures

Tables

Series Editor's Preface

Increasing numbers of children face changes in their family worlds: separation of parents, single parenthood, the entry of stepparents into children's lives, and the presence of step- and half-siblings are now common experiences for children. What do these changes mean for children's development and adjustment? Opinions about the consequences of family transitions are firmly held – and differ markedly. But how far are these various views supported by research evidence? And what can account for the notable differences in the responses of children to family change?

In this book, Jan Pryor and Bryan Rodgers give us a remarkably clear and judicious guide through an enormous literature on family change – providing summaries and signposts, always with an eye on the quality of the studies from which they draw. They begin with the changes in demographic and legal contexts of family transitions, and the shifts in attitudes to parental separation, with a sweep that covers the UK, North America, Australia, and New Zealand. They frame their review in terms of different explanatory accounts, and at the end of the book consider how well the research evidence supports these various theoretical accounts. We are given a strikingly thorough analysis, for instance, of the evidence on the impact on children's emotional, behavioral, and educational development of family change: a succinct presentation of the findings of key research projects, which shows both the size of the effects found, and the quality of those different studies. Fathers, stepparents, single parents, the perception of children themselves are all considered with characteristic scholarship and care. The goals of this series, "Understanding Children's Worlds," are to make available to a wide audience the recent developmental research on key issues for children, and to give developmental scientists an opportunity to write freely and at length about their ideas and perspectives on these issues. These goals are admirably achieved by the focus of *Children in Changing Families* on such an urgent social issue, with the writers' exemplary scholarship, questioning of received views, and their clear account of what we know, and what we need to know about children's family worlds.

Judith F. Dunn

Acknowledgments

In deciding to write this book we were enormously encouraged by the support of several colleagues, notably Paul Amato, Judy Dunn, Robert Emery, Rhonda Pritchard, and Martin Richards. They and several others made the task of finding material considerably easier. We want, in particular, to thank Judy Dunn for her unfailing patience and assistance. We also want to acknowledge the help of the Australian Bureau of Statistics, Julia Brannen, Robin Fleming, Kath Kiernan, Jo Medway, Bren Neale, the Registrar General's Office of Northern Ireland, the Joseph Rowntree Foundation, Carol Smart, Anne Smith, Statistics New Zealand, and many others who provided copies of publications and material in press.

The quotation from "Coming" by Philip Larkin, which forms the epigraph to this book, is reprinted from *The Less Deceived* by kind permission of The Marvell Press, England and Australia.

Finally, without the tolerance and understanding of our own family members and of colleagues, it is doubtful this book would have happened. We thank them all.

Glossary of Studies Frequently Referred to in the Book

Australian Institute of Family Studies (AIFS) Consequences of Marriage Breakdown Study. Random stratified sample of 575 divorced couples interviewed in 1984; one group divorced in 1981, the other in 1983. In 1987, 523 were reinterviewed. In 1988, 105 children of parents in the study were interviewed; 49 whole families were interviewed at this time.

Avon Longitudinal Study of Parents and Children (ALSPAC). Longitudinal study of 13,995 families; all women who gave birth in the county of Avon, UK, between April 1991 and December 1992, their partners, and an index child. In some studies older siblings are included.

Child Health and Education Study (CHES) – 1970 British Birth Cohort. Longitudinal follow-ups of an original cohort of children born in the United Kingdom during the week 5–11 April 1970, recontacted at ages 5, 10, and 16 years. The initial sample (including births in Northern Ireland) comprised 17,588 children (98 percent of all births in the week), but only those living in Scotland, England, and Wales were followed up in the longitudinal study.

Children in Families Study. Australian Institute of Family Studies study conducted in 1982–3; 422 families involved; 33.6 percent intact families, 44 percent stepfamilies, 50.2 percent lone-parent families.

Christchurch Health and Development Study. Longitudinal study of 1,265 children born in 1977 in the Christchurch urban region of the New Zealand South Island, followed at annual intervals until the age of 18 and at longer intervals thereafter.

Exeter Family Study. Cross-sectional study of 76 children from separated families and 76 matched comparison children from intact families in two age groups (9–10 years and 13–14 years) living in Exeter, UK in 1991–2.

High School and Beyond Study (HSB). Approximately 50,000 students (sophomores and seniors) from 1,000 US high schools interviewed in 1980, and a subset reinterviewed in 1982, 1984, and 1986.

Iowa Studies. Sample pooled from two related studies, the Iowa Youth and Families Project (IYFP) and the Iowa Single-Parent Project (ISPP). The IYFP is a panel study of 451 families commencing in 1989, all with two parents, one adolescent child, and a second sibling within 4 years of age of the target child. The third wave of the panel took place in 1991 (N = 407 families). The ISPP is a panel study of 207 mother-headed families containing adolescent children of similar age to those in the IYFP. The mothers had divorced from the biological parent of the adolescent child in the past 2 years at the commencement of the study.

National Child Development Study (NCDS) – 1958 British Birth Cohort. Longitudinal follow-ups of an original cohort of children born in Wales, Scotland, and England during the week 3–9 March 1958, recontacted at ages 7, 11, 16, 23, and 33 years. The initial sample comprised 17,414 children (98 percent of all births in the week); 12,537 remained in the study at age 23 and 11,407 at age 33. The sample has been recontacted at age 42.

National Longitudinal Study of Young Men and Women (NLSY). Nationally representative study of 14,000 young men and women in the US born between 1958 and 1965, interviewed between the ages of 14 and 21 years old in 1979, and reinterviewed annually.

National Survey of Children (NSC). Longitudinal study of 2,301 children originally aged 7–11 years in 1976–7, based on a national probability sample of households in the US. Follow-ups were completed in 1981 when the children were aged 12–16 years (N = 1,423) and in 1987 at ages 18–22 years (N = 1,147).

National Survey of Families and Households (NSFH). A national cross-sectional probability sample of 13,017 adults in the US, recruited in 1987–8.

National Survey of Health and Development (NSHD) – 1946 British Birth Cohort. Longitudinal follow-ups of a stratified sample of children born in

England, Wales, and Scotland during the week 3–9 March 1946. Data collection took place at intervals of no longer than 2 years until early adulthood and less often thereafter. The stratified sample comprised 5,362 children at age 2 years; 3,362 remained in the study at age 36 and 3,322 at age 43. The sample has been recontacted at age 53.

Panel Study of Income Dynamics (PSID). Nationally representative longitudinal study of 5,000 US families. First interviews were in 1968; original panel members have been interviewed annually since then.

Stanford Custody Project. *Study 1*: 1,100 divorcing families recruited in 1984–5 in two California counties, interviewed three times over three and a half years. *Study 2*: 522 adolescents of the families in Study 1, interviewed by telephone when between the ages of 10 and 18.

Study of Marital Stability Over the Lifecourse. 2,033 married individuals interviewed in 1980, 1983, 1988, and 1992. In 1992, 471 offspring 19 years or older were included, and reinterviewed in 1995.

Virginia Longitudinal Study of Divorce and Remarriage (VLSDR). Initial sample involved 144 families; 50 percent were divorced and headed by custodial mothers, length of time since divorce 12–18 months; 50 percent nondivorced. Half had a target son, half a target daughter, 4 years old. Six waves of assessment: 2 months, 1 year, 2 years, 6 years, 11 years, 20 years post-divorce. At wave 4, 180 extra families added evenly distributed across nondivorced, divorced nonremarried mother custody, and stepfather families. At wave 5 the sample expanded to 300 families, and at wave 6 to 450 families similarly balanced.

West of Scotland Twenty-07 Study. Longitudinal study of three cohorts aged 15, 35, and 55 years, commencing in 1987–8. Only analyses based on the 15-year-old sample are referred to in this book. Originally, around 1,000 people in each age group were selected for interview from 52 post-code sectors of the Central Clydeside Conurbation that includes the City of Glasgow. Follow-ups of the youngest cohort were carried out by interview at age 18 and by postal questionnaire at age 21.

. . . And I, whose childhood
Is a forgotten boredom,
Feel like a child
Who comes on a scene
Of adult reconciling,
And can understand nothing
But the unusual laughter
And starts to be happy.

Philip Larkin, "Coming"

Introduction

Families at the beginning of the twenty-first century are going through changes at a pace that is bewildering to both observers and family members themselves. Relationships between parents are, for several reasons, less stable than in past times; parent–child bonds are now often more enduring and less dispensable than partnerships. When partnerships fail, children and their parents experience family transitions, and adults and children alike find themselves adapting to changes in family relationships and household structure. Although almost "normal" in a numeric sense, family structural changes are usually not anticipated by children, and nor are they sought. For them there is an element of involuntariness involved both in the dismantling of their original family structure, and in the formation of new households. Neither are family transitions usually solitary events; the probability is that one will lead to another.

Change calls for reorganization at several levels. Structurally, there are household, school, neighborhood, and financial changes. In terms of relationships, especially, there are major adjustments; some are lost, some are gained, and many are changed. At the individual level, changes in self-perception and perceptions of others are likely to take place. It is safe to say that some children weather these crossings better than others, and those who in the medium and long term are adversely affected clearly justify our consideration and concern.

One way of addressing this concern is to advocate banning such risky passages by, for example, making divorce more difficult to obtain, or making it a source of social shame. This has been tried; until comparatively recently the Anglican Church would not marry divorcees, and in Ireland divorce was only recently made legal. But such measures do not prevent parents from separating and repartnering, although they can add the burden of stigma to families already struggling. It has become increasingly unrealistic, as well, to hope to return to the era of traditional nuclear families. In order to do so we would need to bring about changes in the labor market, reduce women's access to education, and change the provision of social welfare to families. Nonetheless, the risks posed to children by family instability need to be addressed, and there may be better ways of addressing parental separation that include social and economic incentives and support rather than the threat of social, economic, or religious excommunication.

If parental separation cannot be prevented, then a more constructive course is to try and understand the experiences of families and, especially, to tease out the reasons why some children appear to be resilient to the stresses of change while others are not. This book is one attempt to do so, by looking at evidence from research and putting it into some explanatory frameworks. In writing it, however, we have been acutely aware of the impossibility of doing this task in any complete way. First, no book can cover the immensity and complexity of families, theories about families, or research on families. So, we have had to be selective and use an analytic lens that is appropriate to one book. Two examples of our selective process are the absence of a specific focus on children born to lone mothers (although they are often encompassed in groups of children in lone-parent families in studies); and the inclusion of a chapter dealing with fathers in families, but not one that specifically addresses mothers in families.

This leads to a second consideration in writing such a volume – selection is always, in the end, a subjective process. So is the perspective taken on what we have chosen to include. The topic of families may be the one that authors are least able to approach objectively, since researchers, readers, and writers are daughters, sons, siblings, and parents. In short, we all have our unique and idiosyncratic experiences of family life. As researchers and writers we have tried to step back and view our material dispassionately. If we have been even partially successful then we shall be pleased.

One set of facts is, however, too unambiguous and compelling to dismiss as subjective. Families are immensely diverse, and perhaps at no time more so than at the beginning of the twenty-first century. Because the present rate of change in family structures is high, we cannot, and indeed must not, assume that most children spend their childhood in one house with two biological parents and their biological siblings. Simply put, they do not; and unless we acknowledge that fact we fail significantly to understand the diverse contexts in which children grow up.

Demographically and statistically, change and diversity are well documented; anecdotally, the richness of this variation is perhaps better appreciated. Some years ago an officer on a cargo vessel trading around the coast of Australia developed a relationship with a prostitute who had a 10-year-old son, and both went from port to port to be with him. (Details here are changed for obvious reasons.) Eventually they married, and had two children of their own; however, when the children were 9 and 11 years old the parents separated. The mother went back to her former profession, the father introduced a new, 18-year-old partner into the household, and the children remained in their care. A year later two things happened: the mother approached the court to increase her visiting times with the children, and the father left the household, leaving the children with the 19-year-old, now ex-partner. Back into the picture and the household came the mother's older son, now 25 years old. He developed a relationship with the young ex-partner, and custody (as it was then) was awarded to the children's half-brother and their father's ex-partner. The children's social father was their half-brother, and their social mother an unrelated young woman from a different ethnic background. The moral of this (true) tale is not particularly obvious; it does illustrate rather well, though, the danger of making assumptions about children's families.

A second, equally pervasive feature of family transitions is that separation does not occur out of the blue (although it may seem that way to children); it is preceded by stress and distress in families. At least one parent is sufficiently unhappy to initiate separation, and often both are embroiled in conflict that impinges on all family members. Following separation, a series of changes takes place that varies in its configurations from family to family. Most compellingly, we know when we look around our families, friends, and communities that some children suffer in the medium and long term and others recover and thrive. Unfortunately for social science and family research, and for professionals and families, there are no simple ways to identify those who will thrive and those who will not. If we are seeking ways to maximize children's chances of thriving then multifaceted approaches are needed that include both minimizing the risks associated with family transitions, and optimizing the contribution of factors that promote resilience.

This book starts by addressing some relatively uncontestable facts about demographic change, legal contexts, and attitudes to separation and divorce. We then outline some of the major theoretical and conceptual frameworks used to make sense of family change and individual pathways. These frameworks are returned to later when we discuss the research evidence. In chapter 3 we consider the findings of the now considerable body of research that has examined medium- and long-term outcomes for children whose parents separate. In 1998 we reviewed studies in the UK that had addressed these issues (Rodgers & Pryor, 1998). In this book we extend our cover to incorporate research from North America, Australia, and New Zealand.

Research is almost always carried out by adults and, in the main, adults make decisions about and on behalf of children. There is now increasing recognition of the fact that children have their own views and perspectives, and are well able to articulate them. They are also beginning to be accorded rights in matters concerning them, notably by the United Nations Charter on the Rights of the Child. Chapter 4 considers children's perspectives and understandings of families and family change, and looks at experiences of family transitions from their own viewpoints.

Chapter 5 focuses on processes that accompany and follow parental separation. It covers the changes in financial circumstances of families before and after separation, differences in the family environment between lone-parent and two-parent families, and the external risk factors and resources that impinge differentially on different types of families.

Parents who separate do not usually stay by themselves for long. Children are just as likely to experience stepfamily living after their parents have parted as to stay living with a lone parent, and chapter 6 addresses the burgeoning body of research about this complicated and challenging family form. It also discusses the little we know about families that have experienced multiple transitions. In chapter 7 we consider fathers in families. The reason they are singled out for specific attention when mothers are not is because it is only comparatively recently that the role of fathers in children's lives beyond that of providers has been taken seriously. It seems important to document the research findings about fathers and children in particular, because it is a topic of intense speculation and controversy, and in order to provide some research-based evidence to inform the debates surrounding it.

In chapter 8 we return to the explanatory frameworks presented in chapter 2, to consider how well they account for the research evidence presented throughout the book. Finally, in chapter 9 we draw some conclusions for policy and practice about family transitions and indicate areas where further research is needed. A major conclusion, of course, is

that there is still an enormous amount we do not know about our changing, complicated, and important topic.

In talking and writing about family structures, it is a challenge to be
consistent in the terminology used. There are many terms that simply do
not convey the range of family arrangements that at first glance seem
straightforward, and the task becomes more complicated when one household structure is discussed in comparison to another. The term "intact" is
a case in point. It is used in comparison with families that are "broken,"
yet the latter term is not now commonly used. It can be argued, too, that
many members of lone-parent and stepfamily households would consider
themselves "intact." We have chosen, then, to use the terms "original" or
"two-birth-parent" to denote households where children live with their
biological or adoptive parents. Of the range of terms available to identify
households where children live with one parent only, we have chosen
"lone-parent," while aware that this does not always indicate that there is
just one adult in the home; grandparents, other extended family members, and friends are often living in lone-parent households. They are,
though, to be distinguished from stepfamily households where there are
two adults in parental roles in relation to the children, one of whom is a
biological parent. The term "stepfamily" is used in general, although stepmother, stepfather, and complex stepfamily households are distinguished
where appropriate in chapter 6.

There is also a risk of tedium if we describe a major study every time
we mention it. In order to avoid this, we have provided a glossary (pages
xiii–xv) that describes the major studies referred to in the book.

1

The Context of Family Transitions

Whilst individual biography is a process of change and becoming, in diverse ways we remain children, held through life, willingly or reluctantly, in the web of parent–child relations. A configuration of many dimensions, the embrace may be symbolic, lodged, for example in the idea of home; cemented over the life course by flows of resources, material and non-material; bonded by normative expectations, rights, obligations and affectivities; or anchored in memory. These strands both invade emotional interiors and influence performance, and hence are shot with tensions which might combine the ambiguities of welcome, resentment, and rejection.

Allatt, 1996

Our children are living in a world that is changing far more dramatically than it was a century or even decades ago. Far more significant than the internet, or the possibilities opened up by genetic engineering, are the transformations in that most fundamental of structures – the family. Family change is not new; some parents have always died or left home, and some children have always been abandoned or suffered the losses of mothers, fathers, and siblings. What is different, though, is that the predominant reason for these losses in the past was death; and chances were that children would know any stepparents that entered their lives. Today children are most likely to lose a parent through divorce, and stepparents are often strangers to them. The rates and numbers of changes that children experience are also considerably higher now than they were in the past.

How are our children faring? The answers to this are not simple and, as with all topics that touch us personally, the debate about parental separation and stepfamilies is both polarized and intense. It rages at personal and political, and at media and moral levels; it is clouded by passionate and often ill-informed rhetoric, and by the complexities of the issues involved. At heart and held in common by all sides, however, is a deep concern for children and the families within which they thrive, or not. It is this common focus on the well-being of children that can guide us through the maze of rhetoric toward a more dispassionate appraisal of research than is possible from a polarized position.

Polarized views on family change can be characterized as follows, and are summarized in table 1.1. One perspective, usually called the liberal position, argues that family change is on balance a good thing. Divorce liberates many adults and children from punitive, unhappy family situations fraught with conflict, power, and control (Stacey, 1993, 1996; Smart & Neale, 1999). It frees people to establish diverse household structures that are adaptive to the social and economic circumstances in which they live. Lone-parent households, lesbian- and gay-parent families, homes in which several related or unrelated adults live and share parenting roles, and stepfamily households give children and adults the opportunity to function in ways that nurture all family members. Diversity, in this view, is adaptive for children.

Another central aspect of the liberal position is the view that children are essentially resilient, given the right circumstances. They are capable of, and often willing to, articulate their views and to take considerable power in the decision-making of families. Moreover, their views should be given serious consideration both at the individual and interpersonal levels within families, and at the public and legal levels. Some would go so far as to say that children's views should be paramount in decisions made about their living arrangements.

The opposed perspective takes a conservative and more pessimistic view of change, equating family change with family decline. The functions of families have been pared down by social change to childrearing and provision of affection for family members, and even these are seen to be under threat as further social change occurs. Children, it is argued, need a stable two-biological-married-parent family in which to be adequately nurtured. Within that family, stability is most assured when mothers concentrate on childrearing and fathers on economic provision and discipline. One commentator describes this view as "the family consisting of a heterosexual, monogamous, life-long marriage in which there is a sharp division of labor, with the female as full-time housewife and the male as primary provider and ultimate authority" (Popenoe, 1993). The greatest danger to families, according to this perspective, is the rise of individualism as people act according to their own needs and desires rather than giving family and children, in particular, precedence. From this perspective children are seen as in need of caretaking and guidance by adults; their views should not be given the same credence as those of adults. The rise in

Table 1.1 Areas of debate about families from two perspectives

Topic of debate	Conservative perspective	Liberal perspective
Divorce as process or event	Divorce or separation is an event with direct causal impact on children's outcomes	Divorce or separation is part of a process starting some years before and continuing after parents separate.
Frameworks for explaining outcomes for children	Damage to children caused by a single factor such as loss, trauma, or abandonment	Risks to children come from multiple factors including life-course processes and contextual factors
Mothers	Mothers are the key to the well-being of families, and should put childrearing before a career. If parents separate, children should properly be with their mothers	Mothers are better parents and individuals if their lives are balanced between family roles and the workforce
Fathers	Fathers should be present in families as economic providers and heads of the household	Fathers are not crucial for children's well-being. If other factors are positive, children can thrive without fathers.
Children	Children are dependent and vulnerable, and should be protected and treated as "children."	Children are resilient and agentic, and should have equal say with adults in decisions regarding their lives
Marriage	Marriage should be legal and binding, and divorce actively discouraged	Divorce should be allowed without judgment where a marriage has failed
Stepfamilies	Stepfamilies are weak family forms, violating biological imperatives; children are imperiled by living in stepfamilies	Stepfamilies are an adaptive family form that is diverse and potentially functional
Diversity	Family diversity is potentially bad for children and society	Diversity of family forms allows individuals to adapt to current social and economic circumstances

divorce is seen as a consequence of individualism, and as almost always damaging for children. Stepfamilies, too, are poor substitutes for original biological families and pose significant dangers for children (Popenoe, 1994). This leads to the recommendation that the rate of family change be slowed by several means, which include making both marriage and divorce more difficult. One example of this is the introduction of covenant marriages in some states of the United States, in which couples undertake premarital counseling, and where divorce is both more difficult to obtain and fault-based. Another conservative approach to reinforcing families is to argue for the reinstatement of men as authority figures in the lives of their families (Blankenhorn, 1995; Popenoe, 1996), based on the premise that fatherlessness is a major cause of family and social decline.

Just as these perspectives lead to different implications about what should be done about family change, so they invite rather differing explanations for one point about which they often agree – high rates of parental separation and stepfamily formation pose elevated levels of risk for children who go through these transitions. The conservative view, for instance, tends to see parental separation as an event that *causes* children to be damaged, and that the damage done is linked to separation through the loss of, or abandonment by, a parent. An obvious remedy, then, is to prevent parents from separating. The liberal argument, conversely, is that separation is one part of an ongoing process that begins long before a parent leaves the home. Any risks to children have multiple causes, of which divorce is just one, and many of these are modifiable. Divorce, in this view, can be a great liberator for families.

We have presented simplistic and somewhat extreme depictions of the major positions in the debate and, of course, the situation is far more complex than that offered by either view. In this book we will consider evidence from research that will support and refute some aspects of both sides of the argument and, we hope, provide a more accurate perspective on family change. Even a consideration of research, though, is not straightforward and can lead to simplified and sometimes misleading claims, especially in the media. As an example, a feature article in the Sydney *Morning Herald* (Arndt, 1999) presented a detailed account of several research studies on outcomes for children from separated families with a focus on educational achievement. It drew heavily on research in the United States conducted by McLanahan and Sandefur (1994), and largely supported the interpretation that financial hardship accounts for a large part of the disadvantages shown by children in lone-parent families. However, the article did not consider research on other outcomes for children from separated families where financial hardship is not so closely implicated, nor did it point out the several weaknesses of the financial hardship explanation even in relation to educational disadvantages. Yet, the front page of the newspaper carried the banner "The Truth about Divorce and Kids."

Similarly, Melanie Phillips, a journalist with the British *Sunday Times* and previously with the *Guardian* and the *Observer*, said on National Radio in New Zealand that "you have got to lay out before people the truth about this [i.e. the effects of parental divorce on children]." Her version of the truth, however, is very different from that presented by Bettina Arndt in Australia. Phillips attributes the poorer outcomes for children of separated families to the effects of "abandonment": "as far as the child is concerned one of the people who made *me* has chosen voluntarily not to live with me while I am growing up," and this is very often internalized in a sense of guilt (Phillips, 1998b).

Although both these interpretations contain some parts of the "truth," neither encompasses the complexity of the situations families are in. In our view, no one theory or perspective accounts for the evidence available (although some do a better job than others of doing so). Neither does a single factor, such as divorce or economic adversity, account by itself for the risks posed to children by family change. In the rest of this book we will use the liberal and conservative positions, broadly construed, as scaffolds for discussing and evaluating conceptual frameworks and research findings. The hope is to find a synthesis that can take us further in understanding and helping children in changing families.

Why are Families Changing?

Unquestionably, families are undergoing change at alarmingly high rates. It is helpful to have an understanding of what has led to the current era of family transformation in order to put into perspective the family diversity we see today. The present rate of change has been likened to two earlier periods of upheaval (Skolnick, 1997). The first, in the early part of the nineteenth century in the USA, was the move from a family-based economy with the home as the primary workplace, to an industrialized economy in which home and work were clearly separated. The household became the haven for family members, with a woman at its center as men increasingly worked outside the home. The second change, early in the twentieth century, was driven by several factors including the politicization of women and their movement by choice into the wider workforce (although in many poor families women never had the option of being home-based mothers). Emerging from this upheaval, Skolnick suggests, was the model of the companionate marriage where gender expectations, if not realities, were more equitable. The current turmoil is characterized by three factors. The first is an increase in longevity that introduces strains on partnerships potentially lasting far longer than in earlier times. There is also the impact on families of longer-living elders who need emotional and sometimes economic support. Second, economic changes have brought about the decreased dependence of women on partners, and the increasing need for both parents to work. Third, there is the impact of "psychological gentrification," encompassing increased levels of education at all socioeconomic levels, and a demand for emotional and psychological fulfillment in relationships. All of these serve to increase the vulnerability of marriages.

Other explanations for the current rapid rate of family change have also been suggested. Predominant amongst these is a focus on changed economic structures for families. The delineation between home and the workplace meant that the household is no longer a primary source of income, so economic reasons for its existence are reduced (Booth, 1999). More dramatic, though, has been the entry into the workforce of women (Cherlin, 1992; McLanahan & Sandefur, 1994). Although it is not clear whether increased levels of maternal employment predict separation, or whether women in troubled relationships spend more time at work, it is true to say that women's relative economic independence makes it easier for unhappy couples to separate. Both these changes mean that children are not exposed to the work environment of their parents, and that their mothers are more likely than not to be outside the home and in the workplace for significant amounts of time.

Related to women's higher rates of employment, at least in the US, is the decline in men's relative earning power. This is evident both in the decline of young men's incomes in comparison with their parents', and in the closing of the gap between the earnings of men and women especially since 1970 (McLanahan & Sandefur, 1994). In economic terms this considerably lessens both the attractions of marriage, and the disadvantages of leaving them for women.

Another group of explanations centers on psychological and emotional factors. One of these is the often-discussed rise of individualism in Western countries (Popenoe, 1993), and the push for self-fulfillment that exists increasingly at the expense of commitment to family and the institution of marriage. For both structural and psychological reasons the nature of the relationships between individuals in families has changed strikingly, with a transition from the *positional* family with its emphasis on hierarchy, obedience, and rules, to a *personal* family where autonomy and egalitarian roles are emphasized (Bernstein, 1970). No longer are obligations to family and kin based on commitments of blood relationship; rather, they rest increasingly on "negotiated commitments" worked out by family members (Finch & Mason, 1993). Giddens, writing about intimacy between adults, describes the emergence of the "pure relationship" that refers to a situation where a social relation is "entered into for its own sake, for what can be derived by each person from a sustained association with another; and which is continued only in so far as it is thought by both parties to deliver enough satisfactions for each individual to stay within it" (Giddens, 1992, p. 58). Inasmuch as this is the case in modern families, stability becomes vulnerable to disaffected parents whose reasons for staying in a marriage are reduced.

When parents part, negotiations and agreements about commitments become even more complicated as immediate family ties are not confined to one household, and involve potentially competing obligations. This is especially apparent in stepfamilies where children have strong connections with adults and sometimes siblings in two or more households.

What might these changes in the nature of family relationships mean for children? First, the relative certainty about commitments to family members defined by blood relationships has gone; it is no longer so clear to whom one turns for support and to whom one has obligations. Rather, these relationships may need to be discussed and agreed rather than taken for granted. Second, if families are becoming more egalitarian, then children might expect and indeed be expected to have some influence on decisions made, in both trivial and important matters.

Despite these quite profound changes in the nature of relationships in

> The relative certainty about commitments to family members defined by blood relationships has gone; it is no longer so clear to whom one turns for support and to whom one has obligations. Rather, these relationships may need to be discussed and agreed rather than taken for granted . . . [I]f families are becoming more egalitarian then children might expect and indeed be expected to have some influence on decisions made, in both trivial and important matters. Despite these quite profound changes in the nature of relationships in families, however, family matters remain overwhelmingly important in people's lives.

families, however, family matters remain overwhelmingly important in people's lives (Scott, 1997). In 1989, Thornton suggested that "while most people are now more accepting of a diversity of behavior, they still value and desire marriage, parenthood, and family life for themselves" (Thornton, 1989, p. 873). For children, there is little choice. Their family is their sole source of survival and nurturance, at least in the early years.

Public Attitudes toward Family Change

Have attitudes toward families, marriage, and divorce changed as family transitions become more commonplace? There were some changes in public attitudes toward family matters from the late sixties until the early eighties last century (Thornton, 1985, 1989; Cherlin, 1992). In the US in the late seventies, approximately 60 percent of people surveyed agreed that married people were happier than those who were single, and there was little change by 1985 (Thornton, 1991). In Australia in the early nineties, though, fewer thought that married people were happier – only 37 percent agreed (De Vaus, 1997). More men than women, and older people rather than younger, believe that married people are happier than singles. Attitudes to childlessness in the US, however, became more accepting between 1962 and 1980, and by 1985 only about 40 percent of respondents agreed that all couples should be parents if they could. In Australia, nearly half those asked felt that a childless marriage is incomplete (De Vaus, 1997).

Attitudes toward work and family roles for women changed markedly in the US between 1970 and 1989 (Cherlin, 1992). In 1970, 80 percent agreed that it is much better for everyone involved if the man is the achiever outside the home and the woman takes care of the home and family. By 1989, only 26 percent agreed. Similarly, approximately 73 percent in 1970 felt that a preschool child would suffer if their mother worked; by 1989 only 38 percent agreed. In Australia, feelings about women with children working are less approving. Sixty-eight percent agreed that women should stay at home with preschoolers (De Vaus, 1997). Overall, 73 percent of Australians surveyed felt that if a woman works her main responsibility is still to home and family.

In the US, attitudes toward divorce became more liberal in the late 1960s and 1970s (Thornton, 1985; Cherlin, 1992). Paradoxically, though, feelings about divorce laws are less liberal than attitudes toward divorce. In 1989 a majority (53 percent) of people surveyed in the US thought divorce laws should be tougher than they are, and in Australia 70 percent of those asked agreed that it is too easy to get a divorce.

Being married and having children, then, are not seen to be as important now as they were several decades ago. Divorce and working mothers have become more acceptable in the public view. Do attitudes bring about behavioral change, or does divorce bring about a change in attitudes? Some evidence suggests that the experience of divorce predicts changes in attitudes (Thornton, 1985). Thornton found that attitudes to divorce at an earlier time did not predict subsequent divorce but that attitudes were predicted by one's own divorce as well as by church attendance and age at marriage. However, there is also some evidence that attitudes predict later divorce (Amato, 1996), although other factors such as interpersonal skills were more important than attitudes in predicting whether or not people divorced.

Childhood and Changing Families

Beliefs about childhood, and the ways in which children are seen in relation to contemporary families, are central to an understanding of children's lives when parents separate or when they enter a stepfamily. "Childhood" is not a fixed entity, but a constructed pattern of beliefs and ideas about children that changes with economic, social, and political change. In parallel with the changes in family structures and dynamics, the concept of childhood has also been transformed in the last century. A great deal has been written about the history of childhood (Ariès, 1970; De Mause, 1974; Cunningham, 1995), and historians agree that by the end of the nineteenth century families were largely child-oriented. Until then, the need to have children in the laborforce meant that they were treated as minor adults, with few concessions to "childhood." During the first half of the twentieth century several factors contributed to the continuation of a process by which children increasingly became the focus of their parents' "sentimental" world. One of these was their removal from the laborforce and into compulsory schooling (Ariès, 1970). These changes meant first that they were economically dependent, and second that in many cases they were better educated than their parents. Dramatic reductions in child mortality and in fertility rates also enhanced children's emotional value, to the point that scholars now refer to the "priceless child" (Cunningham, 1995).

The twentieth century has been called the "century of the child"

(Cunningham, 1995). In the first part of that century, the growth of science made specific contributions to the understanding of childhood by studying children's development and assessing it, by examining their instincts (this was done chiefly by Freud), and by focusing on the origins of criminality in childhood experiences – hence the establishment of child guidance clinics. In the UK and elsewhere, child health and mothering became a major focus. At the same time, parents increasingly turned to "experts" for guidance on how to raise their precious and increasingly assertive children, so that childhood and childrearing achieved major prominence in the eyes of both parents and society.

The second half of the twentieth century saw increasing permeability of the boundaries between childhood and adulthood. In part this was due to a collapse of adult authority; it was also driven by an increase in children's consumerism as, paradoxically, children's spending power has increased despite their economic dependence on parents. In contrast to the eras when children's earnings contributed to family and household income, children now spend what they earn on themselves and in consequence are primary targets for marketers. More importantly, however, the adjustment of power between children and adults is an emotional one. There is no economic rationale now for explaining why parents have children; instead, children are sources of emotional and psychological gratification that give meaning to their lives and provide a means of expressing generativity, or of contributing to following generations (Beck & Beck-Gernsheim, 1995). In this regard, parents are dependent on their children in complex ways – emotionally, parents need children as much as children need parents.

At the same time, the increase across generations in levels of education has contributed to children's ability, and probably their expectations, to be participants in family matters. Parallel to this has been the gradual process of recognition of children's perspectives and of their rights in relation to family transitions. This is best exemplified by the 1989 United Nations Charter on the Rights of the Child in which children are accorded rights to have a say in decisions affecting their lives.

What does this mean for children who experience divorce and who enter stepfamilies? First, their roles in families have changed with the transition from positional to personal forms where management within families is by negotiation rather than command (and this is reflected in the styles of parenting discussed in chapter 2). These changes are relevant to the views of children, and divorce reflected in the liberal and conservative positions toward family change. The conservative perspective is articulated by those who believe that children have a right to be children and to be protected by adults as far as possible, and in this view children are vulnerable and easily harmed by family transitions such as parental separation. They are also unwilling or unable to make decisions, and their best interests usually coincide with those of their parents. The liberal perspective argues that children hold views that may be independent of their parents' and have both the competence and the right to have them heard. Trinder suggests, "it is argued [that] it is harmful to children to ignore these views, and beneficial to children to participate in decision making" (Trinder, 1997, p. 293). This perspective sees children as both competent and resilient in the face of family transitions.

A second implication of the changes in family dynamics and children as family members is that the positioning of children as precious and emotionally priceless resources for parents will lead to parents fighting to retain emotional connections with their children. Although the battles over living arrangements after separation are often complex and involve several factors, there is little doubt that strong feelings relating to children are usually predominant.

At the beginning of the twenty-first century, views of childhood are in flux. In parallel with attitudes toward families and divorce, and with demographic changes, they reflect increasing diversity and, at the same time, a reluctance to relinquish the core aspects of family that encompass the socialization of children and mutual provision by family members of affection and support.

A more extensive discussion of the liberal/conservative debate over the positions of children is offered in chapter 4. It is safe to say, however, that at the beginning of the twenty-first century, views of childhood are in flux. In parallel with attitudes toward families and divorce, and with demographic changes, they reflect increasing diversity and, at the same time, a reluctance to relinquish the core aspects of family that encompass the socialization of children and mutual provision by family members of affection and support.

The peculiarity of the late twentieth century, and the root cause of much present confusion and angst about childhood, is that a public discourse that argues that children are persons with rights to a degree of autonomy is at odds with the remnants of the romantic view that the right of a child is to be a child. The implication of the first is the fusing of the worlds of adult and child, and of the second the maintenance of separation. (Cunningham, 1995, p. 190)

Legal Changes

Family changes and transitions take place within the wider structure of a legal framework put in place in order to regulate the social lives of citizens. For children, the force of law is partly indirect through its regulation of parents' ability to divorce and remarry. Increasingly, though, its impact is also direct, as children become involved in proceedings surrounding their parents' separation. Legal change and reform, then, is an important aspect of understanding the experiences of children whose parents divorce and remarry.

The belief that divorce is now easy to obtain in comparison with the past is only partly supported by historical research. In Europe, Roman Catholicism imposed doctrines of the indissolubility of marriage that, with few exceptions, limited the possibility of divorce until the Reformation. Legal divorce was then introduced in many Protestant countries, although the Church of England resisted liberalization of divorce law until the mid-nineteenth century. In European countries that remained Catholic, divorce was not introduced until the twentieth century – in Italy in 1970, Portugal in 1910, and Spain most recently in 1981. The Irish Republic did not have legal divorce until the mid-1990s, and indeed it was not permitted by the country's constitution between 1937 and 1986. This backdrop illustrates the moral, social, and legal traditions of the various immigrant groups that flowed into the United States, Canada, New Zealand, and Australia and influenced the development of those same traditions in those countries where the legal system was derived predominantly from English law.

During the early settlement of North America, divorce was available in some colonies. Although many of the settlers were of English origin, the Puritans obviously departed from the traditions of the Anglican Church, and Phillips (1988) points out the possible significance of the founders of Plymouth Colony spending over a decade in Holland (where the law permitted divorce) before they emigrated again to America. The statutes of the colonies allowed divorce but under very limited circumstances: typically the grounds of adultery and desertion that were common in the laws of European Protestant countries at the time. Often, only the innocent party was allowed to remarry when divorce was granted on the grounds of adultery. In the late eighteenth and early nineteenth centuries, following American independence, divorce through secular courts became more common in the legislation of individual states although, as now, there was a great deal of diversity in state provision. Where divorce was available, adultery and desertion remained the principal grounds until the second half of the twentieth century.

In Canada (with the exceptions of Nova Scotia, New Brunswick, and Prince Edward Island) and Australasia, the availability of divorce took a similar path to that of England, and divorce laws in New Zealand and Australia were not enacted until the second half of the nineteenth century. By that time Canada had become a Dominion (in 1867), and agreement on national provision was problematic given the French Catholic background of most of the population of Quebec. Divorce by individual statute (the only means of divorce in England before 1857) was used in Canada until well into the twentieth century. New Zealand first had its own legislation in 1867 and some states of Australia had legislation before and after that time, prompted by the changes in England. National divorce law in Australia became possible after Federation in 1900.

The overall history of the introduction of divorce laws in these countries is that, with the exceptions of some parts of the United States and certain areas of Canada, divorce was not generally available until much more recent times than was the case in Protestant Europe and, in certain instances, later even than in some Catholic countries. Furthermore, the grounds for divorce were very restrictive and largely limited to adultery and desertion.

A significant and major liberalization of these laws occurred in the second half of the twentieth century, with the introduction of no-fault legislation. In principle this meant that a divorce could be obtained on the grounds of the failure of the relationship, without blame being cast on either parent. The availability of no-fault divorce means that parents whose marriages have failed can divorce without the need to incriminate each other as part of the process, although it is usually the case that no-fault divorces take longer to obtain than fault-based divorce, in the hope that couples will reconsider their decision and work to resolve their differences.

Cohabitation

Despite the pervasive view of marriage as the proper arena for having a family, a large number of children are now born out of wedlock. The fact that increasing numbers of adults choose to form families outside a formal legal structure is significant, and particularly notable given the pejorative terms used until recently to refer to children born outside marriage – terms like "bastard" or "illegitimate."

How common is cohabitation? Although there have always been couples who have not formed legal unions, there has been a remarkable increase in the rate of cohabitation and childrearing outside marriage in recent decades. In the US, the rise in the number of cohabiting couples has been 46 percent in the 7 years between 1990 and 1997 (Casper & Cohen, 2000). In Canada 1 in 7 couples were cohabiting in 1996 (Statistics Canada, 1999b); in Australia nearly 1 in 10 were cohabiting (Australian Bureau of Statistics, 1998); in New Zealand a quarter of partnerships were not legal marriages in 1996 (Statistics New Zealand, 1998). In the UK in 1996 12 percent of women and 16 percent of men between the ages of 25 and 29 were cohabiting (Kiernan, 1999a). Of women in the 20- to 39-year age group, over half cohabited in their first relationship, although for 26 percent this was a prelude to marrying their partner.

Not all cohabiting couples have children, but many do. Of the one-third of children in the US born outside marriage, nearly 40 percent are born to cohabiting parents. In New Zealand nearly half of all children are born outside marriage, and it is likely that the majority of these are born into couple rather than lone-parent families. In the US, Canada, and Australia about one half of cohabiting couples have children, either those they have had together or brought to the union. Similarly, in the UK about one-third of all children are born outside marriage, and 17 percent of first-born babies are born to cohabiting mothers (Kiernan, 1999b). A number of children are in cohabiting families as a result of their mother moving in with a partner either before or after their birth and the partner is not always their biological father. Children in stepfamilies, too, are more likely than not to enter a cohabiting stepfamily household although parents often marry subsequently (Bumpass, 1995).

It is difficult to be clear about what children's lives in cohabiting families might be like in comparison with living with married parents, because both the rate and nature of cohabiting families are changing at a bewildering pace. As Seltzer puts it, "studies of nonmarried families focus on a moving target" (Seltzer, 2000). There are, too, few studies that consider children's views about the legal status of their parents' partnerships. One aspect of cohabiting unions that is potentially important for children is that they are less stable than legal marriages. In the US, 29 percent of cohabiting couples, compared with 9 percent of married couples, break up in the first year of union (Bumpass & Sweet, 1989), and 5 years after forming partnerships, over half of cohabitations end (Bumpass & Lu, 2000), although many of these turn into formal marriages. However, co-habiting couples who have children are less likely to break up than those who remain childless (Wu & Balakrishnan, 1995). In the UK, couples who cohabit are also more likely to part than those who marry (Kiernan, 1999a). However, for those who cohabit and then marry their partner, the risk of dissolution in European countries is no higher than for those who enter marriage directly.

Household income in cohabiting families is higher than in single-parent families (Manning & Lichter, 1996; Carlson & Danziger, 1999) since cohabiting couples are more likely to pool resources if they have a child (Winkler, 1997). They are, though, still more likely to be poor than children with married parents in the US.

We have little evidence upon which to draw in considering relationships within cohabiting families. In the UK, both fathers and mothers who were cohabiting in a large-scale community study reported less positive relationships with children than married parents (Dunn et al., in press b). Children in this group did not, though, see parent–child relationships differently if their parents were cohabiting. The children were between the ages of 4 and 17, and age differences in their perceptions were not noted. But in the Stanford Custody Project in the US, adolescents said they felt closer to their stepparents if they were married to their biological parents. Adolescents may be more aware of marital status than younger children, and see marriage as a commitment to the family by the stepparent. We know almost nothing about how younger children see marital status, nor how adolescents view cohabiting and married biological parents.

There are some implications for children of cohabiting parents when their parents separate. In the US, paternal obligations are less for nonmarried than for married fathers, and the former are less likely to pay child support or to see their children after separation than legally divorced fathers (Seltzer, 1991; King, 1994b). In New Zealand the distinction between cohabiting and married fathers is less apparent at separation since both are legal guardians of their children if they were living with their partner at the child's birth and have the same rights and responsibilities when partnerships fail. Fathers who are cohabiting with their children's mothers rather than married to them are less likely to see their children frequently after separation, but just as likely to maintain phone or written contact with their children (Cooksey & Craig, 1998). It would be interesting to compare postseparation contact between unmarried fathers and stepfathers when parents separate. Biological considerations would suggest that unmarried biological fathers would stay in closer contact; on the other hand, legal and formal ambiguities, especially in the US, are similar for both, and may mean that levels of involvement are comparatively low for both groups.

It is predicted that in the future many more children will be raised in cohabiting families, as younger cohorts of adults that endorse cohabitation move through to childbearing years. We need to know a great deal more about how they fare. In the meantime, as families form outside the law, legal structures are being put in place to regulate these important relationships for families, especially when they break down.

Changes in Divorce Rates

What is the evidence that family changes have happened in different countries? The first point to note is that divorce rates have been rising substantially for as long as statistics have been available. It is only comparatively recently, though, that the rates have become sufficiently high to bring about major shifts in the profiles of family types in most countries. Figures for England and Wales provide an excellent illustration of the change, particularly because of the availability of information going back to 1857, when divorce became available through secular courts and no longer required a Private Act of Parliament (Stone, 1990). Divorce rates in the later part of the nineteenth century and early part of the twentieth century were low by contemporary standards, yet they still showed substantial relative increases. Figure 1.1 shows the changes from 1911 up to 1960, a period over which rates multiplied by a factor of over 20 with even higher intermediate rates, particularly in the late 1940s.

The figure uses "refined" divorce rates, where the number of divorces is expressed as a proportion of the number of married couples in the population at the time. These are more informative than "crude" divorce rates where the number of divorcing people is expressed as a proportion of the total number of adults in the population, whatever their marital status. In the 50 years prior to 1911, the rate had roughly doubled from 0.04 divorces per 1,000 married couples to 0.09 per 1,000 (Stone, 1990), but it increased five-fold between 1911 and 1921 and further in subsequent decades.

The picture for the United States is somewhat different; divorce rates were much higher. Figure 1.2 shows refined divorce rates from 1920 to 1960.

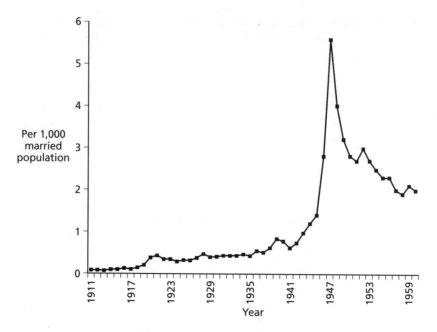

Figure 1.1   Divorce rates for England and Wales, 1911–60

The rates for the 1920s were about 20 times as great as those for England and Wales over that same period. Like England and Wales, the rate of divorce in the US has risen since records have been kept, beginning in the mid-1880s; however, the relative rise before the Second World War was not as marked as in England and Wales. During the Great Depression, too, the number of divorces fell in the US but not in European countries. Phillips (1988) suggests several reasons for the fall in the United States, including easier access to welfare assistance and other relief for families with children, the particular problems of women obtaining employment, and the reduced prospects of remarriage at the time. A similarity that is apparent in the two graphs is the sharp peak in divorce rates following the Second World War. This has been attributed to such factors as the eventual legal termination of marriages that had already broken down during the war, the difficulties experienced by couples reunited after involuntary wartime separation, and the fragility of more recent rushed marriages (Goode, 1993).

In New Zealand in the early twentieth century, divorce rates were about 10 times as high as in England and Wales and, even in the years immedi-

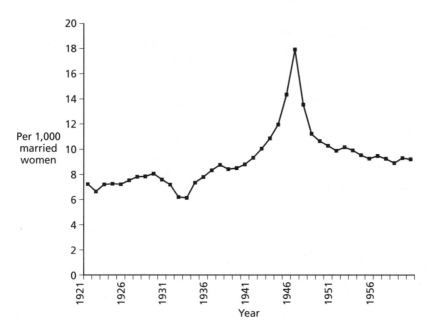

Figure 1.2   Divorce rates for the United States, 1921–60

ately preceding the war, were still over 3 times as great (Phillips, 1981). These levels (3.0 decrees per 1,000 marriages in 1939) were still less than half the rates in the United States at that time, however.

Figure 1.3 shows the rates for the United States and for England and Wales up to the late 1990s and includes information from other countries. The substantial increase in divorce rates over the 1960s and 1970s is strikingly common in all countries shown. There are differences, however, in the times at which these leveled out. The highest rate for the United States was in 1979, but other countries did not reach a maximum until later: Canada in 1987, England and Wales in 1993, and Australia in 1996 (although there is a dramatic but short-lived peak in 1976 in Australia). There is no indication yet of a leveling in New Zealand's divorce rate, with the latest figures for 1998 being higher than in any previous year, although the graph shows that rates have been close to the present level throughout the 1990s. The short-term fluctuations in figure 1.3, occurring at different times in different places, appear to overlay more general trends that are remarkably similar across countries. The divorce rates for Canada, England and Wales, Australia, and New Zealand were closely

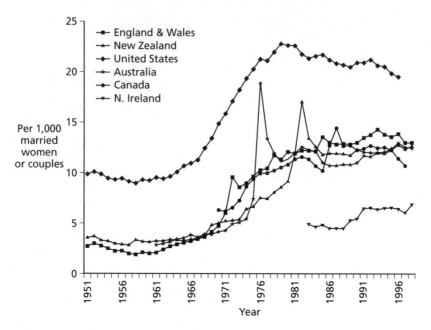

Figure 1.3   Divorce rates in Anglo-American countries, 1951–98

comparable in the mid-1960s, and were again very close in the 1990s. In the United States, a similar increase in divorce rates was seen, with a doubling of the divorce rate between 1967 and 1979. However, the absolute level of the divorce rate was always much higher in the United States, with rates in the 1970s being 2 to 3 times those found in the other countries.

There are some peaks in these graphs that occur at different times in different countries, and tend to be following legislative changes in divorce law. For example, a rise in England and Wales in 1971–2 followed the implementation of the Divorce Reform Act 1969. The very high rate in Australia in 1976 followed the introduction of the Family Law Act 1975 and there was a similar sharp increase in New Zealand in 1982 arising from the Marital Proceedings Act 1980.

There is some debate about whether legal changes precipitate behavioral change such as divorce (Nakonezny et al., 1995; Glenn, 1997, 1999) and this has been addressed by examining the divorce rates of individual states of the US before and after the introduction of no-fault legislation (Nakonezny et al., 1995). Divorce rates were indeed higher in the first 3 years following introduction compared with the 3 years beforehand. However, to interpret this as a causal relationship between legal change and rising divorce rates is contentious (Glenn, 1997, 1999). The higher rates in England and Wales in the 1970s, following similar reforms, could not be ascribed to the availability of no-fault divorce since after the 1969 Act the large majority of divorces continued to be granted under provisions for demonstrating fault by one or both parties. In 1996, 70 percent of dissolutions in England and Wales were still awarded on grounds of adultery, unreasonable behavior, or desertion (Office for National Statistics, 1998). Overall, there is a general long-term upward trend that is probably propelled by social and economic changes interacting with legal reform. To some extent at least, the peaks in figure 1.3 are likely to be reflecting the formalization of separations that had already occurred before legal changes.

Several countries in mainland Europe have substantially lower divorce rates than those shown in figure 1.3, particularly the southern European countries including Spain, Italy, and Greece. However, even those Catholic countries where legal divorce was not possible until relatively recently have shown increases in rates (Haskey, 1992; Goode, 1993; Clarke & Berrington, 1999). Few European countries have higher divorce rates than England and Wales, and these are all northern countries. Sweden has had the highest rates in Europe for some time, and these are now approached by figures for Norway and Finland. Denmark, which has had relatively high divorce rates historically (almost 3 times the rate for England and Wales in the 1950s), had rates in the 1990s somewhat lower than those of England and Wales and the Scandinavian countries (Clarke & Berrington, 1999).

The steady rise in divorce rates that we have discussed here does not give a complete picture of the demographic changes in families that are likely to have an impact on children. Our discussion here does not, for instance, include the separation of cohabiting parents and, as we have seen, increasing numbers of children live with parents who are not married. Neither do the statistics include parents who have separated but do not formalize their separation by legal divorce. Finally, not all divorces involve couples with children.

Where do Children Live?

Although the majority of children still live with two biological parents, as divorce rates rise so do the proportions of those who live in a home with just one parent. Recent figures indicate that in the 1990s 27 percent of children in the US lived with one parent (Saluter, 1996), and in the UK the figure was over 18 percent (Haskey, 1994a). In New Zealand, Canada, and Australia between 18 and 20 percent lived with one parent (Statistics New Zealand, 1998; Australian Bureau of Statistics, 1999; Statistics Canada, 1999a). In sum, there has been a rapid increase in the proportion of lone-parent families in all these countries in the latter part of the 1900s. By the end of the century, about 1 in 5 families with children were lone-parent families.

Most children who live in a lone-parent family do so as a result of their parents' separation after either marriage or cohabitation. Most, too, live with their mothers. In the 1990s in the US, about 14 percent of children in lone-parent families lived with their fathers (Rawlings & Saluter, 1996); in the UK and in Australia less than 10 percent did so. In New Zealand and Canada 17 percent of lone-parent families were headed by fathers in the late 1990s.

How many children live in stepfamilies?

For many children, the divorce or separation of their parents is not the only change. The majority of adults repartner after separation, with two-thirds of women and three-quarters of men marrying after divorce (Bumpass et al., 1990). In the USA in 1994 1 in 2 marriages involved a partner who had previously been married (Hetherington & Henderson, 1997) and in the UK, Australia, and New Zealand over one-third of remarriages include one divorced partner (Haskey, 1994b; Funder, 1996; Statistics New Zealand, 1998). Not all remarriages, though, involve children and more importantly, not all stepfamilies contain married parents. In the US, for example, at any one time a quarter of stepfamilies are cohabiting, and 53 percent of stepfamily couples cohabit before marrying (Thomson, 1994).

In the 1990s between 9 and 11 percent of children in the US and the UK lived in stepfamilies (Cherlin & Furstenberg, 1994; Haskey, 1994b). The chances of entering a stepfamily during childhood are, however, considerably higher. It has been estimated, given current rates of divorce and remarriage, that 35 percent of children born in the 1980s in the USA will enter a stepfamily before the age of 18 (Glick, 1989). In the UK, similar estimates suggest that 20 percent of children will become part of a married or cohabiting stepfamily by the age of 16 (Haskey, 1994b). In New Zealand, over 18 percent of a cohort of children in Christchurch entered a stepfamily at least once before the age of 16 (Nicholson, 1999). Based

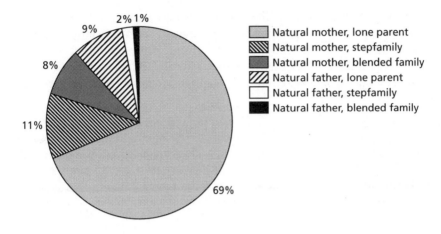

Figure 1.4 Families of children with one original parent living elsewhere, Australia, 1997

on these figures, between 1 in 3 and 1 in 5 of all children will be part of a stepfamily at some time in their childhood. This includes children born to lone mothers who form partnerships; for children whose parents separate, the odds of entering a stepfamily are even higher. For example, in the Stanford Custody Project, 4 years after separation nearly 30 percent of children were living in a stepfather family, 12 percent in a stepmother family, and 5 percent in dual residence where at least one parent was repartnered. In total, 47 percent of young people were spending at least some time living in a stepfamily (Buchanan & Maccoby, 1996). In the Australian Institute of Family Studies (AIFS) project, 52 percent were living in a stepfamily of some kind 5 to 8 years after their parents separated (Funder, 1996), and only 13 percent of children had no stepparent in their lives.

More detailed information on proportions of children in various family arrangements in Australia was provided by a special Family Characteristics Survey carried out in 1997 by the Australian Bureau of Statistics (1998). This survey identified the children who lived with one original parent and whose other parent lived elsewhere, and described their living arrangements. Of all children less than 18 years old, over 27 percent had one original parent living elsewhere. Figure 1.4 shows the proportions of these children living in the various family types according to whether they were usually resident with their natural mother or natural father. A large majority of these children lived in lone-parent families (78 percent for lone-mother and lone-father families combined) and a very large majority lived with their original mothers (88 percent) rather than their original fathers (12 percent). The term "blended family" refers to complex step-families where there are children brought to the family by both parents.

Snap-shots of where children live tell us that about 1 in 5 live with just one parent, and 1 in 10 live in a stepfamily. It is important to note, though, that these situations are far from static. Children whose parents separate are as likely to enter a stepfamily as they are to stay with one parent. Furthermore, of those who do enter a stepfamily a significant number will see the dissolution of their parents' second partnership.

About 1 in 2 children whose parents separate are likely to enter a stepfamily within 4 to 8 years after parental separation. Life in stepfamilies, however, is not necessarily permanent. The rate of breakdown of second marriages is higher than it is for first marriages, with 54 percent of remarried women and 64 percent of remarried men ultimately divorcing again (Martin & Bumpass, 1989). Put another way, 37 percent of remarriages dissolve after 10 years, compared with 30 percent of first marriages in the USA (Bumpass et al., 1990). In a New Zealand cohort of families with children, 50 percent of children were born into or entered a lone-parent family by the age of 16; of those, 71 percent reentered a two-parent house-hold within 5 years (Fergusson et al., 1984); 53 percent of those house-holds dissolved within 5 years. Overall, 27 percent of children in the cohort had experienced two family situations by age 9, and 18 percent or nearly 1 in 5 had experienced three or more by that age.

In summary, snapshots of where children live tell us that about one in five live with just one parent, and one in ten live in a stepfamily. It is important to note, though, that these situations are far from static. Children whose parents separate are as likely to enter a stepfamily as they are to stay with one parent. Furthermore, of those who do enter a stepfamily a significant number will see the dissolution of their parents' second partnership.

Overview

Families and households have been changing steadily and in response to social and economic factors, as well as to changes in the nature of relationships within families, and these changes have been accompanied by changes in legal structures and public attitudes. A particularly significant change has been the transformation of children from subordinate and economically important members of hierarchical families into emotionally highly valued individuals with rights equal to those of adults. Children now live in an increasingly diverse range of family forms, many of them outside a formal legal structure.

Those who take polarized positions on the implications of these changes have in common a deep concern for the well-being of children. However, their interpretations of family change fundamentally differ. In this chapter we have chronicled the diversity of family life for children, and the specific changes that trouble those who hold a conservative perspective. Fewer children today, for example, live in stable, married, two-parent households with both biological parents. For many, fathers are absent and mothers are in the workforce. Marriage is decreasingly either legal or binding, and 1 in 4 children live in what are seen by some as inherently undesirable stepfamily households. Some aspects of the liberal perspective, that diversity is to be encouraged and that children have rights and power, are supported in the sense that there is greater diversity in family structures, and children have moved from positions of relative dependency to relative power in families. Whether or not these changes are good for children is another question, and in the chapters that follow these and other questions arising from the debate will be addressed.

2

Frameworks for Understanding Family Transitions

We believe that there are multiple views and perspectives that can justifiably compete for a place in our knowledge reservoir . . . scholarly views regarding the effects of divorce will covary with the prevailing beliefs in a particular culture and/or in a particular historical era.

Fine & Demo, 2000, pp. 152–3

Introduction

Whenever we attempt to understand complex phenomena such as children's lives after separation, we bring to our investigation patterns of values and beliefs that may not be entirely conscious. When these phenomena have personal meaning for us, as is the case with children and family transitions, individual experiences and concerns are as likely to influence our interpretation of the "facts" as are theoretical frameworks. Few people have not witnessed at close hand the breakdown and reconstitution of families, either one's own or those of friends or relatives. Stories of family change are depicted in literature, the arts, and other media, and each depiction carries its author's selective interpretation.

As far as research and researchers are concerned, the same confusion of values, interpretations, and theories applies (Fine & Demo, 2000). Not only is a welter of information available, but it also comes from a wide range of disciplines including sociology, psychology, psychiatry, education, criminology, epidemiology, economics, law, and social policy. Each comes with its own peculiar traditions of theory, methodology, and terminology. Scholars span the continuum of the debate from conservative to liberal viewpoints, and not only bring these subjectively based frameworks to their work but also run the danger of utilizing research information selectively in order to support their view. The challenge is to bring information to bear on the perspectives we hold, in an attempt to be more objective, since the frameworks we construct from our broader experience and from available information have important implications for the way we approach policy and professional practice related to children's well-being. Academic writers are guilty, often, of not being clear about the conceptual frameworks they are using to guide their work, and this has implications for both what they do and what they convey. It is hardly surprisingly then, that views expressed by journalists in the media and by lay people, who often rely in on what is written by scholars, are sometimes confusing. In this chapter we intend not only to outline the major frameworks presented in the literature, but also to encourage readers to think about their own beliefs and opinions. In this way, it will be possible to evaluate these ideas against the summary of research findings presented in following chapters.

We will outline frameworks that are used for explaining the outcomes for children who have experienced family transitions. We have grouped them under the two main headings of "Trauma Theories" and "Life-course Theories." Trauma theories are, at least implicitly, a component of a conservative perspective that encompasses the notion of parental separation as a distressing and potentially traumatic *event* for children, and feature prominently in artistic and media depictions and in lay views. Life-course theories, in contrast, see outcomes for children as being the result of cumulative factors occurring over time, and parental separation is seen as only one aspect of a process that begins long before separation and continues thereafter. The liberal view that divorce in itself is not of primary importance for children's outcomes is largely encompassed in a life-course perspective.

We have included a third framework that does not sit easily in either trauma or life-course models. It is referred to as a "stresses and resources" model, or alternatively a risk and resiliency model. "Stresses and resources" tends to address the whole family unit, whereas "risk and resilience" takes an individual approach to children. Both consider the balance between positive and negative aspects of children's lives and experiences.

The distinction between trauma and life-course theories is reflected in the common usage of the terms "parental loss" and "parental absence." At first sight, this may appear a minor distinction, as loss and absence of a parent typically go hand-in-hand for children of separated families, and the second is a logical and frequent consequence of the first. Nevertheless, the important conceptual difference can be illustrated by considering two quite different circumstances for children. At one extreme, we can imagine a child whose parents remained together through most of her childhood years and then divorced not long before she is due to leave the parental home. We would not expect this child to show serious adverse outcomes as a consequence of parental absence, but she could be affected by the experience of loss. In contrast, a child whose parents separated when he was in very early infancy (or one who was born to a single mother) and who spends an entire childhood in a lone-parent family would not suffer as a result of loss, but would be susceptible to any consequences of parental absence. These examples serve not only to point out the quite different meanings behind the terms *loss* and *absence*, although they are used almost interchangeably, but also highlight the diverse experiences of children who live in separated families.

We want to understand what factors (in children themselves, their families or the wider environment) are the most important in influencing child development in different types of families and how these factors operate in relation to each other. Second is the need to account for how it is that the disadvantages shown by some children of separated families persist not only through their childhood years but also into their adult lives. Third and equally important is to try and identify what helps many children to be resilient in the face of change.

Although absence is frequently used in both academic and lay literature, it does not fit any specific theoretical framework. Richards and Dyson (1982), in an early review, criticized the indiscriminate use of the term and highlighted failures to acknowledge confounding parental absence and both reasons for, and other consequences of, family disruption. Its widespread use continues, however, and has given rise to even further confusion. For example, McLanahan (1999) has recently referred to "father absence *per se*" as being responsible for some of the differences between children in one- and two-parent families. It is not clear what is meant by "*per se*," given that father absence typically involves a range of adversity for children. These include a fall in parental supervision, lower economic resources, and a reduction in social capital through the links a parent figure has with extrafamilial resources (e.g. extended families and institutions).

Before we discuss the conceptual and theoretical models found in the research literature, it is helpful to consider what it is that we expect from such explanatory frameworks. First, we want to understand what factors (in children themselves, their families, or the wider environment) are the most important in influencing child development in different types of families and how these factors operate in relation to each other. Second is the need to account for how it is that the disadvantages shown by some children of separated families persist not only through their childhood years but also into their adult lives. Third is to try and identify what *helps* many children to be resilient in the face of change.

Trauma Theories

The most readily identifiable aspect of parental separation is the point at which a parent leaves the family home. There is no doubt that this event is generally experienced as deeply distressing by all family members. When asked to rate the significance of different kinds of events, adults place the breakdown of a marriage alongside such instances as the death of a loved one, as one of the most stressful of all (Henderson et al., 1981; Tennant et al., 1982). Trauma theories maintain that events such as these, especially those occurring in childhood, have direct effects on psychological outcomes later in life *independent* of intervening experiences. The impact for some people may not be seen at the time, but may remain latent and emerge later. In the context of parental separation this has been termed a "sleeper effect" (Hetherington, 1972; Wallerstein & Corbin, 1989; Rodgers, 1994).

Loss

The idea that events early in life can have marked and enduring consequences for psychological development has a history going back over millennia (Clarke & Clarke, 1976), but it was the psychoanalytic tradition in the early twentieth century that emphasized the particular importance of parental loss and its implications for mental health. Sigmund Freud (1913; 1940) and others, notably Abraham (1927), discussed the relevance of loss within a broader theoretical model that considered relationships with parents in early infancy to be of special significance for the development of neuroses in adult life. At the time these ideas developed, parental loss effectively meant parental death, which was much more common than parental separation. It was not until some decades later that systematic studies – either based on patients receiving psychiatric care or using samples from the general population – were actually carried out to determine whether parental loss was indeed associated with adult mental illness.

However, the lack of empirical evidence did not prevent the permeation of psychoanalytic ideas into both scientific and nonscientific thinking. The legacy of this remains strong today.

Freud himself had insight into the difference between a typical clinician's viewpoint and the picture that could be obtained from a scientific perspective, and anticipated the findings of later surveys and epidemiological studies:

> So long as we trace the development from its final outcome backwards, the chain of events appears continuous, and we feel we have gained an insight which is completely satisfactory or even exhaustive. But if we proceed in the reverse way, if we start from the premises inferred from the analysis and try to follow these up to the final results, then we no longer get the impression of an inevitable sequence of events which could not have otherwise been determined. (Freud, 1955, p. 167)

Freud's observation opens up the possibility that intervening events may have a role in influencing the connection between early environment and later outcomes, rather than assuming that there is a direct link between an early event, such as loss of a parent, and a later outcome. One mechanism by which early loss might affect later well-being is the possibility that loss in childhood may leave children with a greater vulnerability to loss events in adult life.

What would a loss perspective predict? First, if loss in itself were most important, then children who lose parents by death and by separation would be similarly affected. Second, we would expect worse outcomes for children who lost their mothers or fathers at an early age than those who lost them at later ages. Another prediction from theories of loss is that children from separated families should be substantially more disadvantaged than those from original two-parent families, *after* separation has occurred but not before. It may also be possible to consider loss as a continuum rather than as an all or nothing event, so that some children experience greater loss if they lose all contact with a parent compared to those who maintain a regular and lasting relationship after parental separation.

Although absence cannot be considered a trauma theory in the sense of it being an event, predictions from research findings are similar to those outlined above for parental loss. Parental death and separation at an early age would be considered important, and a particularly thorough test would be to investigate the total time children spend in a lone-parent family in relation to outcomes. We might also expect an increase in disadvantages after separation in comparison with those before parents part.

Abandonment

The notion of *abandonment* implies an actual or a perceived deliberate act by a parent, and makes a distinction between parental separation and parental death that is not made for *loss*. Because an absent parent is still alive after separation, the potential for contact that may not occur can imply, to the child, that he or she is not wanted. Abandonment is referred to in scientific papers as well as in lay discussions of parental separation (Phillips, 1998a, 1998b), and some specific features can be derived from individual research reports. Wallerstein and Kelly (1980) has suggested that the consequences of abandonment include feelings of rejection and low self-worth in children, and a fear of further abandonment, particularly by the remaining parent.

It is uncertain what predictions can be made using an abandonment model. The most obvious areas in which it might be important apart from the distinction between death and divorce would be in regard to outcomes for children whose nonresident parents either did or did not initiate the separation. Central to this would be a question of whether or not a child perceived that the nonresidential parent had left the household intentionally and without regard for their relationship. If a child believed that the parent had chosen to leave her, we would expect that the consequences would be worse than if the child did not blame the parent for leaving. It might also be expected that outcomes would be worse following, compared with before, separation.

Attachment theory

The major feature of attachment theory that goes beyond psychoanalytic views is the emphasis on the quality of the relationship between infants and parent figures during the first few years of life. John Bowlby (1969), the originator of this theory, described patterns of behavior between infants and caregivers (especially their mothers) which he likened to forms of attachment observed by ethologists in some species of birds and mammals, characterized by the young seeking proximity to an attachment figure. The quality of attachment formed in early life, initially described as one of three types (secure, insecure-avoidant, and insecure-ambivalent) (Ainsworth et al., 1978), is believed to have implications for future social relationships, especially close relationships, and for associated mental health problems, including delinquency and depression. The link between early attachment types and later well-being was seen to be the development of internalized *working models* of interpersonal interactions between the self and others. In this way, attachment theory straddles both trauma and life-course frameworks, since its account of long-term outcomes (extending into adulthood) has characteristics of a life-course theory in the sense that working models serve as links between events and outcomes. This aspect was discussed further in Bowlby's (1988) later writing. The relevance of working models in the context of life-course theories is discussed later in this chapter.

Although attachment theory has been used to predict social competence and other aspects of children's well-being generally, it is not easy to derive precise predictions when parents separate. For example, young children usually form attachments with both parents; when one leaves the home, does the attachment to the residential parent compensate for the loss of the nonresident parent, or does the child suffer because of the loss of one of his or her attachment figures? And how important is the *nature* of those early attachments? Is it worse for a child to lose contact with a person to whom she or he is securely rather than insecurely attached, or not? Furthermore, it is not clear what constitutes the loss of an attachment figure since often the child retains at least sporadic contact with the nonresident parent.

There are two areas in family transition research where one might expect attachment theory to have made significant contributions, yet it does not appear to have been as influential as anticipated. An important part of the development of attachment theory was the description of the short-term and medium-term effects of parental separation on children. This was observed specifically in children admitted to hospital, and Robertson and Bowlby (1952) described typical reactions of children and age differences in these reactions, outlining three stages of protest, withdrawal, and detachment. These stages would seem to be relevant both to the distress children experience at the initial separation of their divorcing parents, and also to reactions at the time of handover between parents who have been living apart for some time. However, as we will see later (chapters 3 and 4), the acute effects of parental separation on children have not been well studied in comparison with long-term outcomes.

Life-course Theories

Frameworks that take a life-course perspective include considerations of time, agency, and process in proposing explanations for children's outcomes. In contrast with trauma models in which one event by itself is seen to cause subsequent disadvantage, time and process interact with factors specific to the individual child (agency). Factors preceding and following family transitions, for example, interact with structural changes such as divorce and stepfamily formation, so that any outcome is a result of a dynamic process involving many components. An outcome, too, can itself become a factor contributing to later well-being so that, for example, leaving school early becomes a risk factor itself for unemployment and poor economic conditions in adulthood. Such a chain of events has been called a cumulative process of disadvantage; children can also experience cumulative processes of *advantage* where, for example, attaining high educational goals leads to better employment and income. However, these chains of events are not inevitable. Change, in the form of specific events such as stepfamily formation, has the potential to shift children's development in both positive and negative ways.

Another important feature of developmental pathways is that they occur in social, economic, and community contexts that have a potent influence on how they are manifest in children. This *contextual* aspect of development has led to the development of ecological frameworks of explanation. Taken together, life-course or pathway models, and ecological or contextual models, complement each other and provide a two-dimensional framework for thinking about outcomes for children within which key factors of time, individuality, process, and context can be integrated.

But these models do not, because of their comprehensiveness, offer specific predictions about children's outcomes. They offer a framework for the study of children in families that overarches particular hypotheses. Fundamental to children's development within these life-course frameworks is parenting, since parent-child relationships are the keystone for children's development. Later in this section we will look at some specific models of parenting and of parenting styles.

The contribution of life-course models to the understanding of family transitions can best be understood by considering four key principles of life-course theory (Elder, 1994). They are: (1) historical time and place; (2) timing within lives; (3) human agency and individual difference; and (4) linked lives. The last is able conceptually to incorporate ecological theories, so they are also discussed within the broad framework of life-course principles.

1   Historical time and place

This principle emphasizes the facts that a child is born and develops within a delimited span of historical time and in a particular geographical place. Both time and place have characteristics that provide specific contexts for developmental pathways. A primary example of this is that families exist in frameworks of social beliefs, customs, and sanctions that vary by time and place. The ways in which divorce, "illegitimate" children, lone parents, and stepfamilies are viewed, for example, have changed significantly in most countries in the last few centuries, and vary still across cultural and ethnic groups.

The legal context in which family change occurs is also a critical factor in determining how children are treated at times of family transitions, and we have discussed this in chapter 1. The changes in the legal approach to divorce from fault to no-fault systems in recent decades are one example of how laws relating to divorce might have an impact on children's experiences. Similarly, the use of family mediation (Emery et al., 1994, and in press) and the establishment of Family Courts dedicated to family matters have changed the context within which family transitions occur.

The consideration of children's rights and wishes has, too, become a more frequent component of decision-making about living arrangements, with children over the age of 12 years considered in the US to be fit to hold legitimate views. As we shall see in chapter 4, children considerably younger than 12 have clear opinions on matters to do with families and their well-being, and there is debate in legal and sociological literature about the extent to which children's views should be taken into account. There is, too, considerable cultural variation in the extent to which children's rights are recognized. In Pacific cultures, for example, children's status comes far below that of the church, the community, and elders and other adults, so that the concept of children having rights in these groups is viewed with skepticism (Perese, 1999).

The belief in most Western countries through most of last century that children should always live with their mothers after parental separation is also changing. Children are more likely than they were 20 years ago to reside with their fathers, although still only about 12 percent of men have custody of their children after separation (Maccoby & Mnookin, 1992; Simpson et al., 1995). Economic changes, too, have a bearing on children's living standards and economic and educational opportunities. Although lone-parent households headed by mothers are more likely than any other household form to experience poverty, child support measures are being introduced in many countries that are intended to redress this situation. In earlier times, and in countries where little or no attempt is made to provide economic support for lone parents, parental separation is often associated with severe deprivation for parents and children.

> The consideration of children's rights and wishes has, too, become a more frequent component of decision-making about living arrangements, with children over the age of 12 years considered in the US to be fit to hold legitimate views. . . . [C]hildren considerably younger than 12 have clear opinions on matters to do with families and their well-being, and there is debate in legal and sociological literature about the extent to which children's views should be taken into account. There is, too, considerable cultural variation in the extent to which children's rights are recognized. In Pacific cultures, for example, children's status comes far below that of the church, the community, and elders and other adults, so that the concept of children having rights in these groups is viewed with skepticism.

Another source of temporal and geographical difference lies in rates of family dissolution. As we saw in chapter 1, the prevalence of divorce has grown internationally in recent decades, although it varies still across countries. In the past, family breakdown was common for children but was overwhelmingly the result of parental death rather than separation. The possibility of being stigmatized because of living in a lone-parent household is less if a parent is lost by death than by parental separation; it is likely, though, that in times and places where divorce is more common the stigma will be less.

For children, then, social beliefs, legal frameworks, stigma, and the extent to which their views are valued, are aspects of time and place that impinge on their experiences of family change. As Elder puts it, "the life-course of the individual is embedded in the historical times and places they experience over their lifetimes" (Elder, 1998, p. 3).

2 Timing within lives

The timing of life changes is a pivotal aspect of development that interacts with other aspects of an individual's experience. Elder describes the principle of timing within lives as follows: "The developmental impact of a succession of life transitions or events is contingent on when they occur in a person's life" (Elder, 1998, p. 3). Although, as we shall see later in the book, age at the time of separation is not by itself a powerful predictor of long-term outcomes for children, this principle suggests that the age at which major life transitions occur in general is important. Children's age and developmental stage at the time at which family transitions occur will, for example, determine to a considerable extent how they will comprehend and react in the short term to changes such as parental separation and stepfamily formation. The meanings that families, parenting, and change have for children are only now being examined systematically; not surprisingly they vary according to children's levels of understanding (see chapter 4). The developmental challenges of adolescence, too, are such that it may be harder for young people in this age group to accept the monitoring role of a stepparent than it would be for a preschooler, since the teenage years are the time when young people are starting to move away from monitoring and to develop their own autonomy.

The ages at which children's subsequent transitions in their own lives take place may also be important. Early school leaving, partnering, childbirth, and parenting are, for example, more likely in young people who have experienced separation and stepfamily life (Kiernan, 1992), and these early transitions to adult roles will have implications for their future well-being including socioeconomic status, partnership breakdown, and further transitions. Such early timing of adult roles has led to the concept of pseudomaturity as a way of explaining poor outcomes such as drug abuse and psychopathology, because of the effects of facing experiences before young people are sufficiently mature to cope well (Newcomb, 1996). Another aspect of pseudomaturity has been called parentification, where because of increased autonomy for children in lone-parent households and the emotional needs of lone parents, a kind of role reversal occurs and children become confidants and comforters of their parents (Kalter, 1987; Hetherington, 1999).

The principle of timing in lives predicts that the early assumption of adult roles will have adverse consequences for young people. Early school leaving, for example, makes it less likely that a young person will undertake tertiary education and, in turn, will enter relatively low-paid employment, which has consequences for socioeconomic well-being in adulthood. Similarly, early dating and partnership may lead to youthful parenting. These two transitions, early school leaving and youthful pregnancy and childbirth, have been found to be linked (Fergusson & Woodward, 2000); young women who leave school early are also likely to become pregnant as teenagers. Parentification, too, might be expected to lead to difficulties in adulthood, largely as a result of the person not having completed the normal adolescent tasks of separating emotionally from parents, and being closely involved with peer groups (Kalter, 1987). Conversely, the early assumption of responsibility and of adult roles may serve to help young people to feel competent (Amato, 1987b; Arditti, 1999).

3   Human agency and individual difference

The principle of human agency suggests that "individuals construct their own life-course through the choices and actions they take within the opportunities and constraints of history and social circumstances" (Elder, 1998, p. 4). Clearly, individuals behave in very different ways within the same set of circumstances. For example, perceptions of events, responses to change, and choices made, vary between people. Sources of individual difference are diverse; some are genetic, others arise from early experience, and some we do not yet understand. Some factors have been identified that are important aspects of individual differences, and make significant contributions to the life-courses of children who experience family transitions.

One is temperament, or behavioral style. It is now widely accepted that temperament varies in children, and that they appear to have specific and different behavioral styles from an early age. The categories most commonly identified are "easy," "difficult," and "slow to warm up" (Thomas et al., 1963; Thomas & Chess, 1977). Difficult children find change particularly challenging and their low threshold for frustration means that they are liable to elicit negative reactions from people around them. Conversely, children with happy dispositions who are relatively unfazed by change and lack of routine may cope better with adversity.

A second source of difference lies in a child's appraisal of a situation, which may determine to a large extent how he or she will perceive and react to an event or series of events, for example episodes of conflict (Grych, 1998). Appraisal incorporates different coping styles, too, that may be used by children. Some take a constructive, problem-solving approach while others use avoidance to cope with stressful events (Armistead et al., 1990; Drapeau et al., 1999). Another aspect of appraisal that has been studied is locus of control. Early conceptualizations of locus of control saw it as a bipolar construct, with an external locus involving a belief that outcomes are determined by external factors, and an internal locus attributing causality to one's own actions and responses (Lefcourt, 1976). Broadly speaking, a child who perceives at least some aspects of the events associated with family change as manageable may cope better in terms of psychological well-being, since there is evidence from other research that locus of control mediates the association between stress and mental health in children (Fogas et al., 1992).

An obvious way in which relationship styles might be relevant to family transitions for children is in the intergenerational transmission of relationship problems. The distress surrounding parental separation often diminishes a parent's ability to parent effectively and consistently, and if as a result of this persisting over a long or crucial part of their childhood a child develops a low sense of self-worth and distorted expectations of relationship partners, then their own relationships are likely to be jeopardized *unless* subsequent factors such as therapy, consistent subsequent experiences of optimal parenting, or having a supportive partner enable them to make fundamental adjustments to their ways of forming relationships.

A third source of individual difference is the way in which relationships are formed and sustained. One aspect of attachment theory, for example, is the nature of the attachments formed. It argues that the specific *patterns* of interaction that occur between caregivers and infants in the first few years become internalized as working models of the self and of others, and become increasingly inaccessible to consciousness and to modification as the young person gets older. These original patterns of relating then serve as templates for subsequent relationships. A child who has experienced rejecting or insensitive parenting early in life may internalize a sense of self as unworthy, and of partners in interaction as unreliable or unable to be trusted, and thus carry a vulnerability to poor or failed relationships. Similarly, a consistently responsive and sensitive parent arms a child with a strong positive sense of self, and an ability to form effective relationships. It is in this way that attachment theory can be seen as a life-course model since working models are both persistent and dynamic. Their establishment is not a discrete event but part of a process over several years, and they are subject to modification (albeit less readily with age). More generally, experiences and expectations of relationships may be specific to individuals, and thus be an aspect of agency that predicts the formation and possible fragility of adult relationships.

An obvious way in which relationship styles might be relevant to family transitions for children is in the intergenerational transmission of relationship problems. The distress surrounding parental separation often diminishes a parent's ability to parent effectively and consistently. If, as a result of this persisting over a long or crucial part of their childhood, a child develops a low sense of self-worth and distorted expectations of relationship partners, then their own relationships are likely to be jeopardized. However, subsequent factors such as therapy, consistent subsequent experiences of optimal parenting, or having a supportive partner may enable them to make fundamental adjustments to their ways of forming relationships.

Another aspect of individual difference comes from genetics. The possibility that the associations between parental separation and children's outcomes may be mediated at least in part by genetic factors has recently been examined (Emery et al., 1999; O'Connor et al., 2000). The impetus comes from the understanding that family factors present before parents separate account for a considerable proportion of the risks faced by children and, in turn, that these family factors may be linked to vulnerabilities in parents and their children. So, for example, personality disorders or traits in parents that have a degree of genetic determination may set up negative family processes related to separation, *and* may be passed on through genetic mechanisms to children who, similarly, contribute both to family processes and to their own negative outcomes. The task of teasing out the contributions of environmental factors in families to children's problems, from possibly genetically mediated links, is formidable. One approach is to study siblings in one family who share some but not all their parents' genes, and to examine the quality of relationships between genetically related and unrelated children and adults (Hetherington et al., 1999). Another is to look at the impact of divorce on genetically related (biological) and unrelated (adoptive) families (O'Connor et al., 2000).

Human agency as an explanatory framework would predict that children in similar circumstances experiencing similar events would show different levels of adjustment depending on some aspect of demonstrable difference between them. For example, children already vulnerable to stress because of difficult temperaments would be expected to fare less well through family transitions than children who have easy dispositions that attract support, and who feel some control over their lives. Similarly, a child with a secure sense of worth and early experiences of supportive relationships would be predicted to have comparatively little trouble in establishing and maintaining relationships in adulthood.

4   Linked lives

The component of life-course theory that is perhaps most significant for family transitions is the linking of lives. In Elder's words, "lives are lived interdependently, and social and historical influences are expressed through this network of shared relationships" (Elder, 1998, p. 4). Although it might seem unnecessary to emphasize such an obvious aspect of families, developmental psychology in particular has at times been guilty of paying little attention to factors beyond the individual person. The notion of linked lives provides a structure for a systematic consideration of the relationships within which a person functions. These interrelationships extend *through* time, across generations, and also extend *outward* in the present, from the individual to family members, friends, peers, and the community as a vital part of the context in which children develop.

Taking account of contexts, particularly social contexts, in which children live and grow, has given rise to a group of theories that can be characterized as ecological theories. Although strictly speaking they are not life-course or pathway models since they do not emphasize the passage of time, they explicitly address the idea of interdependent lives. They are (i) Bronfenbrenner's Ecological Theory, (ii) Social Capital, and (iii) Family Systems Theory. Patterns of parenting will also be discussed in this section, since parenting is a vital component of parent–child relationships.

i) Bronfenbrenner's ecological theory

Bronfenbrenner's ecological model emphasizes the fact that children are from birth embedded in a social context, and that their development and well-being cannot be understood outside that context. Bronfenbrenner describes four levels, or systems, within which individuals function. The first is the *microsystem*, which encompasses the immediate set of relationships for a child, usually within the family. The second level is the *mesosystem*. This comprises the links between the child, the family, and other systems within which the child operates, for example daycare, school, sports and other community groups, and health professionals.

The third level, the *exosystem*, involves contexts in which the child does not directly participate but which have an impact on the child. The most obvious example is the parents' workplace, where flexibility of hours, attitudes to parental leave, and time off for children's needs such as holidays and illness, are relevant. Finally, the *macrosystem* is the wider culture or community within which families live, and in particular the attitudes, beliefs, opportunities, and policies encompassed in that community or culture.

Bronfenbrenner's ecological theory puts particular emphasis on the links between these systems. Home and school communication is an example of a link that is salient for children. When family transitions occur, there are changes to the microsystem within which the family functions; equally important are disturbances of the links between the family and the community, or mesosytem. Changes in children's schools, community groups, and friends, through moving house when parents separate or stepfamilies form, are likely to be associated with well-being in children.

ii) Social and economic capital

Social capital is a term that has acquired wide but somewhat ambiguous use in the social sciences. Its relevance to family change lies in its precise definition and use by James Coleman (1988), who distinguishes it from physical capital (machines, computers, other equipment) and human capital, which is generated by mechanisms that enable the acquisition of skills and knowledge, such as education. Social capital exists in the relationships between persons and, in this case, both *within* families and *between* family members and the community, thus overlapping with Bronfenbrenner's micro- and mesosystems. "Capital" is seen as existing in the investment made in children through these relationships, and as social resources upon which they can draw for their well-being. These relationships offer three aspects of social capital. The first are sources of information children may need; the second includes a sense of obligation, trustworthiness, and expectations; and the third an understanding of norms and effective sanctions when they breach those norms. Within families, social capital is represented primarily by the parent-parent and parent–child relationships, and is dependent on both the presence of, and attention from, parents. If, for example, parents are present but not emotionally invested in their children, then the supply of social capital is small. Emotional investment includes love and support, while social investment incorporates monitoring, aspirations, and concern for physical well-being.

Community social capital includes schools and other educational resources, and other families in the community. Central to community social capital are the links between a child's family and other families, and between the family and school. Coleman uses the term "closure" to describe the monitoring resources available for children where, for example, other parents know them and their parents, and their parents have good communication with schoolteachers through activities such as attending school meetings. So, if family–community links are strong and maintained, and if the resources available are of good quality, then the amount of community social capital available to children is enhanced and their well-being is better served.

In stepfamilies, social capital may be in reduced supply. The biological parent–child relationship has to adapt to the presence of another adult in the parent's life, and the stepparent–stepchild relationship is fragile in its formative phase. Because stepfamilies are "instant" families there is often not the development of community involvement that comes through partnership formation, pregnancy, birth, and preschool activities and that integrates original families into their neighborhoods. The community social capital account, then, may also be in debit for stepfamilies, at least in the early years of family establishment.

Coleman's conceptualization of social capital has, however, been criticized for being too ethnocentric, and for ignoring the contribution of children to their own developmental pathways (Morrow, 1999). It also suggests that lone-parent families are in deficit, without taking into account the contributions of the nonresident parent, nor of other adults including extended family and friends.

A social capital framework predicts associations between family relations and community links, and children's outcomes. These include parent–child relationships, investment of time and support for children in families, aspects of school–family communication such as parental attendance at meetings, and familiarity with other families in the neighborhood. A wider interpretation of the concept would include support for resources outside household and biological relations, for example grandparents, teachers, and mentors.

Economic capital, although not addressed by Coleman, is also critical to a discussion of family transitions. The reduction in household income that usually follows, and sometimes precedes, parental separation, is potentially a key factor for explaining risk. Although there is not a specific conceptual framework coming from social science, an obvious prediction from a consideration of economic resources would be that reduced resources will be associated with risks indirectly through the stresses experienced by families who find it hard to manage financially, and directly by a paucity of resources such as access to good education, computers, and extracurricular activities.

iii) Family systems theory

Family systems theory approaches the concept of linked lives at a level beyond that of interindividual connections, since it proposes that outcomes for individuals can be understood best by considering the network of interdependent relationships in families (Minuchin, 1974). The family system is made up of subsystems comprising members of, for example, the same generation (as in parent–parent relationships), the same sex (e.g.

fathers and sons), or function (parent–child). The key relationships that interact with each other to form a relational subsystem are contained by boundaries. These can be diffuse or permeable, so that information flows freely between subsystems. Family members, at the extremes of diffusion, can become enmeshed with each other so that, for example, generational boundaries between mothers and daughters may blur the extent that a daughter is burdened with emotional issues normally appropriate for adults. Boundaries can also be rigid, so that little information exchange or engagement occurs between relational subsystems. An example of rigid boundaries exists where a parent–stepparent relationship excludes or reduces the interaction of the parent with a child. Family systems theory assumes that families are usually self-regulating, and that they establish rules and structures to stabilize family roles and functions. When parents separate and when stepfamilies form, a reorganization of the system of relationships occurs and subsystems outside the household become important for children, especially with nonresident parents. So, for example, nonresident parent–child relationships become a part of a family subsystem that includes relations within the household. Stepfamily formation is especially amenable to examination using family systems theory (Hetherington & Clingempeel, 1992; Hetherington et al., 1999) since there is a juxtaposition of new and existing relationships, some of which are involuntary for children. The process of integrating relationship subsystems into a functioning family is a major challenge for stepfamily members. Family systems theory predicts, then, that children's well-being is linked with associations between relationships. It does not, though, predict the precise interplay of relationships and allows for the possibility that different patterns of relationships might be more or less optimal in different family situations.

iv) Patterns of parenting

The most fundamental and direct influence on children's development and well-being is the parenting they receive. Of particular interest to this book is the likelihood not just that children may be parented by only one adult after parental separation, but also that the *ways* in which parents behave toward children are liable to change around the time of family transitions. When stepfamilies are formed, too, there are additional challenges for parenting as family members adjust to new and changed relationships, and stepparents and stepchildren establish relationships with each other.

Parenting styles have been well studied, and links between differing styles and children's outcomes established. One model of parenting has been developed by Belsky (1984), who suggested that parenting is multiply determined by three major influences. These are parental characteristics and resources; the social context in which the family lives, and the support available in this context; and characteristics of children. He proposed that, of these, parental characteristics are the most important.

Belsky believes that the spousal relationship is the most potent source of support for competent parenting; and indeed, it has been shown to be more crucial than social network support for parents of 12-year-olds (Simons et al., 1993). This may be important when parents separate and repartner, as the quantity and nature of partner support is inevitably changed. It would not be surprising, then, to find that the quality of parenting is diminished during family transitions at least partly because this source of support is reduced or changed.

A second model of parenting that has been widely examined involves combining dimensions of parenting to identify parenting styles (Baumrind,

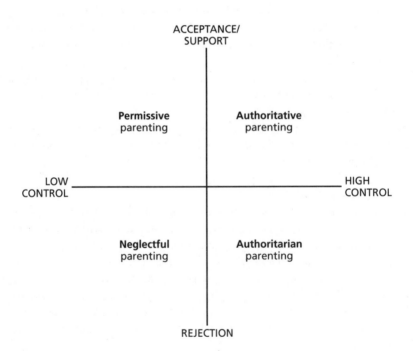

Figure 2.1   Parenting styles along two dimensions

1971; Maccoby & Martin, 1983; Baumrind, 1991). Early formulations of these parenting styles used two dimensions: acceptance and support, and control and monitoring. Figure 2.1 shows the parenting styles developed according to these dimensions.

Two similar dimensions of warmth and control, also referred to as care and protection, have been used to develop the Parental Bonding Instrument (PBI) (Parker, 1979) and the Swedish instrument, the EMBU (Perris et al., 1980). Using these instruments, adult affective symptoms and in particular depression have been reported to be linked with parenting that is low in care and affection and high in control, i.e. affectionless control (Perris et al., 1986; MacKinnon et al., 1993; Rodgers, 1996a).

An interesting aspect of later formulations is that they introduced a third dimension, called psychological autonomy (Steinberg et al., 1991), incorporating parents' efforts to encourage individuality and use democratic methods of discipline. Authoritative parenting that includes this dimension is high on acceptance, control, and the facilitation of psychological autonomy. Authoritarian parenting is high on control and low on acceptance and psychological autonomy; and permissive parenting is high on acceptance and psychological autonomy but low on control. Neglectful parenting is low on acceptance and control, and around the median for psychological autonomy (Avenevoli et al., 1999). (See table 2.1.) The incorporation of the dimension of psychological autonomy reflects the change in children's positions of power in families (we discussed this in chapter 1); the encouragement of autonomy would not have been a desirable aspect of parenting in hierarchically organized families.

Although these parenting styles have been developed by researchers the vast majority of whom are adult, children's and adolescents' perceptions of parenting styles are very similar (Amato, 1990), and Maccoby and Martin (1983) have also referred to parents as being both responsive and demanding, terms that reflect the two-way interaction between parents and children where parents respond to children as much as children respond to parents. Parenting is not unidirectional; aspects of children contribute as much as do those of adults.

In the US, authoritative parenting has been found across socioeconomic status, ethnic groupings, and different family structures to be linked with children's well-being in areas of social competence, behavior, and academic performance (Steinberg et al., 1989; Baumrind, 1991; Lamborn et al., 1991; Steinberg et al., 1991). There are, however, a few exceptions to this generalization. For example, authoritative parenting has been found to predict academic performance in White US adolescents but not in

Table 2.1   Parenting styles according to three dimensions of parenting

Parenting style	Acceptance	Control	Psychological autonomy
Authoritative	↑	↑	↑
Authoritarian	↓	↑	↓
Permissive	↑	↓	↑
Neglectful	↓	↓	●

Asian-American or African-American young people (Dornbusch et al., 1987), and has only marginal impact for Hispanic-American youth.

We can predict, in general, that where lowered levels of parental warmth and reduced partner support accompany family transitions then children will be adversely affected. Control or demandingness as a dimension of parenting by itself is less straightforward to specify as a predictor of well-being. High monitoring in an atmosphere of low support is likely to be a negative factor; however, lack of monitoring in itself might also be linked with poor outcomes.

Stresses and Resources

Another framework for taking an overview of children's situations focuses on the *balance* between positive and negative factors in their lives. Amato has suggested that individual children's situations can be better understood and outcomes predicted if we know what aspects of their lives are stresses, and what are resources for them (Amato, 1993). This allows the inclusion of both human (e.g. relationship) and material (e.g. economic resources) factors. Other writers, for example Rutter, conceptualize this balance as risk and protective factors (Rutter, 1987). For both risk and protection, there are three main sources of influence. *Individual* or *child-based factors* include temperament, genetic makeup, cognitive factors, and (a risk factor) being male. *Sociocultural factors* encompass socioeconomic status and household income, neighborhood characteristics, school factors, and peer groups. *Family factors* include cohesion and support, conflict, discipline methods, sibling relationships, and parental mental health (Deater-Deckard & Dunn, 1999). In the context of this book, family transitions are likely to include risks particularly in sociocultural and family domains. In some cases, though, transitions may be protective for children by removing them from conflicted or violent households or by restoring levels of household income.

Some risk and protective factors precede a family transition and are cumulative by interacting with currently occurring factors. Those that are brought to a transition include age, gender, genetically linked characteristics, the impact of previous experiences, and "selection" factors associated with household change. There are, for example, circumstances known to put parents at risk for separation such as young age at partnership or marriage, low educational levels, and socioeconomic disadvantage (Fergusson et al., 1984; McLanahan & Sandefur, 1994; Hanson et al., 1996). Similarly, adults and children forming stepfamilies are very likely to have experienced elevated levels of conflict, parenting difficulties, a drop in household income, and high levels of psychological stress in parents, as a result of having gone through a parental separation. Human agency in general encompasses antecedent factors, whereas concurrent factors include many of the contextual elements mentioned earlier, such as family relationships, present conflict, and family-community links. Current household income is also a key component of the context in which families live.

Because a stresses and resources perspective overlaps with several aspects of other frameworks, it is difficult to make precise predictions, although the apparent simplicity of adding factors on either side of the balance is beguiling. However, as Amato (1993) points out, there are interactions between stresses and resources such that the presence of one resource, for example a supportive parent, may compensate for low household income. The total configuration of stresses and resources is important for assessing a child's situation; it does not, though, help to make precise predictions about children's well-being in the medium and long terms.

Overview

The lens through which we view families and family change is fashioned by several influences. These include the time in which we live, and the social conditions and attitudes that are dominant in that era. They also include the paradigms, both implicit and explicit, within which we think about families and children. Perhaps most influential are our own experiences and value systems. Another crucial influence is, or should be, the input of research findings; although, as we noted earlier, scholars may bring their own perspectives to bear on their work. It is a major challenge for researchers, commentators, professionals, and writers to be aware of particular subjective frameworks and to test theories against available evidence.

The frameworks we have discussed in this chapter overlap with each other, and the distinctions we have made between them are at times arbitrary. We can, though, take some generalizations from them. Trauma theories suggest, for example, that single events constitute a major risk for children and that divorce, in particular, causes the risks and problems children face. This perspective is sympathetic with the conservative view that we outlined in chapter 1, although a conservative position would also include the likelihood that separation *precipitates* a chain of subsequent events and conditions in a causal way, so that a life-course process begins at that point. It would also acknowledge the importance of the social context in which families live, and would see legal frameworks, for instance, as pivotal in affecting the lives of families. The agency of children would receive less acknowledgment since families, in a conservative view, function better with clear lines of authority starting with a father. Similarly, authoritative parenting that encourages psychological autonomy might fit uneasily with a conservative perspective.

Life-course frameworks provide an understanding of developmental trajectories over time, including family contexts before parental separation. They allow for the interplay between a multiplicity of factors, and include the possibility that separation might be a positive event for children – a position with which a liberal perspective would have more sympathy. The life-course perspective also emphasizes the potential for developmental trajectories to be modified either by characteristics of children themselves or by external factors. The contribution of children to parent–child relationships and to their development is more readily acknowledged by liberal than by conservative perspectives. There is then, a flexibility and complexity in life-course frameworks that is more in tune with liberal perspectives on family change.

The rest of this book will discuss evidence from research that addresses families and family transitions, as it relates to some of these questions. In chapter 8 we will evaluate the frameworks discussed in light of the research described.

3

Family Transitions and
Outcomes for Children

*Only fanatics can continue to deny that divorce has harmful effects
on children. . . . If this were a medical disease, it would prompt
demands for a national campaign of eradication.*
Editorial, the Telegraph, June 24, 1998

Divorce is the single greatest liberator of our times.
Polly Toynbee, the Guardian, June 24, 1998

Introduction

The fundamental question that is most often asked about family transitions is whether they harm children. The belief that divorce and stepfamily
living is harmful underpins the perspective of conservative commentators
who see these transitions as events that usually cause subsequent problems for children. The liberal view is that there are few differences between children in original and separated families, and that any differences
that might exist are too trivial to be important. A second aspect of the
liberal perspective is that where differences are shown, they are not caused
by the *event* of parental separation. Both conservative and liberal perspectives cannot be right; however, the differences between them are
often in degrees of emphasis. In this chapter we turn directly to research
that addresses outcomes for children, as a way of bringing information to
the debate. We will look at what differences may exist, and later, in chapter 8, will consider the possible causes of the differences.

We noted in chapter 2 that researchers are not immune from the intrusion of their own value systems into their work, and that questions are
often asked and data interpreted within their particular subjective frameworks. However, a consideration of a wide range of studies carried out in
several countries, from within a variety of disciplines, and over a period
of time spanning a large part of the twentieth century, enables us to take

a comparatively objective perspective on outcomes for children. Paradoxically, another important strength in this regard for many of the studies considered is that they were not established with the intention of addressing questions about family transitions. They cannot then be accused of biased sample selection or data collection.

An important first step is to construct an accurate picture of the differences that exist between those who experience transitions and those who do not. The basic question is whether or not children fare less well if brought up in families that depart from the structure of two original parents living with their own children. There are several ways in which this question can be elaborated further. The first is to consider the magnitude of any differences between children from different types of families. The second is to identify the particular areas of social, psychological, and physical development where such differences are most evident. And the third is to determine the time course of these differences; for example, do children of separated families show fewer problems after several years have elapsed compared to the time immediately after separation?

Types of study design

Some studies have looked in depth at samples of children from divorced families, and these have provided valuable scientific and practical information, especially where children have been followed up in longitudinal studies (Wallerstein & Kelly, 1980; Wallerstein & Blakeslee, 1989). However, they have limitations if they do not include a comparison group of children who remain with their original families. A large number of individual studies have made such comparisons and there are several excellent reviews of their findings (Amato, 1993; Emery, 1999; Hetherington & Stanley-Hagan, 1999). Two meta-analyses published in 1991, predominantly of research from the United States, covered 92 and 37 studies of childhood and adult outcomes respectively (Amato & Keith, 1991a, 1991b). There have been many more studies since that time and further studies have been conducted in other countries (Rodgers & Pryor, 1998; Amato, 2000). These research studies fall into three main types, although there are variations within each of these general categories.

First are studies that use samples from the general population and identify children who have experienced parental separation. The children are often subdivided into those now living in lone-parent families and those in stepfamilies. These studies have become more economical to carry out in recent times because of the increased divorce rate.

The second type of study selects a sample, perhaps obtained through court records, of families that have experienced divorce or are going through divorce proceedings, and then recruits a comparison group of intact original families. For example, children matched on age and sex may be selected from the same schools attended by the children from the divorced families. Usually these studies, sometimes called prospective case-control studies, have roughly equal numbers of children from divorced and intact families.

Third are true (or retrospective) case-control studies. These start by recruiting samples of children or adults with particular problems (cases), such as serious behavioral disorders, and a comparison group (controls), and then collect information to see whether the cases have a greater frequency of having experienced parental separation. Usually these studies are interested in a range of risk factors and not just parental divorce.

These three types of studies have different strengths and weaknesses. General population studies have the advantage of using representative samples and therefore give a more accurate picture of circumstances in a particular country or region. Their main weakness is that they are usually general-purpose studies and they typically do not have the depth of information on changes in family structure or on family processes collected by more specialized studies. Prospective case-control studies have the advantages of requiring fewer participants (especially when divorce rates were lower than at present) and being more specialized, but it is harder to obtain representative samples. Families going through the stress of divorce may be reluctant to participate in research, when approached through the courts, and will be more difficult to trace if contact is delayed. An alternative is to identify children from divorced families in some other way, such as through the school system.

Retrospective case-control studies are especially suited to studying a comparatively rare but identifiable outcome, such as suicide, criminal behavior, or serious mental health problems requiring professional intervention. There are limitations to the type and quality of information that can be obtained, particularly when relating to long-past events and circumstances. There may be inherent bias, too, when samples are identified from administrative sources, for instance if children of divorced families are more likely to be referred for treatment or are dealt with in a discriminatory way by the criminal justice system.

In practice, researchers have used a number of variants and refinements of these three basic study designs. The most prominent and useful (applied to the first two study types) is to introduce a longitudinal component, by following the same families over time. This allows further important questions to be addressed regarding factors that influence the longer-term outcomes for children after separation. Longitudinal studies of general population samples are particularly valuable, because some families that were together at the start of the investigation separate during the period of follow up. The outcomes for children from these families can therefore be compared *before* as well as after separation with the outcomes for children from families that stay together throughout the study.

We will not provide here a comprehensive review of all the studies carried out in this area, but can refer readers to previous accounts of studies conducted in North America, the United Kingdom, Australia and New Zealand (Amato & Keith, 1991a, 1991b; Rodgers, 1996b, 1998; Rodgers & Pryor, 1998). We will, instead, describe the findings of key studies that represent the breadth of research across countries, over recent historical time, and covering the variety of measures that have been used to assess outcomes, both in childhood and in the adult years. Preference will be given to studies using samples representative of their target populations, with sufficiently large numbers of participants to yield reliable findings, and employing accurate and valid measures of important aspects of development. These are grouped into seven categories of outcomes: (1) social and emotional behavior in childhood and adolescence; (2) education and socioeconomic attainment; (3) aggressive, antisocial and criminal behavior; (4) substance use; (5) physical health and development; (6) mental health; and (7) family and intimate relationships in adolescence and adulthood (including leaving home, getting married, and having children).

We acknowledge that this categorization has a degree of arbitrariness. It could be argued that substance abuse is linked with antisocial behavior and these areas should, therefore, be grouped together. But no classification would be perfect in this respect and many of the outcomes covered are interrelated to some extent. There are particular reasons for dealing separately with childhood social and emotional behavior and adult mental health, even though some researchers have considered these as being equivalent outcomes that apply at different ages (Cherlin et al., 1998). The label "internalizing" problems or disorders has been used to apply both to withdrawn or shy behavior in childhood and to depression, anxiety and general psychological distress in adulthood. However, longitudinal studies of clinical disorders in children show that internalizing disorders are only weakly associated with adult depressive and anxiety disorders (Morris et al., 1954; Cunningham et al., 1956; Robins, 1966). The continuity found is far less than that for externalizing problems (aggression, antisocial behavior and delinquency) or conduct disorders (Rutter, 1972; Robins, 1979). Similarly, assessments by parents or teachers of children's internalizing behavior are also very poor predictors of adult mental health problems (Rodgers, 1990b). Reports of depression and moodiness from children themselves (especially in later childhood and adolescence) are better predictors of adult depression and anxiety, but these seem to reflect a different dimension of behavior from those obtained through teacher or parent ratings (Rodgers, 1990b).

Children after Divorce: Medium- and Long-term Outcomes

Findings from research studies in each of the areas identified are summarized in seven corresponding tables (tables 3.1–3.7, which are clustered at the end of this chapter). For every outcome in the studies selected, the original results have been used to calculate statistics known as "effect sizes." These are standardized methods of expressing the size of difference found between children from intact families and separated families. The technique allows us to compare the effect sizes obtained from different studies, where different designs and different measures have been used. In each row of the tables, the effect size is given using a rating system, such that plus signs indicate children from intact families have better outcomes than children from separated families and minus signs indicate the opposite. A simple guide to this rating system is given in more detail in the following section, along with the key to some abbreviations used throughout the tables, and a more detailed guide to the effect size statistics is provided in the Appendix preceding the tables (see pages 73–4).

Guide to tables

In tables 3.1–3.7, studies are listed in the order of the average date of birth of the participants who were raised in separated and intact families, so that the first studies involved earlier born individuals (i.e. older cohorts). Within each study, results are ordered in accordance with the mean age of participants at the time the particular outcomes were assessed. The design of individual studies is assumed to be based on a general population sample, unless it is specified as prospective case-control (PCC), true case-control (CC), or nested case-control (NCC). For the latter, the size of sample given is the number of *cases* only. Some studies present findings separately for different subgroups of their samples. Most often this applies to males (M) and females (F), but there are also instances in US research where data have been analyzed separately for Black (B), White (W), and Hispanic groups (H). Most outcomes in these studies are obtained from participants' self-reports or from some independent assessment, diagnosis, or administrative classification. However, other measures come from such sources as parents (P) or schoolteachers (T).

A detailed key to the categorization of effect sizes is given in the Appendix preceding the tables, but a relatively simple way to gain an understanding of the several levels of effect size is given in the table below, where it is assumed that a particular adverse outcome is normally found in 10 percent of children from intact families. The column headed "Range of differences" shows the range of percentages for such an outcome in children from separated families that corresponds to each band of effect size. For example, studies marked with "++" are those where between 17.0 and 23.4 percent of children from separated families show a poor outcome compared with 10 percent of children from intact families.

Effect size categories	Range of differences
—	3.8–5.4% vs. 10%
–	5.5–7.3% vs. 10%
0	7.4–13.3% vs. 10%
+	13.4–16.9% vs. 10%
++	17.0–23.4% vs. 10%
+++	23.5–33.7% vs. 10%
++++	33.8–55.4% vs. 10%

Social and emotional behavior in childhood

Studies that have compared children from separated and intact families in respect of social and emotional behavior during childhood and adolescence are summarized in table 3.1. The most obvious feature of the table is that the effect size column shows either zeros or pluses; none of these studies found that children from separated families were doing better than their peers from intact families. With regards to the magnitude of the differences reported, these range up to the band denoted as "++++" but the most common rating is a single "+", with roughly equal numbers of zeros and "++" on either side. Very typical findings are those from the

British 1958 Birth Cohort Study (Ferri, 1984), where 15.5 percent of children from separated families had behavior problems at age 16 compared with 10.0 percent from intact families, and also from the Australian Mater Study of Pregnancy (Najman et al., 1997), where 15.0 percent of children showed withdrawn behavior at age 5 compared with 10.3 percent of those from intact families. The one study that reported findings denoted as "++++" is the Exeter Family Study in the UK. This study is not widely known internationally but, even though described by the authors as only a pilot study, it received a great deal of publicity in the UK when its report was published in 1994 (Cockett & Tripp, 1994). Its standing has remained particularly high in some sections of the media (Phillips, 1998a). As seen in table 3.1, and in some of the later tables presented in this chapter, the effect sizes from the Exeter Family Study are larger than generally seen in other research conducted in the UK or elsewhere. This may be, in part at least, because the report from this study was selective in presenting detailed results whenever findings indicated a disadvantage for children from separated families, but omitted figures or tables for nonsignificant results. It could also be that the greater than expected differences were chance findings. The sample size was relatively small, even taking account of the study's prospective case-control design, and the margin of error in the results is therefore greater than those for other investigations.

No clear pattern emerges when looking across the range of outcome measures used in research investigating social and emotional behavior. Differences of similar magnitude have been found for a diverse set of behaviors including bed-wetting, withdrawn behavior, habit behaviors (such as nail-biting), social/attentional problems, and other mixed social/emotional problems. There is some suggestion that effect sizes are larger for outcomes reflecting receipt of treatment compared with direct measures of behavior. The strongest example (+++) is the early case-control study of Child Guidance Clinic children carried out in Cambridge (UK) during the Second World War (Banister & Ravden, 1944, 1945). It is possible, therefore, that experience of parental separation increases the likelihood of referral for behavior problems, above and beyond the increased presence of the difficulties themselves. It is also possible, of course, that some referrals are a result of short-term influences of separation on behavior and distress.

There is no indication from table 3.1 of any trend in effect sizes from earlier-born to later-born cohorts, nor any indication of systematic differences between younger and older children. There is also no evidence for a difference in effect sizes across the countries represented in the table, the UK, the US, and Australia.

Education and socioeconomic outcomes in adulthood

Table 3.2 presents the findings from studies looking at educational outcomes in childhood and adulthood and at adult socioeconomic attainment. Again, no studies reported that children from separated families did better in these respects than children from intact families, whereas all but one study (Amato & Booth, 1991) found evidence that children from separated families were disadvantaged. Overall, effect sizes in this area were a little larger than those seen for childhood social and emotional problems. Some typical findings were those from the early study carried out by Nye (1957) in Washington, where 13 percent of children from separated families had poor school grades (Ds or Fs) compared with 7 percent from intact families, and the Avon Longitudinal Study of Pregnancy and Childhood (ALSPAC) in the UK (O'Connor et al., 1999b), where 11 percent of women who had experienced parental divorce as children lived in overcrowded housing in adulthood, compared with just 5 percent of other women. An effect size of similar magnitude was also seen in the US High School and Beyond Study (McLanahan & Sandefur, 1994), where 16 percent of children from separated families dropped out of high school compared with 9 percent from intact families.

There is a very notable feature of the information in table 3.2 when comparing effect sizes across different types of measures. It appears that such outcomes as years remaining in school or full-time education, or attainment expressed in terms of final qualifications received, show larger differences between children from separated and intact families by comparison with direct assessments of educational skills (e.g. reading and arithmetical ability). In the instances of the British 1958 and 1970 Birth Cohort Studies (Ferri, 1984; Wadsworth et al., 1985; Kiernan, 1992; Ely et al., 1999) and the US High School and Beyond Study (Zimilies & Lee, 1991; McLanahan & Sandefur, 1994), this distinction was observed within the same samples of students. This pattern is necessarily reflected in comparisons between measures obtained for children of different ages, as final qualifications and years in education can only be obtained from older students, whereas younger students are often assessed by educational testing or reports of progress from teachers. The different effect sizes seen when comparing the two approaches to assessing educational outcomes could reflect extrinsic constraints on children from separated families completing their education (and fulfilling their potential). These include the lack of socioeconomic and other resources in such families that facilitate full-time study, and the greater likelihood that children who have experienced parental separation will leave the parental home at an early age (see table 3.7).

As with the studies of childhood social and emotional problems, there is no indication that effect sizes for educational and socioeconomic outcomes have increased or diminished over successive generations. The study by Ely and her colleagues (1999), using the three British Birth Cohort Studies, addressed this issue by direct comparison and concluded that there had been no significant historical trend for cohorts born from 1946 to 1970. Again, the magnitude of differences between children from separated and intact families appears fairly robust across geographical locations.

Aggressive, antisocial, and criminal behavior

Of all the measures in all of the studies summarized in table 3.3, there were only two instances where children from separated families were better off than those from intact families (Whitehead, 1979; Rodgers, 1994). In one of these two instances, the finding for aggression in girls aged 13 in the British 1946 Birth Cohort Study was counterbalanced by a finding in the opposite direction for antisocial behavior in the same girls subsequently assessed at age 15 (Rodgers, 1994). Such negative findings are best viewed as anomalous and arising by chance. Overall, the magnitude of effect sizes for aggressive, antisocial, and delinquent behavior are again rather modest. The most typical findings for the US were from the National Health Examination Survey of 1966–70, where 15 percent of adolescents from separated families had had two or more contacts with the law compared with 8 percent of their peers from intact families, and the National Survey of Children 1976–87, where equivalent figures for ever being suspended or expelled were 11.3 percent and 5.4 percent, respectively. For the UK, Sweeting and colleagues' (1998) study in the Glasgow area reported that 10.7 percent of male 18-year-olds from separated families had committed theft, compared with 5.5 percent of those from intact families. However, in spite of the median effect size appearing much the same for aggressive and antisocial behavior as had been found for educational and socioeconomic outcomes, there is an indication that the former have a greater proportion of effect sizes rated as "+++," but these are balanced by studies with effect sizes close to zero. Several of the "+++" outcomes were from different follow-ups of the same study – the Cambridge Study in Delinquent Development in the UK, although other studies found comparable effect sizes particularly for criminal behavior.

There is no general tendency in table 3.3 for outcomes indicative of criminal behavior to show greater effect sizes than those seen for non-criminal aggressive or antisocial behavior. There is also no obvious pattern regarding the implications of family separation for severity of offending, although an earlier review did conclude that "the broken home was more strongly related to minor offenses than more serious offenses" (Free, 1991). The US National Surveys of Youth (Rankin, 1983), shown in table 3.3, indicated that parental divorce is linked more with running away from home and truancy rather than criminal acts (Rankin, 1983). However, a British investigation found an equally large effect size for more serious crimes as for relatively trivial offences (Wadsworth, 1979) and these differences were greater than those seen for teachers' assessments of antisocial behavior in the same sample (Rodgers, 1994).

The effect sizes in table 3.3 do not vary systematically with time of birth, age of assessment, or geographical location of the studies. The stability across generations of differences between children from separated and intact families was noted previously by Wells and Rankin (1991) in their meta-analysis of delinquency and broken homes. There is one very striking pattern in the findings, however, in relation to gender. Of 17 instances where studies presented separate findings for male and female members of their samples, only one study reported a "+++" outcome for females, whereas 13 reported effect sizes of this magnitude for males. Of course, aggressive, antisocial, and delinquent behavior is more common in males than females, but this does not in itself explain why differences between children from separated and intact families are larger for males. The statistics used in our tables take into account such differences in base rates. It seems likely, therefore, that males are more susceptible than females to the influence of circumstances surrounding parental separation in relation to aggression, antisocial behavior, and delinquency.

Substance use in adolescence and adulthood

The findings for substance use in adolescence and adulthood are shown in table 3.4. On average they reveal effect sizes that are smaller compared with the previous two tables and similar to those for the social and emotional outcomes in table 3.1. A very typical finding was that from the US National Health Examination Survey 1966–70 (Dornbusch et al., 1985), where 14 percent of women from separated families were found to be regular smokers compared with 9 percent from intact families. Effect sizes of very similar magnitude were also obtained from two national studies where alcohol use was assessed. In the US National Comorbidity Survey (Kessler et al., 1994; Kessler et al., 1997), alcohol dependence (ever in lifetime) was found in 18.2 percent of adults who had experienced parental separation as children compared with 13.1 percent of those from intact original families. In the British 1958 Birth Cohort Study, 18.1 percent of men whose parents had divorced during their childhood were heavy drinkers at age 33 years, compared with 12.2 percent of their peers from intact families (Hope et al., 1998).

Looking across the different forms of substance use covered by these studies, it appears that effect sizes are larger for use of illicit substances than for use of tobacco, alcohol, and analgesics. The median effect size for the latter fell at the lower end of the "+" range, whereas it was a little into the "++" range for illicit substances. Alcohol use has been assessed in a number of different ways across several studies, including the simple distinction between drinking and not drinking, typical consumption level (usually in a one-week period), identifying heavy drinking or other signs of abuse, and indications of dependence. However, there seems to be no systematic difference in effect sizes for different methods of assessment.

As has often been the case for other outcomes, the differences between children from separated and intact families seem invariant across generations, age at assessment, and geographical locations. There is an exception to this pattern, however, specifically for alcohol use. Studies of teenagers and young adults (up to their mid-twenties) typically find no differences in drinking between those from separated families and those from intact families, whereas studies of samples aged over 30 years find, on average, differences corresponding to the middle of the "+" range. This divergence was observed in one longitudinal study where the participants were assessed at age 23, when effect sizes were found to be very small, and then again at age 33, when effect sizes were noticeably larger (Estaugh & Power, 1991; Hope et al., 1998). This gradual emergence in adulthood of risk associated with parental separation appears to fit the criteria for the notion of a "sleeper effect" (Hetherington, 1972; Wallerstein & Corbin, 1989; Rodgers, 1994), although substance use is not usually discussed in this context.

Physical health and development in childhood and adulthood

Fewer studies have examined physical health outcomes for children from separated and intact families, by comparison with investigations of social and psychological outcomes. The nature of the outcomes (table 3.5) is also more diverse in this area than in the areas covered by previous tables, ranging from use of health services in early childhood (e.g. immunizations for infectious diseases) through to self-reported illness and disability in adulthood. There is, therefore, less justification for considering the average effect size for these outcomes. Generally, however, the magnitude of differences between children who experienced parental separation and those from intact families is smaller than seen for social and psychological outcomes. The most typical finding would be from the US National Health Interview Survey on Child Health (Dawson, 1991), which reported that 17.5 percent of children from separated families had suffered an accidental injury in the past year compared with 13.4 percent of their peers. Again, it is notable that the effect sizes from the UK Exeter Family Study (Cockett & Tripp, 1994) were substantially larger than those found in other investigations in this field.

One report that could not be reanalyzed to suit the format of the table – from the Terman Life Cycle Study (Tucker et al., 1997) – found increased mortality rates in adults who had experienced parental separation as children, so the pattern seen in table 3.5 may also hold for more serious outcomes, such as premature death. Generally, however, there are insufficient studies of physical health and development to be able to draw conclusions as to whether any specific outcome measures reveal greater effects than other measures.

As was found for social and psychological outcomes, there is no indication that effect sizes vary over historical time or geographical location for physical health and development. There is also a dearth of such studies looking at outcomes in adulthood.

Mental health and well-being in adolescence and adulthood

The traditional interest in parental loss as a factor contributing to poor adult mental health produced some very early research in this area, especially studies that used retrospective case-control designs and focused on more serious mental health problems leading to specialist treatment. Many of these early studies were concerned more with parental death than with divorce, simply because the former was more common at the time, and often the reports did not distinguish between different types of loss (Granville-Grossman, 1968). However, several studies did separately identify loss due to marital breakdown (Oltman et al., 1952; Koller & Williams,

1974; Roy, 1978, 1985). Case-control studies continue to be important in this area, especially for rare outcomes such as serious suicide attempts (Beautrais et al., 1996), but there have also been many investigations using large general population samples, such as the US National Comorbidity Survey (Kessler et al., 1994; Kessler et al., 1997).

The effect sizes shown in table 3.6 are very similar in magnitude to those described earlier for educational and socioeconomic outcomes, and also for aggressive and antisocial behavior. The most typical finding for mental health outcomes came from the Avon Longitudinal Study of Pregnancy and Childhood (O'Connor et al., 1999b) in the UK. High depression scores were found for 17 percent of the mothers in this study who had experienced parental separation during childhood compared with 12 percent of the mothers who had not.

Studies in this area tend to focus on outcomes within the sphere of "negative affect," i.e. depression, anxiety, worry, and general psychological distress, and so there is little scope for considering variations in effect sizes across different outcome measures. Some studies in table 3.6 included assessments of positive affect, i.e. life satisfaction and happiness, and the differences between children from separated and intact families for such measures appear a little smaller than those for negative affect measures. However, more studies would be needed to establish whether there is a true variation in this respect.

Similarly, there have been too few studies of adolescents to compare adequately the relevant effect sizes with those for adults. As mentioned earlier, studies of children and adolescents have tended to utilize measures based on teacher or parent ratings (see table 3.1) rather than self-reports of mood and distress. The existing studies that have obtained self-reports from teenagers show rather varied findings.

Yet again, the overall pattern of results in table 3.6 indicates the invariant nature of effect sizes across time and place. Two studies, one in the US (McLeod, 1991) and one in the UK (Rodgers, 1994), did report larger differences in depression for women than for men, and both confirmed this with statistical tests of interactions between parental separation and gender. Although these studies had large and representative samples, however, this pattern of results has not been replicated in other research, and several reports have described similar effect sizes in men and women.

Family and intimate relationships in adolescence and adulthood

Findings relating to family and intimate relationships in adolescence and early adulthood are summarized in table 3.7. The effect sizes for these outcomes are larger than those for all the other areas covered in previous tables, with over half falling into the "++" and "+++" bands. The most typical findings included McLanahan and Sandefur's (1994) results from the US Panel Study of Income Dynamics, where 13 percent of women from divorced families of origin had a nonmarital birth compared with 5 percent of women from intact original families. In the UK National Survey of Sexual Attitudes and Lifestyles, Kiernan and Hobcraft (1997) found that 15 percent of men who had experienced parental divorce, had their first child before age 22, compared with 8 percent of men who did not experience parental divorce.

Looking across different outcome measures, the effect sizes are rather larger for having children at a younger age than for entering partnerships (including marriage) at an early age, or for self-reported quality of marital relationships. The largest effect sizes, however, are for own divorce in adulthood, with 12 out of 14 falling into the "++" and "+++" bands.

Outcomes in the family and intimate relationships area follow the established pattern of showing similar effect sizes over different cohorts and different countries. They are also very similar for males and females.

Children from separated and intact families: summary

The overriding impression from this compendium of studies, spanning several domains of outcomes, is that differences between children from separated and intact families are seen in all areas considered as important aspects of individual social, psychological, and physical development, but the size of these differences is not large. There is some variation in the strength of relationships observed, these being somewhat weaker for childhood social and emotional behavior and for substance abuse in adolescence and adulthood, and somewhat stronger for family and intimate relationships in adolescence and adulthood. Children from separated families typically have from one-and-a-half times to double the risk of an adverse outcome compared to children from intact original families. For some outcomes, patterns of results vary with the age or gender of participants but, generally, findings are remarkably robust across time, geographical location, and subgroups within the populations studied. The disadvantages associated with parental separation are not only seen in childhood but are notably persistent. There are even circumstances, such as alcohol use, where effect sizes appear larger later in adulthood. The larger differences seen for outcomes in the domain of family and intimate relationships are also more pertinent in adult life than childhood, and this adds to the seeming divergence between children from different family types as they grow older.

Although the magnitude of overall differences between children from separated and intact families is very modest, such differences can still be of immense importance at the population level in terms of the implications for services and other social costs of poor outcomes. This is especially so in recent times because of the greater proportion of children who experience parental separation. Other forms of childhood adversity, such as physical or sexual abuse, may be far more detrimental for the individuals concerned, but their impact may not be so important at the population level because of the relative rarity of their occurrence. The public health significance of parental separation can be assessed by taking account not just of effect sizes associated with this risk factor but also with the proportion of children who experience family transitions.

A statistical tool used in epidemiology, known as *population attributable risk* (PAR), provides a valuable way of estimating the importance of parental separation for social policy and the cost of providing services. If we assume, as for some outcomes summarized in this chapter, that children from separated families have roughly double the likelihood of having a poor outcome and also that about 25 percent of children experience parental separation (the proportion currently in the UK, Australasia, and Canada) then we can calculate that 1 in 5 occurrences of that poor outcome in the total population is "attributable" to the increased risk seen in the children from separated families, i.e. a PAR of 20 percent. Correspondingly, if the risk in children from separated families could be reduced to the same level as those from intact families then the burden on society of the poor outcome concerned would be reduced by 20 percent. This is far from trivial in terms of services and necessary public expenditure. In Australia, for example, 20 percent of current government expenditure on mental health services corresponds to a reduction of around AUS$500 million per annum, equivalent to over $32 per head of the adult population each year. Adult mental health is just one domain of the outcomes considered in this chapter, and it would be necessary to combine the measures of PAR and public expenditure across all the areas we have considered to arrive at a more comprehensive estimate of costs. Furthermore, such costs are only those falling on the collective public purse and do not include the social and economic burden borne by individual families.

Children and Remarriage: Stepfamilies versus Lone-parent Families

Table 3.8 summarizes studies where children brought up in stepfamilies have been compared with children brought up in lone-parent families. It should be borne in mind that family structure is a dynamic feature for many children, so that such comparisons are often based on a snap-shot of the type of family children are in at the time the outcomes are assessed. An equivalent rating system is used in table 3.8 as in the previous tables, and pluses indicate instances where children in lone-parent families are doing better than children in stepfamilies. The outcomes are not grouped into subject areas because, as the table shows, there is no systematic variation across different domains. The most striking feature of table 3.8 is that a large majority of effect sizes falls into the "0" category (80) and that the majority of the remaining studies are rated as either "+" or "−" (i.e. there is little overall difference in the outcomes for children from stepfamilies and single-parent families). This is in broad agreement with the conclusion of Amato and Keith's (1991b) earlier meta-analysis of childhood outcomes, although the studies reviewed here contain more examples of outcomes where children from lone-parent families are the better off group (37) compared with instances where children from step-families are better off (15).

With such a small overall difference between these two groups of children, there is little opportunity to consider whether effect sizes may vary across generations or countries. There appear to be no trends of this sort in table 3.8. There is also no clear-cut gender difference when looking at the studies that reported separate effect sizes for males and females, although there was some increased likelihood of finding positively rated effects for males (i.e. those from lone-parent families fared better than those from stepfamilies). This small difference is the opposite to that indicated by some studies reviewed by Amato (1993), where he noted several instances where "the presence of a stepfather improves the well-being of boys but either has little effect or decreases the well-being of girls." The evidence on this issue appears inconclusive to date. As Amato (1993) also pointed out, "future research needs to consider the sex of the stepchild *and* the stepparent."

Multiple Transitions

The high likelihood that parents will repartner after divorce, and the relative instability of stepfamilies in comparison with original families, means that children who have experienced one or two transitions are at some risk for further family change (see chapter 1). Do further transitions also increase the chances that children will experience adverse outcomes?

The comparatively few studies that have considered multiple transitions do not always distinguish between two transitions – which usually indicate that a child has gone from an original two-parent to a lone-parent household and then into a stepfamily – and more than two changes, indicating the dissolution of the stepfamily. For example, Najman and colleagues (1997) reported that children whose mothers had changed partners at least once over a 5-year period had 30–60 percent higher rates of behavior problems than those who had lived in stable lone-parent or original families. Many of those children would, though, have been living in stepfamilies.

The total number of family changes is positively associated with levels of offending in 11- to 13-year-olds (Fergusson et al., 1992), and 12-year-olds who have experienced more than two family changes are more likely than those who have none to show disruptive behavior in school (Kurdek et al., 1995). Similarly, children in "redisrupted" families (those who had experienced more than one parental divorce) in the UK reported lower levels of happiness than children from other family types, and lower social self-image than those in original families (Cockett & Tripp, 1994).

Poor educational outcomes are also associated with multiple transitions. Children report more school problems (Cockett & Tripp, 1994), and have lower grades and achievement scores (Kurdek et al., 1995) if they have experienced more than two transitions. There are mixed findings with regard to dropping out of school, with two studies reporting no associations with multiple transitions (McLanahan & Sandefur, 1994; Aquilino, 1996). One study, though, found that those who experienced more than one family change in the previous four years were more likely, when compared with adolescents in original families, to drop out than those who had just one transition (Pong & Ju, 2000). Many of these young people, however, would have entered stepfamilies after a period in a lone-parent family and so would have had two household changes in four years during their adolescence – a time when stepfamily formation is particularly fraught (see chapter 6).

Adolescents who have experienced two or more family transitions are significantly less likely to enter postsecondary education than those in lone-parent families, and are more likely to live independently, to be in the laborforce by the age of 18 (Aquilino, 1996), and to have had an illegitimate child (Wu & Martinson, 1993). In adulthood, those who have experienced more than one parental divorce are comparatively less likely to be close to their mothers, and more likely to have marital problems, marital instability, and to experience their own divorce (Amato & Booth, 1991).

It is apparent from these studies that children and young people who have experienced multiple family transitions are at particularly high risk for adverse outcomes. In comparison with those in original families, stable lone-parent families, and, in many cases, stepfamilies, their education, behavior, and own relationships are more likely to suffer.

Studies of Children Before and After Parental Separation

In the preceding sections we have looked in some detail at the differences in outcomes between children who are currently living or have previously lived in various types of families. However, the picture portrayed is essentially a static one based on analyses where outcomes are examined at only one point in time. An alternative approach, but one that is far less common, is to investigate differences longitudinally. This enables us to tackle important questions that cannot be addressed with cross-sectional information alone, but of course it requires researchers to undertake painstaking studies where children and families are tracked and contacted over a number of years. The crucial issue that concerns us here is whether differences between children in intact original families and those in separated families arise only after the latter group of children experiences the transition of parental separation, or whether they are present in some degree before separation.

Two national longitudinal studies have been especially important in providing answers to this question. They are the 1958 British Birth Cohort study (also known as the National Child Development Study) and the US National Survey of Children (NSC). Each of these studies followed large samples of children over many years; the British study has tracked participants into adulthood. They have routinely collected data on children's outcomes at several stages, and a proportion of each sample experienced parental separation at some point during the follow-up period. This has allowed comparisons to be made between groups of children both before and after separations have occurred. Both studies looked at behavioral problems based on parents' and/or teachers' ratings; the British study also obtained measures of educational achievement. Information from the British study has been independently examined by two research teams and both found that children from separated families did less well on reading and mathematics tests, compared with children from families that stayed together, and also had more behavior problems (Cherlin et al., 1991; Elliott & Richards, 1991a, 1991b). The average differences were not large, being equivalent to a range of about 2 to 5 points on a standardized test (i.e. with a standard deviation of 15 points), and again it should be emphasized that there was substantial overlap in the scores of the two groups. But these differences still mean that children from separated families have a significantly greater chance of obtaining poor scores on educational and behavioral assessments.

The results from the US study were similar, although the girls from separated families were found not to be different from those in intact families once race and socioeconomic status before separation were taken into account (Cherlin et al., 1991). Especially important in the findings from these national studies was that differences between the children of separated and intact families were seen *before* separation, confirming observations made previously from a smaller longitudinal study of children in Berkeley, California (Block et al., 1986). For example, children in the British study who experienced parental separation between the ages of 11 and 16 years already showed disadvantages on the measures obtained when they were just 7 years old (Elliott & Richards, 1991a). Overall, the differences found were similar in magnitude before separation as afterwards, except for mathematics achievement, where the gap between the children for intact and divorced families widened after separation. In other words, factors aside from separation itself, but which are more common in families that separate, contributed to the differences. Furthermore, whatever these factors may be, they have a significant impact several years beforehand. This indicates that specific events precipitating separation or sudden increases in family conflict immediately prior to separation are also not responsible for the differences, but rather that the circumstances present in these families long before separation are important influences on development. Of course, it is possible (and very likely) that individual children are affected by the experience of separation in several respects, including their short-term distress (see chapter 4), but for longer-term outcomes it must be the case that any resulting disadvantages for some children are roughly counterbalanced by benefits for others. Further evidence for this conclusion will be discussed later, in chapter 8, when we also look in detail at what other factors, before and after separation, help explain the differences summarized in tables 3.1 to 3.8.

Other, smaller-scale longitudinal studies have investigated children's progress before and after separation and the findings have been somewhat mixed. Doherty and Needle (1991) measured a number of characteristics in adolescents, initially aged 11–13 years, in 508 families followed up over a 5-year period, and this study also found many differences were present before separation occurred. However, for substance use in boys, the gap between those from disrupted and intact families widened after separation, while for psychological adjustment the gap narrowed after separation.

A study based on the Child Supplement of the US National Longitudinal Survey of Youth examined *changes* in the behavior and educational performance of children over a two-year period, comparing those who remained in an intact family with those who experienced separation in that time (Morrison, 1995). No differences between the groups were found for two measures of reading attainment, either in boys or girls, and no difference was found for behavior problems in girls. Boys, however, were more likely to show worsened behavior if their parents separated (35 percent) than if their parents stayed together (19 percent). As this study only used information collected over two years, it is not possible to say whether this difference reflected short-term distress following separation or whether it would persist over a longer period. A later study of externalizing and internalizing problems in the same sample followed for a further two years concluded, for boys, that "the strongest effects are in evidence when the father has recently exited" (Mott et al., 1997). This may not be such a straightforward issue, however, and findings from the Oregon Divorce Study have suggested that externalizing behavior problems in younger boys continue to increase over time following parental separation, whereas such problems in older boys diminish with time (Forgatch et al., 1996).

One further report, based on the New York Longitudinal Study, adds a further element of complexity into this picture. This study found no significant differences in behavioral adjustment comparing children in always-married families with those in to-be-divorced families, contrary to the findings from several studies outlined above, but it did find significant differences in parental conflict, parental concern, and rejecting behavior (Shaw et al., 1993). This indicates that even when children have similar levels of behavior problems, those that are in to-be-divorced families experience less favorable parenting, and may go on to develop difficulties as a consequence, before separation itself occurs.

Overview

The question, with which we began this chapter, of whether or not family transitions harm children, is only partially answered here. The evidence indicates unequivocally that those children whose parents separate are at significantly greater risk than those whose parents remain together, for a wide range of adverse outcomes in social, psychological, and physical development. Furthermore, the risks are evident across generations and geographical region, and persist into adulthood. A subsequent transition into stepfamily living does not appear to increase the level of risk for children significantly, although the relative paucity of good studies suggests that more, and more sophisticated, examination of this area is needed.

It is always tempting to infer causality from such robust and consistent findings. However, as well as the dangers of concluding that separation causes poor outcomes on the basis of associations, the evidence from longitudinal studies indicates particular caution in coming to this conclusion. Levels of behavior and educational difficulties are higher in children whose parents later separate, than in those whose parents do not; in other words, poor outcomes are in place before separation, suggesting other or additional causes of long-term disadvantage.

How do these findings contribute to the debate between conservative and liberal positions? Undoubtedly, parental separation constitutes a risk for children, but the evidence suggests that it is not *the* major risk factor. Children are not necessarily harmed by family transitions, but neither are transitions benign, risk-free events. In chapter 8 we will return to the question of what factors help to explain poorer outcomes for children who experience family transitions.

Appendix: Guide to Effect Size Statistics in Tables 3.1 to 3.8

The symbols (pluses and minuses) used to denote effect sizes are explained in the following key. The effect size "d" is the difference in mean score between children from separated and intact families expressed as a fraction of the standard deviation of the measure used (i.e. standard scores). The effect size "h" in prospective studies (either general population samples or case-control designs) is obtained from the percentages of particular outcomes found in the two groups, using the *arcsin* transformation of proportions. The same statistic is used for the effect size "h" from true (or retrospective) case-control studies, where the relevant proportions are the percentage of cases and controls that experienced parental separation. The key shows the approximate equivalence of these three indexes. It is not possible to calculate exact translations of these different statistics. For example, the two versions of "h" vary in their relationship to one another, depending on the likelihood of a particular outcome in the population and, to some extent, the likelihood of parental separation. We have estimated equivalent values in the key on the assumption that outcomes investigated in true case-control studies are comparatively rare (i.e. are often around 1 percent in the population or less).

Symbol	d	h (prospective)	h (case-control)
—	−0.55–0.33	−0.27–0.18	???–???
–	−0.32–0.18	−0.17–0.10	???–0.23
0	−0.17–0.17	−0.09–0.10	−0.22–0.22
+	0.18–0.32	0.11–0.20	0.23–0.41
++	0.33–0.55	0.21–0.36	0.42–0.70
+++	0.56–0.86	0.37–0.59	0.71–???
++++	0.87–???	0.60–0.93	???–???

The design of individual studies is assumed to be based on a general population sample, unless it is specified as prospective case-control (PCC), true case-control (CC), or nested case-control (NCC). Other abbreviations used in the table relate to subgroups in the population or to sources of information, as follows: males (M), females (F), Black (B), White (W), Hispanic (H); parents (P), schoolteachers (T).

Table 3.1 Children from separated versus intact families: social and emotional behavior in childhood and adolescence

Reference	Study	D.O.B.	Ages (mean)	N	Outcome	Effect size
Banister & Rauden (1944; 1945)	Children at the Cambridge Child Guidance Clinic and controls from local schools (UK): 1942	1929–36	6–13	112 (CC)	All referrals to Child Guidance	+++
Douglas (1970; 1973); Rodgers (1994)	National Survey of Health and Development – British 1946 Birth Cohort (UK): 1946–61	1946	6	3,393	Bedwetting[a]	++
			8	"	Bedwetting[a]	++
			11	"	Bedwetting[a]	++
			13	1,473	Sociability (M)	0
			"	"	Withdrawn behavior (M, T)	0
			"	"	Habits (M, T)	+
			"	1,489	Sociability (F)	0
			"	"	Withdrawn behavior (F, T)	0
			"	"	Habits (F, T)	0
			15	3,393	Bedwetting (P)[a]	+
			"	1,473	Withdrawn behavior (M, T)	0
			"	"	Habits (M, T)	+
			"	1,489	Withdrawn behavior (F, T)	0
			"	"	Habits (F, T)	0
Whitehead (1979); Ferri (1984)	National Child Development Study – British 1958 Birth Cohort (UK): 1965–91	1958	7	1,400	Withdrawal syndrome (M, P)	0
			"	1,400	Withdrawal syndrome (F, P)	+
			16	5,722	Behavior problems (M, P)	+
			"	"	Behavior problems (M, T)	++
			"	5,445	Behavior problems (F, P)	+
			"	"	Behavior problems (F, T)	+

Table 3.1 (contd)

Reference	Study	D.O.B.	Ages (mean)	N	Outcome	Effect size
Allison & Furstenberg (1989)	National Survey of Children (USA): 1976–81	1965–9	7–11 " " 12–16	1,197	Social/attentional problems (P) Adjustment (T) Distress Distress (P)	+ ++ + 0
Wadsworth et al. (1985)	Child Health and Education Study – British 1970 Birth Cohort (UK): 1975	1970	5	3,543	Withdrawn behavior (P)	0
Zill et al. (1988)	Child Health Supplement to the National Health Interview Survey (US): 1981	1964–78	3–17 4–17	12,373 11,588	Psychological help in past yr Behavior problems index (P)	++ ++
Demo & Acock (1996)	Adolescents of mothers in the National Survey of Families and Households (USA): 1987–8	1969–76	12–18	850	Socioemotional problems (P)	+
Thomson et al. (1994)	Children in the National Survey of Families and Households (USA): 1987–8	1969–83	5–18	3,397	Any behavior problem Internalizing problems Sociability	++ + +

Study	Study details	Years	Age	Sample	Outcome	Effect
Cockett & Tripp (1994)	Exeter Family Study (UK): 1991–2	1977–81	9–14	152 (PCC)	Current or past bed-wetting Low self-esteem Poor social image Unhappiness Unhappiness (P)	++ ++++ +++ +++ ++++
Dawson (1991)	National Health Interview Survey on Child Health (US): 1988	1971–88	0–17	17,110	Bed-wetting in past yr (P) Speech defect in past yr (P) Treated emotional problem (P)	0 0 ++
Zubrick et al. (1995)	Western Australian Child Health Survey: 1993	1977–89	4–16	2,737	Any mental health problem	++
Najman et al. (1997)	Mater-University of Queensland Study of Pregnancy (AUS): 1986–9	1981–4	5	5,110	Withdrawn behavior (P) Social/attentional problems (P)	+ +
Dunn et al. (1998)	Avon Longitudinal Study of Pregnancy and Childhood (UK): 1991–2	1991–2	4	7,366	Emotional problems (P) Peer problems (P) Social/attentional problems (P)	0 + +

[a] Separations in first 6 years only.

Table 3.2 Children from separated versus intact families: education and adult socioeconomic attainment

Reference	Study	D.O.B.	Ages (mean)	N	Outcome	Effect size
Tucker et al. (1997)	Terman Life Cycle Study – followup of children from schools in California (USA): 1921–1	1910	81–	635 497	Years of education (M) Years of education (F)	++ ++
Illsley & Thompson (1961)	Women having their first pregnancy in Aberdeen (Scotland): 1952–4	1910–36	18–42	2,930	Left school at minimum age Manual job pre-marriage Un-/semi-skilled husband	+++ + ++
Amato & Booth (1991)	Study of Marital Stability over the Lifecourse – national sample of married people (USA): 1988	1917–64	18+	1,243	Years of education Occupational prestige Annual earned income Material assets Economic strain	0 0 0 0 0
Nye (1957)	Grade 9–12 high school students in Washington (USA): pre-1957	1940–3	14–17	780	Poor high school grades	+

Reference	Survey	Year	Age	N	Variable	Effect
Wadsworth & Maclean (1986); Maclean & Wadsworth (1988); Kuh & Maclean (1990); Maclean & Kuh (1991)	National Survey of Health and Development - British 1946 Birth Cohort (UK): 1964–82	1946	18	2,223	Unemployed (M)	0
			26	3,681	Any qualifications	+++
			"	"	"A" level equivalent or more	++
			"	"	University or equivalent	+
			36	1,556	Low income (M)	++
			"	"	Unemployed (M)	++
			"	1,454	Manual occupation (F)	++
			"	"	Partner not working (F)	++
McLanahan & Sandefur (1994)	Adults in the National Survey of Families and Households – older cohort (USA): 1987–8	1943–52	35–44	N.K.	Dropped out of high school	++
Svanum & Bringle (1982)	Health Examination Survey (USA): 1963–5	1952–9	6–11	5,341	WISC vocabulary score (W)	+
				"	WISC block design score (W)	+
				"	WISC intelligence index (W)	+
				"	WRAT reading score (W)	++
				"	WRAT arithmetic score (W)	+
				"	WRAT achievement index (W)	++
				768	WISC vocabulary score (B)	0
				"	WISC block design score (B)	0
				"	WISC intelligence index (B)	0
				"	WRAT reading score (B)	+
				"	WRAT arithmetic score (B)	0
				"	WRAT achievement index (B)	+

Table 3.2 (contd)

Reference	Study	D.O.B.	Ages (mean)	N	Outcome	Effect size
Ferri (1984); Kiernan (1992; 1997)	National Child Development Study – British 1958 Birth Cohort (UK): 1974–91	1958	16	11,340	Reading score	+
			"	"	Mathematics score	+
			23	4,546	Left school at age 16 (M)	++
			"	4,536	Left school at age 16 (F)	++
			33	10,138	Any qualifications	++
			"	"	"O"-level or more	++
			"	"	"A"-level or more	++
			"	5,000	Low earnings (M)	0
			"	"	Low family income (M)	+
			"	"	Unemployed (M)	++
			"	"	Social housing (M)	+
			"	"	Low earnings (F)	0
			"	"	Low family income (F)	+
			"	"	Social housing (F)	++
McLanahan & Sandefur (1994)	Adults in the National Survey of Families and Households (USA) younger cohort: 1987–8	1953–67	20–34	N.K.	Dropped out of high school	++
McLanahan & Sandefur (1994)	Panel Study of Income Dynamics (USA): 1968–89	1956–65	24–33	2,900	Dropped out of high school	++

Reference	Study	Dates	Age	N	Outcome	Effect
O'Connor et al. (1999b)	Avon Longitudinal Study of Pregnancy and Childhood (UK): 1991–2	1935–78	14–46 (28)	11,000	No/minimal qualifications	++
					University degree level	++
					Overcrowded housing	++
McLanahan & Sandefur (1994); Sandefur et al. (1992)	National Longitudinal Survey of Youth (USA): 1979–89	1962–5	20–23	5,246	High School Diploma (HSD)	+++
			"		HSD/Gen. Equiv. Dip.	+++
			"		College attendance	+++
			24–27		Dropped out of high school	+++
Zimiles & Lee (1991); McLanahan & Sandefur (1994)	High School and Beyond Study (USA): 1980–6	1964	16	13,532	Achievement test score (M)	+
			"	"	Achievement test score (F)	+
			"	"	Dropped out of school (M)	++
			18	12,188	Dropped out of school (F)	+++
			"		Achievement test score (M)	0
			"	10,400	Achievement test score (F)	+
			22		Dropped out of high school	++
Allison & Furstenberg (1989); Zill et al. (1993)	National Survey of Children (USA): 1976–87	1965–9	7–11	1,197	Academic difficulty (P)	+
			"		Academic difficulty (T)	+
			"		Academic difficulty (C)	0
			12–16		Academic difficulty (P)	++
			"		Academic difficulty (T)	0
			"		Academic difficulty (C)	0
			18–22		Dropped out of high school	++

Table 3.2 (contd)

Reference	Study	D.O.B.	Ages (mean)	N	Outcome	Effect size
Zill et al. (1988)	Child Health Supplement to the National Health Interview Survey (US):1981	1964–75	6–17	9,502 9,897	Standing in class rating (P) Grade repetition	+ ++
Wadsworth et al. (1985); Ely (1999)	Child Health and Education Study – British 1970 Birth Cohort (UK): 1975–86	1970	5 " 16 "	3,543 " 5,499 5,725	Picture Vocabulary score Copying Designs score Any qualifications Five "O" levels or more	+ + ++ +++
Economic and Policy Analysis Division (1993)	Australian Youth Survey – 19-yr-olds: 1989–91[e]	1970–2	19	3,255	Left school without completing Yr 12 and no further qualifications or study	+++
Sweeting et al. (1995b; 1998)	West of Scotland Twenty-07 Study: 1990	1972	18	430 " " " 478 " " "	Left school early (M) Any qualifications (M) Five "O" grades or more (M) Not in employment (M) Left school early (M) Any qualifications (F) Five "O" grades or more (F) Not in employment (F)	+ +++ ++ + +++ +++ +++ +++

Study	Survey	Years	Age	N	Outcome measure	Effect
Demo & Acock (1996)	Adolescents of mothers in the National Survey of Families and Households (USA): 1987–8	1969–76	12–18	850	School grades (P)	+
Thomson et al. (1994)	Children in the National Survey of Families and Households (USA): 1987–8	1969–83	5–11 12–18	1,645 1,641	Rating in class (P) School grades (P)	+ +
Cockett & Tripp (1994)	Exeter Family Study (UK): 1991–2	1977–81	9–14	152 (PCC)	Difficulties with work Special help at school	++ +++
Dawson (1991)	National Health Interview Survey on Child Health (US): 1988	1971–88	0–17	17,110	Ever repeated a grade (P)	++
Zubrick et al. (1997)	Western Australian Child Health Survey: 1993	1977–89	4–16	2,737	Low academic competence (T)	++

Table 3.3 Children from separated versus intact families: aggressive and antisocial behavior, and delinquency in adolescence and adulthood

Reference	Study	D.O.B.	Ages (mean)	N	Outcome	Effect size
Koller & Castanos (1970; 1974)	Short-term and long-term male prisoners in Sydney (AUS): 1967	1922–47	20–55	374 (CC)	Short-term prisoner (M) Long-term prisoner (M)	+ +
Nye (1957)	Grade 9–12 high school students in Washington (USA): pre-1957	1940–3	14–17	780	Delinquency	++
Douglas (1970, 1973); Rodgers (1994); Wadsworth (1979)	National Survey of Health and Development – British 1946 Birth Cohort (UK): 1946–67	1946	13 " " " 15 " 17 21 "	1,473 " 1,489 " 1,473 1,489 2,300 2,291 "	Aggression (M) Antisocial behavior (M, T) Aggression (F) Antisocial behavior (F, T) Antisocial behavior (M, T) Antisocial behavior (F, T) Delinquency (M) Delinquency (M) More serious crime (M)	0 ++ – 0 + + ++ ++ ++
Kolvin et al. (1988)	Newcastle Thousand Family Study (UK): 1947–81	1947	15 33 "	404	Criminal offence by 15 yrs (M) First offence after 15 yrs (M) All offences by 33 yrs (M)	+++ 0 +++

Study	Description	Year	Age	N	Measure	Rating
Koller (1971)	Delinquent girls at institutional training school in Sydney (AUS): 1967	1950–1	16–17	121 (CC)	Delinquency (F)	++
Gibson (1969); West & Farrington (1973, 1977); Juby & Farrington (2001)	Cambridge Study in Delinquent Development (UK): 1961–94	1953	14	411	Delinquency (M)	+++
			15	"	Police record (M)	+++
			18–19	389	Delinquency (M)	+++
			40	409	Juvenile conviction (M)	+++
			"	"	Adult conviction only (M)	+++
Dornbusch et al. (1985)	National Health Examination Survey (US): 1966–70	1949–58	12–17	3,145	Contact with law (M)	++
				"	2+ contacts with law (M)	++
				"	Arrested (M)	++
				"	School discipline problem (M)	++
				"	Truancy (M)	++
				2,857	Runaway (M)	+
				"	Contact with law (F)	+
				"	2+ contacts with law (F)	0
				"	Arrested (F)	+
				"	School discipline problem (F)	++
				"	Truancy (F)	+
				"	Runaway (F)	0
Bell & Champion (1979)	Delinquents in institutions in New South Wales (AUS): 1972–3	1953–8	15–19	214 (CC)	Delinquency	+++

Table 3.3 (contd)

Reference	Study	D.O.B.	Ages (mean)	N	Outcome	Effect size
Rankin (1983)	National Surveys of Youth (USA): 1967 & 1972	1951–61	11–18	2,242	Run away	++
					Truancy	++
					Fighting	+
					Vandalism	0
					Theft	0
					Trespass	0
					Auto theft	0
					Entry	0
					Assault	0
					Threat	0
Kalter et al. (1985)	National Survey of Youth (USA): 1972	1954–61	11–18	522	Truancy (F)	+++
					Larceny (F)	++
Whitehead (1979)	National Child Development Study – British 1958 Birth Cohort (UK): 1965–91	1958	7	1,400	Hostility to adults (M, T)	++
			"	"	Hostility to children (M, T)	++
			"	"	Destructive (M, P)	++
			"	1,400	Hostility to adults (F, T)	0
			"	"	Hostility to children (F, T)	–
			"	"	Destructive (F, P)	0

Reference	Study	Birth years	Age	N	Outcome	Result
Peterson & Zill (1986); Allison & Furstenberg (1989); Zill et al. (1993)	National Survey of Children (USA): 1976–87	1965–9	7–11	1,197	Conduct problems (T)	++
			12–16	"	Conduct problems (P)	++
			"	"	Conduct problems (T)	0
			"	"	Conduct problems (P)	+
			"	"	Delinquency (P)	++
			"	"	Delinquency	0
			"	526	School discipline (M, P)	++
			"	"	Suspended or expelled (M, P)	++
			"	546	School discipline (F, P)	+
			"	"	Suspended or expelled (F, P)	+
			18–22	1,049	Conduct problems (P)	++
			"	"	Delinquency	0
Wadsworth et al. 1985	Child Health and Education Study – British 1970 Birth Cohort (UK): 1975–86	1970	5	3,543	Antisocial behavior (P)	0
Sweeting et al. (1998)	West of Scotland Twenty-07 Study: 1987–90	1972	18	430	Vandalism/violence ever (M)	++
				"	Theft ever (M)	++
				"	Police trouble 16–18 yrs (M)	0
				478	Vandalism/violence ever (F)	+
				"	Theft ever (F)	+
				"	Police trouble 16–18 yrs (F)	+

Table 3.3 (contd)

Reference	Study	D.O.B.	Ages (mean)	N	Outcome	Effect size
Thomson et al. (1994)	Children in the National Survey of Families and Households (USA): 1987–8	1969–83	5–18	3,295	Conduct problems (P)	+
Cockett & Tripp (1994)	Exeter Family Study (UK): 1991–2	1977–81	9–14	152 (PCC)	Truancy/school refusal (P)	++
Dawson (1991)	National Health Interview Survey on Child Health (US): 1988	1971–88	0–17	17,110	Ever expelled/suspended (P)	++
Najman et al. (1997)	Mater-University of Queensland Study of Pregnancy (AUS): 1986–9	1981–4	5	5,110	Aggressive behavior (P)	+
Dunn et al. (1998)	Avon Longitudinal Study of Pregnancy and Childhood (UK): 1991–2	1995–6	4	7,366	Conduct problems (P)	0

Table 3.4 Children from separated versus intact families: substance use in adolescence and adulthood

Reference	Study	D.O.B.	Ages (mean)	N	Outcome	Effect size
Tucker et al. (1997)	Terman Life Cycle Study – followup of children from schools in California (USA): 1921–91	1910	81–	372 " 352 "	Ever smoked (M) Heavy smoker (M) Ever smoked (F) Heavy smoker (F)	+ 0 +++ +++
Oltman et al. (1952)	Patients admitted to state hospital psychiatric service in Newtown, Connecticut (USA): 1946–50	1896–1932	18–50	200 (CC)	Alcoholic states	0
Koller & Castanos (1969); Koller & Williams (1974)	Patients at a special clinic for alcoholism in Sydney (AUS): 1967–8	Pre-1950	18+	210 (CC)	Treatment for alcoholism	+
Kuh & Maclean (1990); Maclean & Kuh (1991)	National Survey of Health and Development – British 1946 Birth Cohort (UK): 1982	1946	36	1,052 1,500	Heavy drinkers (F) Current smoker (F)	++ ++

Table 3.4 *(contd)*

Reference	Study	D.O.B.	Ages (mean)	N	Outcome	Effect size
Tennant et al. (1975)	US Army soldiers stationed in former West Germany: 1971	1947–53	18–24 (22.8)	5,044	Regular alcohol use	0
					Heavy alcohol use	0
					Marijuana use ever	0
					Weekly marijuana use	0
					Amphetamine use ever	+++
					Weekly amphetamine use	++
					Opiate use ever	+
					Weekly opiate use	+
Dornbusch et al. (1985)	National Health Examination Survey (US): 1966–70	1949–58	12–17	3,145	Regular smoker (M)	+
				2,857	Regular smoker (F)	+
Bell & Champion (1979)	Students in high school and other educational and training colleges in New South Wales (AUS): 1971–3	1952–8	15–19 (17.0)	6,999	Current smoker	+
					Current drinker	0
					Analgesic use	0
					Sedative use	+
					Marijuana use	++
					Hallucinogen use	++
					Stimulant use	+
					Narcotic use	+

Study	Description	Year	Age	N	Measure	Rating
Kessler et al. (1994, 1997)	National Comorbidity Survey (USA): 1990–2	1937–76	15–54	8,098	Alcohol abuse not dependence	+
					Alcohol dependence	+
					Drug abuse not dependence	+
					Drug dependence	++
Cowan & Roth (1972)	Public school students (Grades 6–12) in Southeast Michigan (USA): 1971	1954–61	11–18	4,101	Illicit drug use	++
Kalter et al. (1985)	National Survey of Youth (USA): 1972	1954–61	11–18	522	Marijuana use (F)	++
					Other illicit drug use (F)	++
Estaugh & Power (1991); Hope et al. (1998)	National Child Development Study – British 1958 Birth Cohort (UK): 1981 & 1991	1958	23	11,500	Heavy drinking (M)	0
			"		Average consumption (M)	0
			"		Heavy drinking (F)	0
			"		Average consumption (F)	0
			33		Heavy drinking (M)	+
			"		Average consumption (M)	+
			"		Heavy drinking (F)	+
			"		Average consumption (F)	+
Tennant & Bernardi (1988)	Heroin addicts from an in-patient drug clinic in Sydney (AUS): 1986	1960	(25.6)	70 (CC)	Treatment for heroin addiction	++

Table 3.4 *(contd)*

Reference	Study	D.O.B.	Ages (mean)	N	Outcome	Effect size
Sourindhrin & Baird (1984)	Children at clinic for solvent misuse in Glasgow (Scotland): 1978–9	1962–70	9–17 (13.6)	134 (CC)	Attending solvent abuse clinic	++
Ely et al. (2000)	Child Health & Education Study – British 1970 Birth Cohort (UK): 1986	1970	16	6,259 6,081	Current smoker Current drinker	++ 0
Sweeting & West (1995b); Sweeting et al. (1998); Ely (2000)	West of Scotland Twenty-07 Study: 1987–90	1972	15 18	482 " " 527 " " 430 " " 478 " "	Current smoker (M) Current drinker (M) Other drug use ever (M) Current smoker (F) Current drinker (F) Other drug use ever (F) Current smoker (M) Heavy drinker (M) Other drug use ever (M) Current smoker (F) Heavy drinker (F) Other drug use ever (F)	++ 0 ++ ++ – – + 0 0 ++ 0 + +++
Flewelling & Bauman (1990)	School students from household sample in Southeastern US: 1985	1971–3	12–14	2.102	Smoked ever Current smoker Drank alcohol ever Marijuana ever	+ + + ++

Table 3.5 Children from separated versus intact families: physical health and development in childhood and adulthood

Reference	Study	D.O.B.	Ages (mean)	N	Outcome	Effect size
Kulka & Weingarten (1979)	Survey Research Center national general population sample (USA): 1957	Pre-1936	21+	2,051	Physical ill health	0
Kulka & Weingarten (1979)	Survey Research Center national general population sample (USA): 1976	Pre-1955	21+	1,923	Physical ill health	+
Ferri (1984)	National Child Development Study – British 1958 Birth Cohort (UK): 1974–91	1958	16 "	5,577 5,296	School sickness absence (M) School sickness absence (F)	+ ++
Zill et al. (1988)	Child Health Supplement to the National Health Interview Survey (US): 1981	1964–75	6–17	9,502 9.897	School sickness absence (P) Rating of health/disability (P)	0 +
Wadsworth et al. (1983); Ely et al. (2000)	Child Health and Education Study – British 1970 Birth Cohort (UK): 1975–88	1970	5 " " " " " " 15–18	3,543 " " " " " " 3,696	Any accident (P) 2+ accidents (P) Admission for accident (P) Head injury (P) Burns and scalds (P) Suspected poisoning (P) High physical symptoms	+ + + 0 0 0 0

Table 3.5 (contd)

Reference	Study	D.O.B.	Ages (mean)	N	Outcome	Effect size
Ely et al. (2000)	West of Scotland Twenty-07 Study: 1990	1972	15	984	High physical symptoms	0
Cockett & Tripp (1994)	Exeter Family Study (UK): 1991–2	1977–81	9–14 "	152 (PCC)	4 or more health problems GP visit in last 6 mths	+++ +++
Dawson (1991)	National Health Interview Survey on Child Health (US): 1988	1977–88	0–17	17,110	Accident/injury in last yr (P) Asthma in last yr (P) Headaches in last yr (P)	+ 0 +
Australian Bureau of Statistics (1992)	National Health Survey (AUS): 1989–90	1983–90	0–6 " " 1–6 1–6	N.K. " " " "	Diptheria/tetanus immunization Whooping cough immunization Polio immunization Measles immunization Mumps immunization	+ + + + ++

Table 3.6 Children from separated versus intact families: mental health in adolescence and adulthood

Reference	Study	D.O.B.	Ages (mean)	N	Outcome	Effect size
Tucker et al. (1997)	Terman Life Cycle Study – follow up of children from schools in California (USA): 1921–50	1910	40	642	Some problems (M)	++
				"	Considerable problems (M)	+
				548	Life satisfaction (M)	0
				502	Some problems (F)	++
				"	Considerable problems (F)	+
				442	Life satisfaction (F)	0
Oltman et al. (1952)	Patients admitted to state hospital psychiatric service in Newtown, Connecticut (USA): 1946–50	1896–1932	18–50	139	Psychoneuroses	+
				600	Schizophrenia	+
				115	Bipolar disorder	–
				90 (CC)	Psychopathic personality	++
Kulka & Weingarten (1979)	Survey Research Center national general population sample (USA): 1957	Pre-1936	21+	2,044	Very happy	+
				903	Anxiety symptoms (M)	++
				1,145	Anxiety symptoms (F)	0
Koller & Castanos (1968)	Patients presenting at a general hospital in Sydney following suicide attempt (AUS): 1966–7	1900–48	18+	106 (CC)	Treatment for suicide attempt	+

Table 3.6 (contd)

Reference	Study	D.O.B.	Ages (mean)	N	Outcome	Effect size
Koller & Williams (1974)	Patients seen at a hospital psychiatric unit in Sydney (AUS): 1966–7	1900–48	18+	132 (CC)	Treatment for neuroses	+
Kulka & Weingarten (1979)	Survey Research Center national general population sample (USA): 1976	Pre-1955	21+	2,264	Very happy Anxiety symptoms (M) Anxiety symptoms (F)	0 + +
Kessler & Magee (1993)	Americans' Changing Lives survey – national general population sample (USA): 1986	Pre-1961	25+	3,617	Major depression	+
Glenn & Kramer (1985)	General Social Surveys of the National Opinion Research Center (USA): 1973–82	Pre-1964	18+	15,000	Happiness (M) Happiness (F)	+ +
Roy (1978; 1985)	Patients seen at psychiatric hospitals in London (UK) and in Toronto (Canada): 1976–82	1911–64	18–65 (35)	300 (CC)	Out-patient or in-patient treatment for depression	+++

Study	Description	Birth years	Age	N	Measure	Effect
Amato & Booth (1991)	Study of Marital Stability over the Lifecourse – national sample of married people (USA): 1988	1917–64	24–63	1,243	Life satisfaction	0
					Depressive symptoms	0
McLeod (1991)	Detroit Area Study general population sample (USA): 1985	Pre-1967	18+	777	Depressed mood (M)	0
				884	Depressed mood (F)	0
Rodgers (1990a; 1994)	National Survey of Health and Development – British 1946 Birth Cohort (UK): 1959–89	1946	13	1,473	Emotional stability (M)	+
			"	1,489	Emotional sability (F)	0
			16	1,473	Neuroticism (M)	+
			"	"	Introversion (M)	0
			"	1,489	Neuroticism (F)	0
			"	"	Introversion (F)	0
			36	1,613	Depressive state (M)	0
			"	"	Depressive symptoms (M)	0
			"	1,633	Depressive state (F)	++
			"	"	Depressive symptoms (F)	++
			43	1,596	Depressive symptoms (M)	0
			"	1,599	Depressive symptoms (F)	+
Amato (1991)	National Survey of Families and Households (USA) : 1987–8	Pre-1970	18–95 (38)	9,177	Depressive symptoms (W)	0
				2,279	Depressive symptoms (B)	0
				968	Depressive symptoms (H)	0

Table 3.6 (contd)

Reference	Study	D.O.B.	Ages (mean)	N	Outcome	Effect size
Kessler et al. (1994, 1997)	National Comorbidity Survey (USA): 1990–2	1937–76	15–54	8,098	Major depression	+
					Manic episode	+
					Dysthymia	+
					Panic disorder	0
					Agoraphobia	+
					Social phobia	+
					Simple phobia	0
					Generalized anxiety	+
Rodgers et al. (1997)	National Child Development Study – British 1958 Birth Cohort (UK): 1981 & 1991	1958	23	8,635	Depressive symptoms	+
			33		Depressive symptoms	++
O'Connor et al. (1999b)	Avon Longitudinal Study of Pregnancy and Childhood (UK): 1991–2	1935–78	14–46 (28)	10,745	Depressive symptoms (F)	+
					High depression score (F)	+
Allison & Furstenberg (1989); Zill et al. (1993)	National Survey of Children (USA): 1976–87	1965–70	12–16	1.147	Depressive symptoms	+
			"		Life satisfaction	0
			18–22		Depressive symptoms	0
			"		Psychological help (ever)	++

Raphael et al. (1990)	High school students (Yrs 9 & 10) in the Lower Hunter Valley Region (AUS): 1983	1967–9	14–16	1,083 1,054	Consultation for worry or depression (M) Consultation for worry or depression (F)	++ +++
Ely et al. (2000)	Child Health & Education Study – British 1970 Birth Cohort (UK): 1986–8	1970	15–18	4,950	High depression score	+
Beautrais et al. (1996)	Serious suicide attempts in Christchurch (NZ): 1991–4	1967–83	13–24 (19.8)	129 (CC)	Serious suicide attempt	++
Ely et al. (2000)	West of Scotland Twenty-07 Study: 1990	1972	18	924	High depression score	0
Aseltine (1996)	High school students (Grades 9, 10 & 11) in the Boston area (USA): 1989	1971–4	15–18	942	Depressive symptoms	0

Table 3.7 Children from separated versus intact families: family and intimate relationships in adolescence and adulthood

Reference	Study	D.O.B.	Ages (mean)	N	Outcome	Effect size
Tucker et al. (1997)	Terman Life Cycle Study – follow up of children from schools in California (USA): 1921–91	1910	81–	597 448	Own divorce (M) Own divorce (F)	++ ++
Kulka & Weingarten (1979)	Survey Research Center national general population sample (USA): 1957	Pre-1936	21+	2,460	Marital happiness Marriage problems Inadequacy as spouse Own divorce or separation (M) Own divorce or separation (F) Orientation to parenthood (M) Orientation to parenthood (F) Problems raising children Inadequacy as parent	0 ++ ++ + +++ – – 0 0 0
Illsley & Thompson (1961)	Women having their first pregnancy in Aberdeen (Scotland): 1952–4	1910–36	18–42 ,,	2,930	Conceived outside of marriage Teenage birth	+++ +++

Study	Survey	Birth years	Age	N	Variable	Effect
Kulka & Weingarten (1979)	Survey Research Center national general population sample (USA): 1976	Pre-1955	21+	2,264	Marital happiness	0
					Marriage problems	++
					Inadequacy as spouse	+
					Own divorce or separation (M)	++
					Own divorce or separation (F)	++
					Orientation to parenthood (M)	−
					Orientation to parenthood (F)	+
					Problems raising children	0
					Inadequacy as parent	0
Glenn & Kramer (1987)	General Social Surveys of the National Opinion Research Center (USA): 1973–85	Pre-1967	18+	5,830	Own divorce or separation (M)	++
				7,730	Own divorce or separation (F)	+++
Mueller & Pope (1977)	National Fertility Survey (USA): 1970	1925–52	18–45	4,812	Own divorce – 1st marriage (F)	++
Amato & Booth (1991); Amato (1996)	Study of Marital Stability over the Lifecourse – national sample of married people (USA): 1980–92	1917–64	18+	1,243	Marital happiness	0
				″	Spouse interaction	0
				″	Spouse disagreements	+
				″	Marital problems	+
				″	Marital instability	+
				″	Divorced by 1988	+
				1,711	Own divorce in 12-yr period	++
				1,387	Relationship problem score[a]	++

Table 3.7 (contd)

Reference	Study	D.O.B.	Ages (mean)	N	Outcome	Effect size
Douglas (1970); Kuh & Maclean (1990); Maclean & Kuh (1991); Rodgers (1994)	National Survey of Health and Development – British 1946 Birth Cohort (UK): 1961–82	1946	18	2,223	Illegitimate birth (F)	0
			36	1,655	Premarital fathering (M)	+
			"	"	Never married (M)	0
			"	"	Own separation/divorce (M)	+++
			"	"	Married twice or more (M)	++
			"	1,669	Premarital pregnancy (F)	+
			"	"	Teenage marriage (F)	++
			"	"	Never married (F)	0
			"	"	Own separation/divorce (F)	+
			"	"	Married twice or more (F)	++
			43	1,594	Never married (M)	– –
			"	"	Own separation/divorce (M)	++
			"	"	Married twice or more (M)	++
			"	"	Poor emotional support (M)	0
			"	1,591	Never married (F)	0
			"	"	Own separation/divorce (F)	++
			"	"	Married twice or more (F)	+
			"	"	Poor emotional support (F)	0
McLanahan & Sandefur (1994)	National Survey of Families and Households – cohortA (USA): 1987	1943–52	35–44	N.K.	Marriage before 20 yrs (F)	0
					Birth before 20 yrs (F)	+++
					Nonmarital birth < 20 yrs (F)	++

Study	Survey / dataset	Birth years	Age	N	Outcome	Effect
Kiernan & Hobcraft (1997)	National Survey of Sexual Attitudes and Lifestyles (UK): 1990–1	1931–65	26–59	1,606	Sex before 17 yrs (M)	+
				"	Partnership under 22 yrs (M)	++
				"	Child before 22 yrs (M)	++
				2,185	Child pre-first partnership (M)	++
				"	Sex before 17 yrs (F)	+
				"	Partnership under 20 yrs (F)	++
				"	Child before 20 yrs (F)	++
				"	Child pre-first partnership (F)	+++
Kiernan (1992)	National Child Development Study – British 1958 Birth Cohort (UK): 1974–81	1958	23	4,760	Left home by 18 yrs (M)	++
				4,481	Left home by 18 yrs (F)	++
				4,500	Partnership before 21 yrs (M)	++
				"	Child by 23 yrs (M)	+
				"	Extramarital fathering (M)	+
				4,500	Partnership before 20 yrs (F)	+++
				"	Child by 20 yrs (F)	++
				"	Extramarital birth (F)	+++
McLanahan & Sandefur (1994)	National Survey of Families and Households – cohort B (USA): 1987	1953–67	20–34	N.K.	Marriage before 20 yrs (M)	0
					Birth before 20 yrs (M)	+
					Nonmarital birth < 20 yrs (M)	+
					Marriage before 20 yrs (F)	0
					Birth before 20 yrs (F)	++
					Nonmarital birth < 20 yrs (F)	0

Table 3.7 (contd)

Reference	Study	D.O.B.	Ages (mean)	N	Outcome	Effect size
McLanahan & Sandefur (1994)	Panel Study of Income Dynamics (USA): 1968–1989	1956–65	24–33	2,900	Marriage before 20 yrs (M)	0
					Birth before 20 yrs (M)	++
					Nonmarital birth < 20 yrs (M)	++
					Marriage before 20 yrs (F)	0
					Birth before 20 yrs (F)	++
					Nonmarital birth < 20 yrs (F)	++
O'Connor et al. (1999b)	Avon Longitudinal Study of Pregnancy and Childhood (UK): 1991–2	1935–78	14–46 (28)	11,000	Left home before 18 yrs (F)	+++
					Child before 20 yrs (F)	+++
					Never married (F)	+++
					Currently cohabiting (F)	+++
					Married twice or more (F)	0
					Relationships > 2 (F)	0
					Social/emotional support (F)	+
McLanahan & Sandefur (1994); Sandefur et al. (1992)	National Longitudinal Survey of Youth (USA): 1979–89	1962–5	20–23	5,246	Marriage before 20 yrs (M)	0
					Birth before 20 yrs (M)	+
					Nonmarital birth < 20 yrs (M)	0
					Marriage before 20 yrs (F)	0
					Birth before 20 yrs (F)	+++
					Nonmarital birth < 20 yrs (F)	++

Study	Year	Age	N	Variable	Effect
McLanahan & Sandefur (1994)	High School and Beyond Study (USA): 1980–6	1964	22	10,400	Marriage before 20 yrs (M)	0
					Birth before 20 yrs (M)	0
					Nonmarital birth < 20 yrs (M)	0
					Marriage before 20 yrs (F)	0
					Birth before 20 yrs (M)	+
					Nonmarital birth < 20 yrs (M)	+
Raphael et al. (1990)	High school students (Yrs 9 & 10) in the Lower Hunter Valley Region (AUS): 1983	1967–9	14–16	1,083	Sexually active (M)	++
				1,054	Sexually active (F)	++
Flewelling & Bauman (1990)	School students from household sample in Southeastern US: 1985	1971–3	12–14	2,102	Sexual intercourse ever	++
Sweeting & West (1995b); Sweeting et al. (1998)	West of Scotland Twenty-07 Study: 1990	1972	18	430	Intercourse before 16 yrs (M)	++
			"	"	Intercourse before 19 yrs (M)	++
			"	478	Intercourse before 16 yrs (F)	–
			"	"	Intercourse before 19 yrs (F)	++
			"	"	Pregnant before 19 yrs (F)	++
			21	373	Partnership by 21 yrs (M)	+++
			"	434	Partnership by 21 yrs (F)	+

[a] For couples in first marriages only.

Table 3.8 Children from stepfamilies versus lone-parent families

Reference	Study	D.O.B.	Ages (mean)	N	Outcome	Effect size
Glenn & Kramer (1987)	General Social Surveys of the National Opinion Research Center (USA): 1973–85	Pre-1967	18+	298	Own divorce or separation (M)	−
				487	Own divorce or separation (F)	0
Amato & Booth (1991)	Study of Marital Stability over the Lifecourse – national sample of married people (USA): 1988	1917–64	18+	202	Yrs of education	+
					Occupational prestige	+
					Annual earned income	0
					Material assets	−
					Economic strain	−
					Life satisfaction	0
					Depressive symptoms	+
					Marital happiness	0
					Spouse interaction	0
					Spouse disagreements	−
					Marital problems	0
					Marital instability	0
					Divorced by 1988	++
Ferri (1984); Kiernan (1992, 1997)	National Child Development Study – British 1958 Birth Cohort (UK): 1974–91	1958	16	785	Behavior problems (M, P)	+
			"	"	Behavior problems (M, T)	0
			"	774	Behavior problems (F, P)	+

Study	Survey (years)	Cohort year	Age	N	Outcome	Effect
					Behavior problems (F, T)	0
				1,500	Reading score	0
					Mathematics score	0
				748	School sickness absence (M)	0
				742	School sickness absence (F)	0
			23	280	Left school at age 16 (M)	0
					Left home by 18 yrs (M)	+
					Partnership before 21 yrs (M)	++
					Child by 23 yrs (M)	+
					Extramarital fathering (M)	0
					Left school at age 16 (F)	0
				300	Left home by 18 yrs (F)	0
					Partnership before 20 yrs (F)	++
					Child by 20 yrs (F)	+
					Extramarital birth (F)	0
Sandefur et al. (1992)	National Longitudinal Survey of Youth (USA): 1979–89	1962–5	20–23	1.166	High school Diploma (HSD)	0
					HSD/Gen. Equiv. Dip.	0
					College attendance	++
Zimiles & Lee (1991)	High School and Beyond Study (USA): 1980–2	1964	16	1,252	Achievement test score (M)	0
				1,413	Achievement test score (F)	0
			18	1,252	Dropped out of school (M)	–
				1,413	Achievement test score (M)	0
				1,094	Dropped out of school (F)	+
				1,136	Achievement test score (F)	0

Table 3.8 (contd)

Reference	Study	D.O.B.	Ages (mean)	N	Outcome	Effect size
Peterson & Zill (1986)	National Survey of Children (USA): 1976–87	1965–9	12–16	107	School discipline (M, P)	0
				″	Suspended or expelled (M, P)	0
				125	School discipline (F, P)	+++
				″	Suspended or expelled (F, P)	++
Zill et al. (1988)	Child Health Supplement to the National Health Interview Survey (US): 1981	1964–75	6–17	3,762	Psychological help in past yr	0
				3,572	Behavior problems index (P)	0
				2,987	Standing in class rating (P)	0
				3,145	Grade repetition	0
				3,093	School sickness absence (P)	0
				3,800	Rating of health/disability (P)	–
Wadsworth et al. (1985); Ely et al. (2000)	Child Health and Education Study – British 1970 Birth Cohort (UK): 1975–86	1970	5	1,043	Withdrawn behavior (P)	0
			″	″	Picture Vocabulary score	0
			″	″	Copying Designs score	0
			″	″	Any accident (P)	+
			″	″	2+ accidents (P)	+
			″	″	Admission for accident (P)	0
			″	″	Head injury (P)	+
			″	″	Burns and scalds (P)	0
			″	″	Suspected poisoning (P)	0
			″	″	Antisocial behavior (P)	0
			15	1,308	Any qualifications	0

Reference	Study	Birth year	Age	Outcome	Association
Sweeting et al. (1995b, 1998); Ely et al. (2000)	West of Scotland Twenty-07 Study: 1990	1972	170	Five "O" levels or more	+
"	"	"	"	Current smoker	+
"	"	"	"	Current drinker	0
"	"	"	"	High physical symptoms	0
"	"	"	"	High depression score	0
"	"	"	15	Current smoker (M)	0
"	"	"	"	Current drinker (M)	0
"	"	"	"	Other drug use ever (M)	0
"	"	"	"	Current smoker (F)	–
"	"	"	"	Current drinker (F)	–
"	"	"	"	Other drug use ever (F)	+
"	"	"	"	High physical symptoms	0
"	"	"	"	High depression score	0
"	"	"	18	Left school early (M)	+
"	"	"	"	Any qualifications (M)	++
"	"	"	"	Five "O" grades or more (M)	+++
"	"	"	"	Not in employment (M)	+
"	"	"	"	Vandalism/violence ever (M)	++
"	"	"	"	Theft ever (M)	+
"	"	"	"	Police trouble 16–18 yrs (M)	++
"	"	"	"	Intercourse before 16 yrs (M)	++
"	"	"	"	Intercourse before 19 yrs (M)	++++
"	"	"	"	Left school early (F)	+
"	"	"	"	Any qualifications (F)	0
"	"	"	"	Five "O" grades or more (F)	0
"	"	"	"	Not in employment (F)	–

Table 3.8 (contd)

Reference	Study	D.O.B.	Ages (mean)	N	Outcome	Effect size
			"		Vandalism/violence ever (F)	--
			"		Theft ever (F)	0
			"		Police trouble 16–18 yrs (F)	+
			"		Intercourse before 16 yrs (F)	-
			"		Intercourse before 19 yrs (F)	0
			"		Pregnant before 19 yrs (F)	--
			21		Partnership by 21 yrs (M)	-
			"		Partnership by 21 yrs (F)	0
Flewelling & Bauman (1990)	School students from household sample in Southeastern US: 1985	1971–3	12–14	801	Smoked ever	0
					Current smoker	+
					Drank alcohol ever	0
					Marijuana ever	0
					Sexual intercourse ever	0
Demo & Acock (1996)	Adolescents of mothers in the National Survey of Families and Households (USA): 1987–8	1969–76	12–18	413	Socioemotional problems (P)	0
					School grades (P)	0
Thomson et al. (1994)	Children in the National Survey of Families and Households (USA): 1987–8	1969–83	5–18	1,432	Any behavior problem	0
			"		Internalizing problems	0
			"		Sociability	0

Study	Dataset	Year	Age	N	Measure	Effect
			5–11		Rating in class (P)	0
			12–18		School grades (P)	0
			5–18		Conduct problems (P)	0
Cockett & Tripp (1994)	Exeter Family Study (UK): 1991–2	1977–81	9–14	57	Low self-esteem	0
					Poor social image	0
					Unhappiness	|
					Unhappiness (P)	–
					Difficulties with school work	0
					Special help at school	+
Dawson (1991)	National Health Interview Survey on Child Health (US): 1988	1971–88	0–17	3,400	Bed-wetting in past yr (P)	0
					Speech defect in past yr (P)	0
					Treated emotional problem (P)	0
					Ever repeated a grade (P)	0
					Ever expelled/suspended (P)	0
					Accident/injury in last yr (P)	0
					Asthma in last yr (P)	0
					Headaches in last yr (P)	0
Dunn et al. (1998)	Avon Longitudinal Study of Pregnancy and Childhood (UK): 1991–2	1995–6	4	1,617	Emotional problems (P)	0
					Peer problems (P)	0
					Social/attentional problems (P)	0
					Conduct problems	0

4

Children's Perceptions of Families and Family Change

Try to take into account the kids' views because the kids know what they want more than the parents do because they're them.
15-year-old boy (Gollop et al., 2000)

Introduction

It is only relatively recently that what children say about families and family change has been taken seriously. Children are the least likely of all family members to be the initiators of transitions despite being profoundly involved. Yet listening to what children say about family change is a surprisingly contentious issue. There is a deep ambivalence about children's roles and rights of participation in determining their well-being. Why might this be? One answer is that to take children seriously poses a fundamental challenge to power issues within the family and in the wider community. As Roche (1999, p. 72 n. 2) has suggested, "In arguments about childhood and children's rights we are arguing about ourselves and our place in the world: it is an argument about politics." This deeper issue of power and family politics is usually not acknowledged; however, it underpins some more obvious points of contention that are openly articulated, and is an inherent part of the wider debate about family change that we have described earlier. Beliefs held about childhood in general influence our views about children's roles in families and their participation in decision-making. As we saw in chapter 1, there was a remarkable upheaval in attitudes about children and childhood during the twentieth century.

The conservative view of children and their roles sees them as having a right to remain as children and to be protected from pressures to be involved in issues that are properly the business of adults. To ask children to participate in decisions about their welfare is to make unreasonable demands on their maturity. The liberal perspective, in contrast, sees children as willing and capable participants in family decisions that concern them.

There are three specific areas of debate about children's views. The first is whether a child *can* and *does* hold a coherent view of families and of social life in general, and if so, whether or not their opinions are to be taken seriously as valid perspectives. A second issue concerns the relative importance of children's perspectives, and whether or not such views that children might hold have relevance for their well-being against the views of adults who are involved with them. The debate is polarized between those who believe that children have rights equal to those of adults and should be both heard and heeded (the liberationist position), and those who hold the conviction that children should not be free to make autonomous decisions (the caretaking position) (Archard, 1993). The liberationist position argues that children should be treated in exactly the same ways as autonomous adults, with rights to total confidentiality and to legal representation. The caretaking position is based on the view that although children may be able to say what they want, they lack the emotional and cognitive maturity to hold valid opinions and to make proper decisions and need protection even from themselves. These are similar to the positions held by liberal and conservative advocates in the family change debate, and, in turn, reflect the wider disquiet about whether childhood and adulthood are separate domains.

> There are three major areas of debate. First is whether children can hold coherent views of families and of social life in general ... the second concerns the relative importance of children's perspectives and whether they have relevance for their well-being. A third question is whether and to what extent children want to participate in major decisions related to their well-being.

A third question is whether and to what extent children *want* to participate in major decisions related to their well-being. Even if it is agreed that a child can form and hold a valid view that carries significant weight in relation to adult views, there is a question about whether she or he would want the responsibility of taking a major decision-making role in the family, especially at a time of major change.

Associated with all of these is a question of whether or not a developmental perspective on children's views should be assumed. It has been argued, for example, that to posit developmental changes in children's understanding is to objectify children, to undervalue their capacities, and to keep them dependent (James et al., 1991). This argument contains an implicit assumption that developmental phases are quantitatively more or less than each other rather than qualitatively different. As we will see, there do appear to be developmental differences in the ways in which children understand notions of family and family change, and we argue that to ignore these is to jeopardize the ability to empower children in articulating their views.

In this chapter, we will examine children's perspectives on family transitions by looking at how they describe their experiences of their parents' separations. We will then consider the views of wider groups of children and young people about their perceptions of families and family change. Finally, we will discuss some of the implications of these findings for the questions of children's abilities, rights, and desires to participate in decisions affecting their lives.

Children's Experiences of Family Transitions

The increasing interest in children's abilities, perspectives, and rights has inspired several studies that have talked directly to children whose parents have separated. A burgeoning number of UK studies, in particular, are finding that children often (although not always) want to talk about their feelings and do, indeed, have well-formed views about their situation (Morrow, 1998; Brannen et al., 1999b; Lyon et al., 1999). Furthermore, their appraisals of what happens are often quite different from those of adults involved in the same events (Mitchell, 1985). The perspectives that children articulate are remarkably similar across English-speaking countries. In this section findings from studies in the UK (Walczak & Burns, 1984; Mitchell, 1985; Gorrell Barnes et al., 1998; Brannen et al., 1999b; Dunn et al., in press a), Australia (Amato, 1987a; McDonald, 1990; Funder, 1996; Dunlop & Burns, 1998), New Zealand (Smith et al., 1997; Pritchard, 1998), and the USA (Kurdek & Siesky, 1980; Wallerstein & Kelly, 1980; Neugebauer, 1989) have been used to develop an account of how children experience families and family transitions.

How do children feel when parents separate?

Children describe a welter of paradoxical feelings at the time of their parents' separation. Foremost are feelings of sadness (Walczak & Burns, 1984; Mitchell, 1985; Neugebauer, 1989; Dunlop & Burns, 1998; Pritchard, 1998). Sadness and despair at the time his parents separated were recalled three years later by a 15-year-old in a school essay, where he wrote:

The silence was jet black; too deep and wide simply to scan with words. So we just sat numbly, each of us in our own world of thought, or grief, travelling down the long metal road . . . I was stuck, we were all stuck, in that little tin box; inches between us but light years apart . . . and it still seems like we're going down that long black road in that little tin box. I wonder if we'll ever get home. (Pritchard, 1998, pp. 231–2)

Children are often also angry and bewildered. The anger is sometimes directed at the parent who is seen to have "caused" the separation; for younger children, that is the person who leaves the house, regardless of who initiated the separation (Burns & Dunlop, 1999). At the same time, there is an acute longing for the missing parent, and for younger children especially, the fear that they will never see him or her again and that both parents might disappear from their lives (Wallerstein & Kelly, 1980). For some, this fear is realistic, as their fathers' leaving does signal the absolute loss of the relationship. Many children, again especially those who are young, long for their parents to get back together, and hold reconciliation fantasies for a considerable time (Wallerstein & Kelly, 1980; Plunkett & Kalter, 1984; Smith et al., 1997). In the Children in Families Study in Australia, 12 percent of school-age children and 4 percent of adolescents said they wished their parents would get back together (Amato, 1987a). When asked whether or not they think their parents *will* get back together, however, most are sufficiently realistic not to believe that would happen (Kurdek & Siesky, 1980).

Yet the presence of conflict can mean that there is a sense of relief when one parent leaves the house (Neugebauer, 1989; Pritchard, 1998). Some describe a constant state of fear when their parents were together, fear for their own safety and sometimes that of their parents. Reflecting on her childhood, one young woman said

When I hear people saying, "She or he is staying for the children's sake" I can only recall those long lonely nights listening to my parents fighting. That is what I hated the most – Mum and Dad fighting. You could see the fight coming and you couldn't stop it. (Pritchard, 1998, p. 39)

Her ambivalence, though, was evident in her diary entry the day her father left, when she wrote:

when we came home, Dad wasn't there. His clothes, sleeping bag and toilet gear all gone. He had left . . . Hell this is terrible. I always thought this would happen but hoped it wouldn't. (Pritchard, 1998, p. 23)

Children's responses to parental separation are, then, diverse. In a New Zealand study 33 percent of children reported an entirely negative response to their parents' separation, 23 percent had mixed reactions, and 44 percent had neutral or mildly positive reactions (Smith et al., 1997). In the Children in Families Study in Australia, approximately 44 percent of children reported negative responses; 11 percent and 27 percent of adolescents reported neutral or positive responses; and approximately 47 percent said they didn't know how they felt (Amato, 1987a). In general, negative feelings appear to dissipate as time passes; three years after separation children in an Australian longitudinal study expressed significantly lower levels of sadness, shock, and disbelief than they had at the time of the separation, while their feelings of relief and gladness rose (Burns & Dunlop, 1999). In the Children in Families Study there was a reduction in negative and "don't know" responses with time since separation, and an increase in neutral or positive responses with 93 percent of adolescents falling into that category (Amato, 1987a). In the Burns study, feelings at the time of separation were recorded as well as feelings about the separation 10 years later. Children recalled their sadness, disbelief, and shock as being far worse than they had expressed at the time. In the Children in Families group 51 percent were neutral or positive about both their feelings at the time and now, 10 percent were negative at both times, 31 percent changed from negative to positive, and 9 percent changed from positive to negative. It is difficult to know whether children suppressed the true depth of their feelings at the time, or (for those who felt better later) whether there was a bias in their recall and they overestimated their distress because they felt so much better about the separation ten years later.

Blaming themselves
There is some evidence that younger children may blame themselves for their parents' separation (Wallerstein & Kelly, 1980), although only 5 percent in one study said that children were to blame for parents' separation (Kurdek & Siesky, 1980), and those who did so were most likely to be in families where parents had separated very recently. Children whose parents have not separated are also more likely to believe that a child would be to blame if parents separated, than those who have been through the experience (Kalter & Plunkett, 1984). At the time of separation, then, children may blame themselves and even feel they have the power to reconcile their parents, but as time passes they come to understand that they were not the cause of their parents' separation, and most do not seem to blame anyone in particular (Kurdek & Siesky, 1980).

Do children know why their parents separate?
The ways in which children find out that a separation is happening are also varied; only about a quarter know in advance (Neugebauer, 1989; Smith et al., 1997) and only 20 to 30 percent of young people say they knew why their parents were separating (Wallerstein & Kelly, 1980; Neugebauer, 1989). Even some time after the event nearly half the children in Smith's New Zealand group said they still did not know why (Smith et al., 1997). In the ALSPAC study in the UK, 23 percent of children said no one talked to them about the separation; 44 percent said their mothers talked to them, and 17 percent said both parents talked to them (Dunn et al., in press a). Only 5 percent felt they were fully informed, and 45 percent said they were told simply with a blunt statement with no explanation. One young person recalled finding out in the following way:

> we came down, and my father was crying in the chair . . . I just remember him saying something about she'd "gone" – and that was it. I think when you're seven, you probably don't know how to take things like that. You don't believe people "go," you can't: people don't "go," do they? I mean, you're seven. (Gorrell Barnes et al., 1998, p. 55)

This is of particular concern since a study of attributions of control in children whose parents have separated suggests that the dimension indicating attribution to an *unknown* source of control over events is linked with symptoms of distress (anxiety, depression, and conduct disorder) (Kim et al., 1997). The authors suggest that "understanding why events occur, rather than believing in an internal locus of control, is the dimension that buffers stress in children of divorce" (p. 153).

What are the worst aspects of separation for children?

The most immediate change for children when their parents separate is the physical absence of one adult, in most cases their father, from the household. The loss of day-to-day contact with him is the most often-cited factor when children are asked about the worst things about separation (Wallerstein & Kelly, 1980; Kurdek & Berg, 1987; Neugebauer, 1989; Smith et al., 1997). One child in the ALSPAC study said "I don't have a Dad, he doesn't want me any more, he's engaged" (Dunn et al., in press a). Children simply miss their father and the day-to-day contact they have had with him, and this can be made worse by the difficulty they have in admitting their feelings of loss to their mother, who may be experiencing strongly negative feelings about her ex-partner. In addition, the loss of one parent from home is a potent symbol of the loss of the stereotypical family and of a "normal" family identity. The continuing power of the image of a real family as two parents and children, and children's own strong sense of what constitutes family for them, contribute to the distress felt at no longer being a "real" family. One young man expressed it this way:

> My cat died and that cat has been with us for sixteen years and three houses. That symbolized that the family has gone. We are not the dog-cat-parents-three kids any more. (Pryor, 1999)

Another, who was an adult when her parents separated, said:

> I was in a family unit and then all of a sudden there was no family unit and I was out, you know I was "Who am I?" It was – I lost who I was. (Pryor, 1999)

The practical aspects of the absence of a father are sometimes noticed, as well. Another girl reported that she stepped into the gap left by her father:

> I very quickly became the "man of the house." I remember the fuse went and I had to work out how to change it. I clearly remember thinking, "Well, it's me now. I'm going to have to do that." (Pritchard, 1998, p. 40)

Children's responses to conflict and domestic violence

Children react to parental conflict with great distress, and the consequences of being exposed to conflict are well documented (Grych & Fincham, 1990; Cummings & Davies, 1994). Similarly, their exposure to domestic violence is damaging, with outcomes including aggression, behavioral difficulties, anxiety, school problems, attention deficits, and somatic complaints (Holden et al., 1998). When conflict is present in families before separation, children typically express paradoxical feelings of relief and sadness when their parents part. Very little is known, though, about children's feelings when overt physical violence occurs between parents. Interviews with children in temporary residence in a shelter for battered women showed that they abhorred the violence itself, but were ambivalent about the abusive parent (Ornduff & Monahan, 1999) and often expressed a wish for a family reunion. In another group, similar levels of positive attributes were assigned to parents regardless of whether the children themselves had been abused, had witnessed violence, or had no experience of violence (Sternberg et al., 1995); however, abusive parents were perceived more negatively than nonabusive parents.

Indirect reports of children's wishes about contact with an abusing parent after separation were obtained through parents in another study (Chetwin et al., 1998). Children who were seeing their nonresident parents in a variety of supervised and unsupervised settings were reported to enjoy the contact and to look forward to it. Those who had no contact with abusive parents and, presumably, had witnessed serious violence between parents, had mixed reactions, with some settling down happily in conflict-free homes and others missing their parent. Overall, children for whom parental separation occurs in a context of partner violence face particularly conflicting emotions. Anger at a parent for hurting the other can mix with relief at the ending of the violence, sadness at the loss of a parent, and longing for the absent parent.

Where do children get support?

As we noted earlier, parents are not always emotionally available to talk to their children when they separate, as their distress at the time can be a barrier that deters children from asking for support and reduces their ability to provide it. Many children report coping almost entirely alone (Wallerstein & Kelly, 1980; Neugebauer, 1989; Smith et al., 1997), and in the ALSPAC group mothers were ranked only third by children as someone in whom they could confide at an intimate level, although mothers were the most likely people for them to confide in on minor matters (Dunn et al., in press a). Yet children seem to want to talk to their parents. In their UK study, Walczak and Burns found that those people who appeared to be thriving some years after the separation had been talked to about it by their parents. "Good communication at the time of separation," the authors conclude, "helped children cope with separation at the time it happened and served as an insurance policy against effects in the long run" (Walczak & Burns, 1984).

Extended family members, especially grandparents, are a vital source of support for children. A majority of children after separation include maternal grandparents in their family groupings (Funder, 1996), and in the ALSPAC group the people most frequently turned to by children were grandparents or other relatives. Grandparents have been described as having a latent function for children that becomes active at times of stress (Cherlin & Furstenberg, 1986), when they become significant providers of support to them. Grandparents can take the roles of "transition objects" for children that get them through times of difficulty. In the US young people in stepfamilies described closer relationships with grandparents than those in lone-parent families who, in turn, felt closer to their grandparents than those in original families (Kennedy & Kennedy, 1993). This suggests that strong bonds are formed when children are cared for or live with grandparents during family transitions; in Gorell Barnes' interviews with children who had lost a parent by divorce or death, 60 recalled relatives and especially grandparents as playing a significant part in their lives (Gorrell Barnes et al., 1998). Three-quarters of those became closely attached to their relatives, closer in fact than to natural parents or stepparents.

In contrast, children in the ALSPAC group in the UK who lived in original families felt closer to paternal grandparents than those in lone-parent families, and closer to maternal grandmothers than those in stepfather families (Lussier et al., submitted). In general, these children felt closer to maternal grandparents than to paternal grandparents.

Children sometimes feel reluctant to talk with others about their parents' separation. In Smith's New Zealand study only about one-third had talked to anyone (Gollop et al., 2000). Boys, in particular, may find it hard to tell friends even that their parents have parted. One teenage boy told an interviewer that "I just said Mum and Dad are separating and we went off and played cricket or something" (Smith et al., 1997, p. 29). Another said "I don't know if they really gave a shit . . . they asked, and I took it quite hard really you know, they didn't really give a shit when I told them" (Smith et al., 1997, p. 29). In the UK, however, friends were the second most likely group to be turned to for intimate confiding by children, ahead of mothers and fathers (Dunn et al., in press a).

Talking with teachers or school counselors helps some children; however, others are wary of confidentiality in a school situation and see school as a haven where family issues can be escaped. In the ALSPAC group counselors were rarely used as confidants. Sometimes, too, counseling can be an invasive experience, especially if the child has not sought it. One young woman said:

> It was terrible. I felt manipulated into saying things I didn't really feel, and there was a whole lot of unnecessary trauma associated with it . . . [I felt] almost violated by the way I was having to reveal myself. (Pritchard, 1998, p. 42)

Do children see any gains when their parents separate?

Separation is not a time when children are likely to see any positive aspects in the upheaval they typically experience. An exception to this might be when there are high levels of conflict that are reduced by their parents' separation, and this is often endorsed as being an advantage of separation by children in the USA (Kurdek & Berg, 1987). As time goes on, some other advantages can emerge. For example, a close and strong relationship with mothers often develops which might not have happened had their parents stayed together. This seems to be especially apparent in the first two years after separation, and to be articulated in particular by adolescents (Kurdek & Berg, 1987). Positive aspects of their mothers' vulnerability and need for support in lone-parent households have even been described by some young adults (Arditti, 1999), who found that caring for their mothers led to close friendships, especially as the children became older. Arditti suggests that the closeness engendered by mother–child (especially daughters) friendship can be positive and provide a sound basis for the development of autonomy in older children. Linked with this are feelings of psychological growth, maturity, and independence that are found often in children whose parents separate (Amato, 1987b; Kurdek & Berg, 1987; Pritchard, 1998). Not only do they take on practical responsibilities comparatively early; they also feel as if they mature rapidly and that this is a positive experience. Some have described their good understanding of people and relationships as something they might not otherwise have had (Walczak & Burns, 1984). However, the assumption of responsibility for parents' well-being can lead to the blurring of boundaries between child and adult roles that we discussed in chapter 2. Children can and often do provide emotional and practical support for distressed parents, and some talk about the burden this can be (Kurdek & Berg, 1987; Pritchard, 1998). They can see (usually) their mother as in need of support, and this, in turn, leads to feeling responsible. As one young woman said:

> She didn't really talk about it. But I knew she was really upset, and I'd do a lot of work around the house and put dinner on because I knew it would be easier on her. She was always in a bad mood – for about eight years. (Pritchard, 1998, p. 90)

The adults interviewed by Walczak in her British study also talked of the uneasiness they felt if their residential parents appeared not to be coping (Walczak & Burns, 1984). Children, then, sometimes feel they benefit and at others feel weighed down by the burden of responsibility for parents. Overall, so long as lone parents are coping adequately and are not dependent on their children for the majority of their support, then the closeness and friendship that can develop from the parents' needs for some support may lead to increased maturity and understanding that children see as positive as they get older. This has been described by Hetherington (1991) as an "egalitarian, mutually supportive relationship." On the other hand, emotional dependence and use of children as confidants by parents can be a significant burden for children who are trying to develop their own sense of autonomy and independence.

> Children . . . sometimes feel they benefit and at others feel weighed down by the burden of responsibility for parents. Overall, so long as lone parents are coping adequately and are not dependent on their children for the majority of their support, then the closeness and friendship that can develop from the need for some support may lead to increased maturity and understanding that children see as positive as they get older . . . On the other hand, emotional dependence and use of children as confidants by parents can be a significant burden for children who are trying to develop their own sense of autonomy and independence.

Attitudes to marriage in children from separated homes

Contradictory predictions can be made about the possible links between parents' divorce and young people's attitudes to getting married. They may feel cautious and skeptical about their own partnerships after having seen the failure of those of their parents'. Conversely, they may feel that they are equipped by observing their parents' mistakes to do better. Findings, not surprisingly, are mixed. Some studies report that those children whose parents had parted expressed worries about marriage (Wallerstein, 1985) or were less likely to say they wanted to marry (Ferri, 1976; Kinnaird & Gerrard, 1986; Gabardi & Rosen, 1992; Tasker, 1992). In other groups, though, children from separated homes were just as likely to want to marry as those whose parents had stayed together (Coleman & Ganong, 1984; Willetts-Bloom & Nock, 1992). Young people who are wary cite their parents' experiences as causing them to be pessimistic about the likelihood of establishing successful partnerships. Those who are not cautious say that as a result of their parents' experiences they have identified pitfalls and problems, and feel able to enter partnerships more thoughtfully. Children of separated parents are more likely to endorse cohabitation as an alternative to marriage (Tasker, 1992) and to consider the possibility of their own divorce than those from original families (Coleman & Ganong, 1984; Kinnaird & Gerrard, 1986; Mazur, 1993), both of which make their own partnerships particularly vulnerable. Indeed, adults whose own parents separate are at heightened risk of dissolution of their own partnership (Amato, 1996). Adding to the risk is the fact that children whose parents separate are more likely to begin sexual relationships, to partner, and to become parents earlier than those from original families (Kiernan & Hobcraft, 1997) – all of which are risk factors for their own separation or divorce.

A developmental perspective on children's reactions to parental separation

Children's reactions to separation vary by circumstances but also by age, and there is a developmental sequence in the ways in which they are most likely to respond. This is particularly well demonstrated in an in-depth study of children whose parents were separated and who were attending counseling, carried out by Wallerstein and Kelly (1980). Children under the age of 5 are most likely to feel fear and anxiety that both parents may abandon them. At this stage their ability to understand what is happening is comparatively limited. Their attachment to the parent who leaves the household is particularly vulnerable since their capacity to sustain the relationship through days and often weeks of absence is limited. Not surprisingly young children will evince the symptoms of lost attachments that are akin to grief – anger, sadness, and disbelief. They may also fantasize about the separation and the missing parent, imagining that he or she will return. The cognitive egocentricity typical of young children means that they may also blame themselves for their parents' breakup.

Younger school-aged children (5- to 8-year-olds) typically react with sadness, but are less likely to use fantasy than preschool children do to give themselves hope that parents will reconcile. Their understanding of the situation is sufficient that they may be scared of concrete aspects of deprivation such as insufficient food, and loss of toys. They describe yearning for their absent parent, and may still blame themselves for the separation.

Slightly older children (9- to 12-year-olds) are likely to have a better understanding of what has happened, and to feel some mastery of the situation. They still describe feelings of sadness, and may use anger as a way of masking their more painful feelings of helplessness and sadness. Children in this age group may also align themselves with one parent or another.

Adolescents often feel vulnerable in the domains of relationships, because these are the issues they are themselves confronting, and because they are aware of their parents' subsequent relationships and their sexual component. Some demonstrate an accelerated maturity both emotionally and intellectually, while others pull back from the usual adolescent challenges of increasing autonomy and peer orientation. A similar contrast is sometimes found between those who detach themselves from the situation in order to cope, and others who become overly involved often in support of one or other parent. In general, adolescents are more likely than younger children to see separation as positive or neutral after a time (Amato, 1987a).

A widely ignored group are those who are in early adulthood when their parents part. They find the experience no less distressing than younger children and adolescents (Pryor, 1999). Parents tend not to protect them from loyalty conflicts, and they are called upon by both mothers and fathers for support and help. Fathers who have not initiated the separation are especially vulnerable in this middle-aged group, and call on their adult children for explanation and support. Despite the fact that they may have left home, young adults grieve the loss of a family home. The sale of their childhood belongings, for example, and the loss of "their" bedrooms, can signify painfully the collapse of a family that they had taken for granted. They find themselves reassessing what they had thought was a happy family in childhood, after a parent confides in them about the marital difficulties they have had in the past.

Time since separation occurred is also an important factor in children's responses. Recall that in Burns and Dunlop's Australian study, levels of distress reduced five years later while relief and gladness increased (Burns & Dunlop, 1999). Similarly, although this is not so well documented, gender differences can be apparent with boys more likely than girls to be angry and to withdraw as a way of coping in adolescence and adulthood, and girls more likely to be anxious and to become overly involved in their parents' distress (Pryor, 1999).

What can we conclude?

Children's accounts of their experiences reveal a picture of diversity and, often, resilience. Although there may be little that could prepare children adequately for their parents' separation, they are not often told that it is going to happen and nor are they given helpful explanations. They are initially bewildered, sad, and angry, yet what is impressive is their adaptability and resilience to changes that are unwanted and beyond their control. It is apparent from their accounts that explanations and support from parents would help them to cope at the time of separation. We know much less about the long-term consequences of their immediate experiences of and reactions to separation. We need studies that identify possible links between these short-term responses and long-term outcomes for children.

> Children show diverse responses to separation, and are usually ill prepared and ill informed about it. Nonetheless, after initial sadness and confusion they can show remarkable resilience to the changes involved. There are age-related responses to the loss of their original family. From their accounts it is apparent that appropriate support and information would help them to cope at the time.

Children's Views of Family and Family Transitions

Children's reactions to parental separation take place in the context of the meanings that families in general have for them. The impact of changes in family structures may depend on children's sense of what a family is, and how that changes with transitions. Their understanding will be influenced both by their own experiences, for example living in an extended, lone-parent, originally two-parent family or stepfamily; and by cultural and media depictions of family – the "family mythology" that exists in their communities, cultures, and countries.

The meaning of "family"

In New Zealand, Anyan (1998) examined the frequency with which several criteria were mentioned by 17- and 18-year-olds in defining families for these young people. Her findings are shown in table 4.1. For these adolescents, affection was named twice as often as any other factor in defining what a family means. Biological ties were also named, but cohabitation and the presence of children were relatively unimportant and legal ties were the least important of all.

Table 4.1   Percentages of 17- and 18-year-olds mentioning criteria in defining families

Criterion	% mentioning it
Affective factors	80.0
Blood relations	41.5
Living together	35.3
Presence of parents and children	29.9
Legal ties	12.1

Note: N = 224
Source: Anyan, 1998.

Another way of approaching the question of how children view families is to ask them whether specific household structures constitute "real" families. This has been done in studies that have questioned children in different age groups, and a developmental pattern emerges that indicates changes in their understanding and acceptance of different households and their characteristics (Gilby & Pederson, 1982; O'Brien et al., 1996; Anyan, 1998). Table 4.2 shows the percentage of children and young people at six different ages who endorsed the households indicated as "families."

Although these studies involved different samples of children, we can nonetheless discern a pattern of understanding that has a developmental sequence. Very young children see families as consisting of two parents with children, who are married and live in the same household. Lone-parent households, cohabiting families, couples without children, and extended family apart from grandparents are unlikely to be seen as families. Children in middle childhood are more likely to include extended family members and lone-mother households, but most still see children as essential to a family. Biological relationships become more important at this age so that nonresident mothers become included (Richards, 2000). For adolescents, families encompass a wide range of groupings, not requiring legal marriage but they are still less likely to endorse family members who are not living together or who do not include children. The majority of young adults include nonresident, biologically related family members but, like all age groups, are less likely to include families without love. Across all ages, then, love and affection are paramount as defin-

Table 4.2   Percentages of children and young people endorsing household types and family members as family at different ages

Family type	6-year-olds	10-year olds	17-year-olds	21-year-olds
Nuclear	90	100	99.6	100
Solo mother plus children	55	80	92.6	95
Unmarried parents & children	20	40	88.4	
Sole father & children	45	75	90	95
Grandparents	60	85	86	100
Aunt, uncle, & cousins	45	80	83	85
Two women & child			80	
Family without love	15	55	64	70
Nonresidential father & children	5	50	63	85
Couple, no children	45	70	62	85
Nonresidential mother & children	10	75	56	90

Sources: Anyan, 1998; Gilby & Pedersen, 1982; O'Brien, Alldred, & Jones, 1996.

ing features of families, and married two-parent households with children are almost universally endorsed.

Children living in different household structures see families in slightly different ways. Lone-parent households are more likely to be seen as real families by children whose parents have divorced (Moore, 1976). Anyan (1998) found that nonresidential parents were less likely to be endorsed as part of their families by young people in lone-parent and stepparent households than were the residential parents of those in original families. In her sample, nearly half of those in lone-parent and stepfamilies had not seen their nonresidential parents in the last year, so that endorsement of

Children's understanding of family

Very young children see families as consisting of two parents with children, who are married and live in the same household. Lone-parent households and extended family apart from grandparents are unlikely to be seen as families. Children in middle childhood are likely to include extended family members and lone-mother households. Biological relationships become more salient at this age and in adolescence and adolescents also include lone-father households and gay parents. Across all age groups, love and affection are paramount as defining features of families, and married two-parent households with children are almost universally endorsed.

parents they saw rarely is less likely. They were more likely, though, than those in original families to endorse gay couples and loveless families as real families.

How do children view parents?

Children's views about their parents and the relationships they have with them differ in significant ways from the assumptions made by many adults. Children tend to be regarded as dependent on their parents, and the parent–child relationship is widely seen as one that is determined principally by the actions of adults. Parenting is conceptualized as something that is "done" to children who are vulnerable and passive (James, 1999). When children are asked how they perceive their relations with their parents, it becomes apparent that they see themselves as proactive in determining what those relationships are like. They regard the relationships as negotiated and interdependent rather than seeing themselves as passive recipients, and they also see themselves as providers of care and support for their parents (Morrow, 1998; James, 1999). This is expressed by a 14-year-old in Morrow's study, who said, "Families are for giving me stuff; food, clothes, presents. Loving, caring for me, and for giving things back to" (Morrow, 1998). More than this, children see themselves as central to their parents' lives, and as major achievements on their parents' part (Allatt, 1996).

Who do children include as family members?

For children whose parents have not separated, the question of who are members of their own family is relatively uncomplicated. Those who live in their household will be included, as will relatives. Parental separation complicates the question of who is family for children, since their biological kin are now in different households and other people such as stepfamily members may become household members. The ways in which children define their families postdivorce offer a window into criteria used for family inclusion; what we find is a great deal of diversity in who constitutes family for children. In the AIFS study, Funder used a family sculpture technique with 105 children in order to explore how children after separation identified family membership (Funder, 1996). She found that nearly 20 percent included original nuclear family members and biological kin only; 41 percent included a wide array of nuclear, extended kin, and stepfamily members; 21 percent included nuclear family and stepfamily members (resident or nonresident); and the rest named an extensive and varied group of individuals including godmothers, mothers' friends, and a dog. Funder came to the following conclusion:

> Children clearly use a variety of criteria in defining family. The criteria appear to be original nuclear family, biological kin, resident household members, membership of the nonresident parent's household, extended stepkin, and people with particular importance to the child . . . the variety within the group cannot be ignored; children conceive of their family in idiosyncratic ways, and use boundaries which may or may not coincide with standard notions of family relationships. (Funder, 1996, p. 66)

Somewhat similar perceptions of postseparation families were found in a study in Canada, where 16- to 18-year-olds who lived in stepfamilies were interviewed about their perceptions of their families (Gross, 1987), and four typologies derived (see the box on p. 130). The largest group (retention) included both and only biological parents as family members. The next biggest group was called augmentation, and included a stepparent and both biological parents. Most lived with their father and stepmother, were comparatively older when their parents separated, and retained close links with both biological parents. One-quarter retained only one biological parent in their definition of family (the reduction group); many of these had little contact with their nonresidential father, and did not get on well with their stepfather. The rest included at least one stepparent and one biological parent as family members. Typically they had no relationship or involvement with their nonresidential father.

Stepfamily typologies formed by Canadian adolescents (Gross, 1987)

Retention (33%): Both and only two original parents included as family members
Substitution (13%): Exclusion of one biological parent, inclusion of stepparent
Reduction (25%): Inclusion of only one biological parent, no stepparent
Augmentation (28): Both biological parents and a stepparent

We do not know why some children extend their concept of family to encompass nonkin and stepfamily members while others include only biological kin as family members. What is important to note is the variety of ways in which children construct their sense of family; we cannot make assumptions about who belongs to an individual child's family in his or her eyes.

There are some strong themes that emerge from these accounts of families and parents by children. Uppermost is the importance of love and affection; also predominant is a normative perception of families as two married parents and their children living together. Children, too, see themselves as active participants in determining the nature of their relationships with their parents. For younger children especially, separation brings with it the violation of their view of what a family is. Co-residence is no longer a fact, and the absence of one parent and the distraction and distress of the other may disrupt their expectations of love and support. Many children, though, adjust their perceptions of family to be congruent with changed household structures and are pragmatic in their conceptions of family. This acceptance of difference was expressed by a 14-year-old in the UK who said, "My family is different from other people's but I don't mind because who says what a family should be like?" (Smart et al., 2000).

As we know, love and emotional support are not always available to children who grow up with two parents in their household. One young woman whose parents had stayed together unhappily throughout her childhood and adolescence remarked that "it would have been better to have one parent there for you than two who were not" (Pryor, 1999). Awareness of the unhappiness of parents can lead to a chronic sense of instabil-

Awareness of the unhappiness of parents can lead to a chronic sense of instability and anxiety in many children, and the experience of children whose parents separate in their early adult years suggests that a lack of emotional support and fear of the family disintegrating pervade their childhoods and impose emotional burdens on children living in intact but unhappy families.

ity and anxiety in many children, and the experience of children whose parents separate in their early adult years suggests that a lack of emotional support and fear of the family disintegrating pervade their childhoods and impose emotional burdens on children living in intact but unhappy families (Pryor, 1999).

Children's understanding of marriage and divorce

Children's understanding of the dynamics of adult relationships such as marriage and divorce are inevitably vicarious since they have not been directly involved. Their impressions will be based on observation of their own parents, other family members, and parents of friends; and on the pervasive cultural and social images of marriage and divorce present in their day-to-day world. Cultural icons that might influence children include the marriage tableau depicted and enacted so widely, and the specter of "broken homes" conveyed by the media and some politicians.

Marriage and divorce
Developmental trends that parallel children's more general understanding of relationships and families are apparent in the ways that children see marriage and divorce (Kurdek & Siesky, 1980; Mazur, 1993). Younger children describe them using physical concepts, including co-residence and things that people do at a practical level. In middle childhood (approximately 7 to 10 years), actions, abilities, and skills associated with marriage are emphasized: for example, raising children and getting things done for the family. As children approach adolescence, they focus on emotional and psychological factors. These include the presence or absence of love, and interpersonal aspects such as compatibility. Young people at this level are able, as well, to understand several perspectives at once, such as those of both parents, and of children and parents (Kurdek & Siesky, 1980; Mazur, 1993).

Age-related *attitudes* to marriage also follow a developmental pattern.

Young children are most likely to say that being married means living happily ever after and that being single is bad (Mazur, 1993). Older children (9- to 10-year-olds) are more likely to believe that an unhappily married couple, with or without children, should get divorced. No differences in attitudes to marriage have been found between young children living in original families and those who experience separation; however, other studies have noted differences in adolescents (Tasker, 1992). In sum, there are few studies upon which to base conclusions and there is a need for more. However, children's understanding appears to follow a predictable sequence based on age and, to a lesser extent, their own experiences.

Causes and consequences of divorce
Children's perceptions of the causes of divorce have been explored with 9- to 11-year-old children, using vignettes (Kalter & Plunkett, 1984). Parental incompatibility was the most likely cause to be mentioned; however, a third of these children also thought that the child in the vignette was the cause of the separation. The most often-perceived consequences of parental separation for children were emotional and behavioral problems, with sadness and preoccupation also frequently mentioned. A similar aged group was asked by the same authors about what they thought children's reactions to parental divorce would be (Plunkett & Kalter, 1984). Three kinds of reaction were derived from the children's responses: sadness and insecurity, active coping (helping, wanting to do better at school), and feelings of abandonment. Children living in original families were more likely than those whose parents had separated to say that children experience abandonment and use passive ways of coping. Those from disrupted homes were less worried about abandonment, and more likely to see active mastery as a way of coping. A very large majority of all children thought that when parents separate, children wish their parents would get back together (95 percent), and nearly 70 percent said that children would feel the separation was their fault. As we saw earlier, though, children whose parents have separated are less likely after some time has passed to blame themselves for their parents' separation.

Children's understanding of the continuity of parenting after divorce
A specific focus on children's understanding of the continuity of parenting after parental separation was taken in an English study of over 300 children between the ages of 4 and 14 years (McGurk & Glachan, 1987). Three levels of understanding were identified, in which the youngest (4-year-olds) were most likely to offer a naive belief in the continuation of

parenting with no logical justification. At the next level, 6-year-olds saw continuity of parenting as conditional on whether the parents lived together. Other factors that were important at this level were affection between the nonresident parent and child, the subsequent marital status of that parent, and the sex of the parent. Mothers were more likely, overall, to be seen as parents after separation. Older children affirmed the continuation of parenthood and based it on the differentiation of parental and marital roles. Again, a developmental progression in understanding is clear; physical ways of understanding give way to psychological bases. Throughout, however is a consistent acknowledgment of emotional components. Children whose parents had divorced understood the continuity of parenthood at a more advanced level for their age than those in intact families (McGurk & Glachan, 1987).

How do children view remarriage?

When children's attitudes to stepfamilies were examined, it was found that a majority of a sample of 119 5- to 10-year olds thought remarriage was good (Mazur, 1993). Younger children were most likely to endorse stepmothers, especially 8-year-olds (70 percent). Even more felt favorably toward stepfathers: 77 percent thought it was "good" to have a stepfather. Older children were not so sure about stepparents; 46 percent thought it was good to have a stepmother and 40 percent felt the same about a stepfather. These attitudes did not vary according to whether or not children themselves lived in a stepfamily. In Anyan's (1998) New Zealand study of adolescents, only 54 percent saw a stepfamily as a real family and stepfamilies were ranked twelfth as real families, below both mother-headed and father-headed lone-parent families. This more cautious endorsement by older children may reflect several factors, including a more realistic understanding of the complexity of families and an increased emphasis on the importance of biological ties.

Children's views about living arrangements after parents separate

As we saw earlier, children whose parents separate nominate the loss of contact with their fathers as one of the worst aspects of parental separation. Arrangements about living and visiting are also usually made for children by adults; in two studies that have examined children's participation, 67 percent (Smith et al., 1997) and 75 percent (McDonald, 1990) of young people said they were not consulted about living arrangements. Although there is some recognition that children might be involved in the decisions arising from their parents' separation, we know little about what children generally think about visiting patterns and living arrangements after parental separation. A few studies, though, have been carried out in Canada, the USA, and New Zealand, that have asked children from the ages of 12 through to young adulthood what their preferred living situations would be (Kurdek & Sinclair, 1986; Derevensky & Deschamps, 1997; Pryor, 1998). Young people were asked in various ways about their views, including vignettes and questionnaires. Between 61 percent (Canada) and 68 percent (New Zealand) of those asked endorsed spending equal time with both parents. There were some age differences: younger children were more likely than those who were older to want to spend equal time with both parents. Only one study reported sex differences: in the US group girls were more likely than boys to want to live with mothers. Findings were mixed with regard to the relevance of young people's own experiences to their attitudes. In the New Zealand study, which used vignettes to ask over 200 adolescents between the ages of 13 and 17 about their attitudes, their own experiences of parental separation or living in stepfamilies made no difference to their responses (Pryor, 1998). The Canadian young people whose parents had not separated were, though, more likely than those who had experienced separation to say they would want to spend equal time with both parents. Only 22 percent of those whose parents had separated said that in retrospect they would have wanted to spend equal time with both parents. The age difference (the Canadian group were university students) suggests that the lifestyles of adolescents better fit the arrangement of living with one parent and visiting another within a flexible schedule. In an English study, children whose parents were both actively involved in their lives after separation were asked about their experiences of co-parenting (Smart et al., 2000). For most, it was a "normal" experience that fulfilled their desire to have regular contact with both parents, although they described problems such as moving clothes from house to house, or difficulties when parents lived far apart. Some also said they missed one parent when they were at the other's house. They talked of being concerned about fairness to their parents and wanted to share their time equally with them. They also expressed a strong desire that their parents respect each other and treat each other civilly. In the ALSPAC group, over half of children regarded moving between houses without negative or with positive feelings. One in four had negative feelings. Positive feelings were more likely if they had had an active role in making decisions about living arrangements, and negative feelings were more likely if communication with parents about problems was infrequent (Dunn et al., in press a).

Children's understanding of transitions

Children's understandings of marriage, parenting, divorce, and remarriage differ by age. Young children see marriage and divorce in concrete terms (e.g. living together or not, doing things, stepparents being good or bad). Children in middle childhood emphasize activities and skills, and parental and marital roles. Adolescents focus on psychological factors such as compatibility, and are more thoughtful about the advantages and disadvantages of stepfamilies and living arrangements after divorce.

Overview

Children experience their parents' separation as a profound disruption to their lives and to their sense of family. Their reactions when it happens are diverse, and reflect variations in their age and understanding, as well as the ways in which the transition is handled by adults. For some it is a release from being in a household filled with tension and argument; for others it is an unwelcome surprise. For most, the experience is mixed and they show remarkable resilience, adjusting their concept of what their family is, and incorporating people from outside their postdivorce household as well as new stepkin. There are some direct messages to be taken from what children say about their experiences. First, they want explanations about what is happening, and access to information and support from parents and others. Second, they find ongoing acrimony between parents painful, especially if they are drawn into the battle. Third, they want to be able to continue their relationships with both parents in as equitable a way as possible.

At the beginning of this chapter three areas of debate about children's views were identified. The first was whether they hold and can articulate views about parents' separation and family change. It is clear when children are asked, that they want adults to listen to their views and feelings about what is happening in their lives. This does not, though, necessarily mean listening to them in the same way as to adults; there are developmental differences in the ways children make sense of families and family change, and *not* to acknowledge these differences may be to fail to empower them by not communicating and listening in appropriate ways. It does, though, mean according them the respect given to adults by listening to them seriously.

Second, the relative importance of children's views is acknowledged in their rights to express their wishes about matters of importance to them that are being recognized in law. At an international level they have been enshrined in legislation in the United Nations Convention on the Rights of the Child. In the UK both the Children Act of 1989 and the Family Law Act of 1996 acknowledge to some extent the rights of children to be heard in law, although the mechanisms by which they might be heard are confusing and ambiguous (Roche, 1996; Lyon et al., 1999). In areas of public law, such as child protection, the law requires that children be consulted in proceedings concerning them. In private law, however, where provisions relating to divorce are located, children cannot at present be independently represented. As early as 1968 in New Zealand, the Guardianship Act stated that the Family Court is required to "ascertain the wishes of the child, if the child is able to express them" (section 23(2)). In the US, the Convention of the Rights of the Child has not been ratified; interestingly, the only other country not to have done so is Somalia, which does not have a recognized government. Children's preferences in the US are generally taken into consideration when the child is "above a certain age (usually about twelve)" (Nolo, 2000). It is notable that of 8 factors listed as being taken into consideration, this comes seventh after other factors including, for example, whether or not the child is exposed to second-hand smoke. In practice, then, mechanisms for taking children's views into account are not particularly systematic, and vary from state to state.

In principle, in many countries the law is in a position to empower children in situations where it is relevant, even if this fails to happen in practice. There are, however, some areas of their lives where the law has no place, or where it is not so evident that their views will be heard or heeded. Where parents make decisions about living arrangements without resorting to legal assistance, for example, the parents' arrangements are rarely challenged. In countries like New Zealand, Australia, and the UK this is the majority of families. As noted by one writer, "the principle of family autonomy prevails over the paramountcy of the child's welfare" (Parry, 1994, p. 4).

A third area of the debate about children's views concerns their wishes about the extent of participation in decision-making. Although it is now usually accepted that children's wishes and feelings should be taken into account, it is not safe to assume that all children want full decision-making powers. When asked, children show the diversity of responses to participation that we have come to expect in family matters. Some, often younger children, want no input into decision-making; 28 percent in one

Children tend to hold "conservative" views of families, seeing them as properly constituted by two married parents who live with each other and their children in the same house. Children would add, however, a crucial caveat – that families should love and support each other. When families do break down, their responses are diverse but generally reflect their distress at losing what they know as an ordinary family. What is remarkable is the degree of resilience and adaptability shown by children. The are able, especially with the help of contextual factors such as good communication and close relationships with both parents, to survive and even thrive in rearranged family forms and to adapt their understanding of families to these realignments.

UK study felt this way (Brannen et al., 1999a), and younger children in another English group thought parents should decide (Smart & Neale, 1999). A similar percentage think that children should make decisions alone (Brannen et al., 1999a). Most, though, feel that parents and children together should make decisions about living arrangements after separation, and make a clear distinction between participation and self-determination (Smart & Neale, 1999). As one young person said:

> I think like your mum and dad like try and push you to make your own decisions . . . I think some decisions you should make for yourself . . . but sometimes there are some decisions that you can't make on your own, you need to like either get your friends involved, or your teachers or your parents, or your family. (Morrow, 1998)

How does this discussion inform the wider debate about family change? Children tend to hold "conservative" views of families, seeing them as properly constituted by two married parents who live with each other and their children in the same house. Children would add, however, a crucial caveat – that families should love and support each other. When families do break down, their responses are diverse but generally reflect their distress at losing what they know as an ordinary family. What is remarkable is the degree of resilience and adaptability shown by children. The are able, especially with the help of contextual factors such as good communication and close relationships with both parents, to survive and even thrive in rearranged family forms and to adapt their understanding of families to these realignments. In this way, children fit a general liberal view of being resilient. The liberal view of children as being agents by holding views and being willing and able to articulate them is also supported by what they say; however, they do not always or even often want to have responsibilities equal to those of adults in making far-reaching decisions about their lives. Overall, it is safe to say that children would like their families to be as an ideal conservative view would portray them. They are, though, sufficiently aware of the nuances in family contexts to know that, where love and support are absent, families can and might be better to change, and children are sufficiently adaptable to survive the transitions with regret and longing, but not necessarily with damage. The ways in which adults handle such transitions are the keys to children's successful management of change.

5

Families that Separate

A family is a group of people which all care about each other. They can cry together, laugh together, argue together and go through all the emotions together. Some live together as well. Families are for helping each other through life.

13-year-old (Morrow, 1998)

A full understanding of children's experience of family change requires a wider view than one focused on children's achievements, behavior, emotional responses, and temperament. The development of children, whether from original, separated, or reconstituted families, occurs in a broad context involving other members of their immediate family and members of their extended family. It is also affected by interaction with peer groups and institutions, such as schools.

In this chapter we are going to prejudge the claims of both liberal and conservative perspectives to some extent. Based on the findings of several longitudinal studies (described in chapter 3), we believe that processes of family change occur over many years, before and after separation itself, and not just around the time of family breakdown. Divorce and repartnering do not occur at random, either in terms of their timing or in relation to the type of families that are affected. It is possible, then, that the development of children who experience such transitions has already been influenced by the different circumstances they live in long before the transitions occur, and also long afterwards. It is also likely that transitions for some children have a detrimental impact on their progress, in the short or long terms, and for others have a beneficial effect. Other children may fare little differently following separation or remarriage, or may only show temporary changes in their behavior and general development. What might explain this diversity of outcomes?

It would be possible to produce an extremely long list of possible differences between families that separate and those that do not. Those aspects of marital relationships and the circumstances of families that predict subsequent divorce are subjects of wide interest (Burns, 1980; Kitson et al.,

1985; White, 1990; Kiernan & Mueller, 1999). The variation in financial and other circumstances of different family types, including original families, lone-parent families, and stepfamilies, has also been researched extensively (Funder, 1996; Maclean & Eekelaar, 1997; Thompson & Amato, 1999). We will start here with a consideration of what family attributes are thought to be the most important influences on children's progress, irrespective of family structure or the experience of transitions, since it is likely that similar factors will be involved across different family types. The likelihood, however, of children experiencing any of these particular risk or protective factors will vary depending on their family circumstances.

Factors Influencing Social, Psychological, and Physical Development

Despite the diversity of characteristics that are influenced by family type, a general pattern emerges from the considerable literature on child-based and childhood environmental factors associated with social, psychological, and physical health outcomes, whether in childhood, adolescence, or adulthood. The following seven domains cover the factors usually thought to be most important:

1 Aspects of family social class or socioeconomic status, including parental education, parents' occupations (or lack thereof), income, and other indicators of financial hardship or material disadvantage, e.g. poor housing conditions.
2 Family environment factors, such as parental relationships including conflict, violence, and other abuse; dimensions of parent–child relationships, such as care and affection, authoritative parenting, intrusive control, and coercion, and mistreatment such as verbal, physical, and sexual abuse; sibling relationships; and the interconnections and dynamics that occur between family relationships.
3 Parental mental disorders, general psychological distress, and substance abuse.
4 Parental antisocial and criminal behavior.
5 Life events and other sources of stress.
6 Social support from peers, siblings, or significant others, such as relatives or schoolteachers.
7 Neighborhood characteristics that constitute community social capital, e.g. measures of social disadvantage aggregated from census or

other household data; official statistics on the incidence/prevalence of social, criminal, or health-related events; the quality of schools; the influence of peer groups; and the disruption of frequent family moves.

As well as these environmental factors, there are also important individual differences between children, such as their gender, intellectual skills, coping skills, interpersonal skills, self-esteem, temperament, and other facets of personality (Garmezy, 1985; Rutter, 1990; Deater-Deckard & Dunn, 1999; Hetherington & Stanley-Hagan, 1999). These characteristics can predispose children to poor outcomes, and may in part reflect genetic as well as environmental differences between them. There is evidence for the *heritability* of many of the outcomes we are concerned with here, i.e. genetic differences between individuals account for some (but by no means all) of the observed variation in social, psychological, and health characteristics in the general population (Kendler et al., 1995).

Although it is possible to separate out different facets of environmental and individual factors into conceptually distinct groupings, there is, in practice, a substantial interrelationship among these dimensions. Children brought up in materially poor circumstances, for example, are more likely to have parents who show antisocial behavior or have substance abuse problems. Those whose parents are less loving and more punitive in their childrearing style are more likely to be physically, verbally, and sexually abused than children whose parents are more caring (Rodgers, 1996a). Even environmental and genetic risks cannot be neatly disentangled, as the likelihood of experiencing adverse environmental circumstances or stressful events is to some degree linked with heredity. This phenomenon, termed the "nature of nurture" (Plomin & Bergeman, 1991), can arise because individuals have influence over their own environments, whether by conscious choice or otherwise, and people of different temperament or personality will vary in their propensities to encounter environmental dangers.

As well as separate risk factors being likely to occur together, there are also possibilities of multiple risk factors having cumulative or even synergistic effects, where their combined impact is greater than would be expected by adding together the effects of individual sources of adversity. Aside from more tragic instances where children are severely abused, the pattern seen across different areas of development is that the children who fare least well are those who experience the greatest number of adverse conditions and events, rather than any particular circumstance or combination of circumstances (Rodgers, 1990a; Mullen et al., 1996).

Mediating and Moderating Factors

In what ways might risk factors be related to outcomes for children? Even if these various groups of risk factors outlined above are shown to be causally related to these outcomes we still cannot conclude that they contribute to differences between children from separated and intact families. Ideally, we would like to have evidence supporting two further steps in the argument. First, that divorced families are more likely than intact families to be subjected to the risk factors concerned and, second, that taking account of such risk factors, individually and collectively, does in fact make a significant contribution to explaining the differences in outcomes for children from different family types. We can deal with the first of these steps now and will return to the second in chapter 8.

It is helpful here to make an important distinction between *mediating* and *moderating* factors (Baron & Kenny, 1986). Mediating factors are those characteristics (of a family or an individual) that are thought to be involved in the causal chain linking an event or circumstance (in this case parental separation) to an outcome. For instance, it may be that financial difficulties experienced by families as a *result* of divorce contribute to poorer educational achievement in the children. Alternatively, low household income before parents separate could make children more vulnerable to what happens afterward, in which case poverty would be described as a moderating factor. In practice, not all factors can be neatly labeled as one or other factor but can be both, as suggested by these examples. A third possibility is that financial difficulties contribute to the likelihood of divorce as well as to poor outcomes for children, such as lower educational attainment, in which case the link between divorce and educational outcome arises from the circumstances already present before separation itself.

Socioeconomic status and financial hardship: hardship in lone-parent families

The association between financial hardship and divorce is widely recognized in developed countries (Maclean & Eekelaar, 1983; Brannen et al., 1989; Thompson & Amato, 1999) and the levels of poverty in lone-parent families are especially high across English-speaking countries (Bradshaw, 1998). In particular, lone-mother families are much less well off than two-parent families, with lone-father families being in between but closer to two-parent families (Garfinkel & McLanahan, 1986; Ford & Millar, 1998; Burström et al., 1999). Stepfamilies are substantially better off than lone-parent families, but are still behind intact, original two-parent families in this respect (Thomson et al., 1994). In the United Kingdom, lone parents are less likely than those in two-parent families to have paid employment (Haskey, 1993) and more likely to have low incomes, receive state benefits, live in rented accommodation, have mortgage or rent arrears, share or lack altogether basic household amenities such as bathroom and kitchen facilities, and report financial hardship (Essen, 1978; Bryson et al., 1997; Benzeval, 1998; Hope, Power, & Rodgers, 1999). They are less likely to have savings, the use of a car, or central heating (Hope, Power, & Rodgers, 1999). In the Avon Longitudinal Study of Pregnancy and Childhood, when the children were aged 21 months, poor housing conditions varied significantly across family type, with a high rate of 35 percent in lone-mother families compared with 9 percent in intact original families (Deater-Deckard & Dunn, 1999). Stepfamilies were intermediate between these two extremes. Benzeval (1998) reported that 65.4 percent of lone-mother families were in the bottom 20 percent of the family income distribution, compared with 41.7 percent of lone-father families and 19.2 percent of couple families, using data from the 1992–3 and 1994–5 British General Household Surveys.

For the US, McLanahan and Sandefur (1994) gave figures from the Bureau of the Census that 45 percent of lone-mother families lived below the poverty line in 1992 compared with 8.4 percent of two-parent families. Their own analyses of families with adolescent children in the Panel Study of Income Dynamics gave poverty rates of 26.5 percent for lone-parent families, 5.3 percent for two-parent families, and 8.7 percent for stepfamilies. In the US National Educational Longitudinal Study of 1988, mean family income for lone-mother families was $18,393 compared with $50,789 for two-parent families and $35,677 for lone-father families (Downey, 1994). There were also substantial differences across these different family types in the proportion that had home computers for educational purposes (16 percent, 32 percent, and 26 percent respectively) and the proportion that had saved money for their children's college education (31 percent, 49 percent, and 42 percent respectively).

In Canada, a supplementary study to the Ontario Health Survey found 46.1 percent of lone-mother families were classified as low income by comparison with 8.7 percent of mothers in two-parent families (Lipman et al., 1998). About two-thirds of the lone mothers identified themselves as being separated or divorced. In a second Canadian sample from London, Ontario, families of separated and divorced single mothers had an average annual income of CAN$22,030 compared with CAN$54,900 for families of married mothers (Davies et al., 1997). A similar picture is seen in Australia, where lone parents are more likely to be unemployed, live in rented accommodation, and have difficulty paying bills and making loan repayments (Australian Bureau of Statistics, 1991; Australian Bureau of Statistics, 1993). Lone mothers in New Zealand, according to the 1996 census, are also more likely to be unemployed and seeking work and less likely to have full- or part-time employment compared with mothers in two-parent families (Statistics New Zealand, 1998). For all lone-parent families in New Zealand (mothers and fathers combined), the proportion living in rented accommodation was 51.4 percent compared with 20.0 percent of two-parent families. These figures may well underestimate true differences in socioeconomic status, as lone parents living with their own parents are classified according to the housing tenure of the total household rather than of their individual family unit.

Socioeconomic circumstances preceding separation

As well as the pervasiveness of these socioeconomic differences across countries and over time, their magnitude is also very striking. Often, lone-parent families are several times more likely to experience financial difficulties than two-parent families. Such differences are far greater than the differences found for children's outcomes, as described in chapter 3 (Rodgers & Pryor, 1998). Given the extent of economic hardship in lone-parent families, it is reasonable to consider a decline in financial circumstances as a significant aspect of the link between parental separation and poor outcomes for children, as suggested by some commentators (Burghes, 1994). However, the picture is rather more complex than this, since financial hardship can precede as well as follow separation.

First, there is an association of divorce with socioeconomic status (or educational background of the parents) measured long before separation. In the 1946 British Birth Cohort study, for example, men and women who had divorced or separated by age 43 were less likely to have had advanced education than those who had married but never divorced (Richards et al., 1997). Similar findings were reported from the 1958 British Birth Cohort, where the risk of partnership breakdown (either marriage or cohabitation) up to the age of 33 years decreased progressively with increasing levels of educational qualifications, such that those with no qualifications at all had a 60 percent greater chance of separation than those with degrees (Kiernan & Mueller, 1999). However, Kiernan (1999) was also able to show that the gradient of risk was accounted for by differences in the *ages* at which people had entered their partnerships. On average, those with lower levels of qualifications started partnerships at a younger age, and this is a well-established risk factor related to subsequent separation across many countries (White, 1990; Bumpass et al., 1991; Bracher et al., 1993). An exception to the pattern that better education and socioeconomic position protect against marital separation is for women in older age groups. They may be more capable of leaving their partner and supporting their family if they are better qualified and more competitive in the labor market. In this case, higher socioeconomic status and education can increase the likelihood of separation (South & Spitze, 1986; Ono, 1998).

Another connection between socioeconomic status and divorce is that *becoming* poor may increase the likelihood of family separation. Reasons given by couples themselves for divorce commonly include financial difficulties (Burns, 1984; Cleek & Pearson, 1985; Gigy & Kelly, 1992), and longitudinal studies in the US and Britain have identified poorer economic resources as a predictor of divorce (Galligan & Bahr, 1978; Kitson et al., 1985; O'Connor et al., 1999a). In the British 1958 Birth Cohort, parents who divorced when their study child was age 11–16 years were substantially less well off than parents of other children in the sample even before their divorce (Elliott et al., 1993). For example, 8.2 percent of parents who stayed together over the following five years reported being seriously troubled by financial hardship, compared to 18.4 percent of those who subsequently divorced. A downward drift or a sudden drop in economic status is, then, a factor leading to divorce for some families. Similarly, in the British Household Panel Survey there was a five-fold variation in the likelihood of subsequent divorce (over a 3-year period) across those couples initially identifying themselves as finding their financial situation "very difficult" in comparison with those who were financially comfortable (Kiernan & Mueller, 1999). In the US the difference in divorce rates between richer and poorer sections of the population has narrowed over time (Kitson et al., 1985). This may not necessarily be the case in other countries, and there is insufficient evidence to draw firm conclusions. The parents of the 1958 British Birth Cohort children and the 1946 Birth Cohort children, however, showed very similar patterns of divorce rates by social class (Maclean & Wadsworth, 1988; Elliott et al., 1993).

Socioeconomic circumstances following separation

Does household income drop after separation? We have seen that poor socioeconomic circumstances often precede divorce; there is also clear evidence of a substantial drop in economic fortunes after separation, particularly for lone mothers with their children. The exact size of this drop has been the subject of some controversy in the US. Holden and Smock (1991) summarize a number of studies that reported declines in the living standards of women after divorce between 7 and 55 percent, and changes in the standards for men from a 19 percent reduction to an increase of 24 percent, two years after divorce. A particularly influential study in California reported a far larger drop for women of 73 percent, in contrast with a 42 percent rise in the standard of living of men after divorce (Weitzman, 1985). However, a reanalysis of the same data suggested an average decline in women's living standards of 27 percent and an increase for men of 10 percent (Peterson, 1996). The reanalysis measured income in relation to financial need, both before and after divorce.

An important aspect of lone-parent families is that their income does not increase at the same rate over time as for original families (Holden & Smock, 1991). Information from the Panel Study of Income Dynamics showed that, five years after divorce, lone mothers' average incomes still represented only 94 percent of their needs, up from 91 percent one year after divorce (Duncan & Hoffman, 1985). Divorced men and couples who remained married received an average of 130 percent of their needs. Repartnering helped, however, and women who remarried almost regained their socioeconomic standing, with incomes averaging 125 percent of needs five years after divorce.

In the UK the pattern of a large and sustained fall in living standards after divorce, especially for lone-mother families, was seen in the British 1958 Birth Cohort Study for separations occurring between 1969 and 1974 (Elliott et al., 1993). In two-parent families that stayed together, financial hardship decreased slightly from 8.2 to 7.4 percent, but for families that separated and where the children remained with their mother, hardship increased from 19.4 to 39.3 percent after divorce. The change was less dramatic for families where children stayed with their father after divorce, with hardship increasing from 15.6 to 22.2 percent over the five-year period. In the British Household Panel Survey, information collected over 1991–4 showed that the net household income of separated mothers fell by 17 percent but, for men, increased by 14 percent (Jarvis & Jenkins, 1998). For children involved in divorces there was an average drop in net income of 14 percent, reflecting the greater likelihood of children remaining with their mothers rather than their fathers. This study also shows considerable individual variability in the change of circumstances accompanying separation. One-quarter of the separating mothers had an *increase* in net income of at least 19 percent, but another quarter showed a drop of at least 38 percent. One-quarter of the separating fathers experienced a fall in net income of at least 29 percent and another quarter increased their net income by at least 47 percent. The economic consequences of divorce are, then, diverse.

In Australia this situation is similar to those in the US and the UK. The Economic Consequences of Marriage Breakdown Survey, conducted by the Australian Institute of Family Studies, found that single women after divorce had household income levels around 53 percent of their preseparation level compared to 82 percent for men, and there was little difference between those who had been separated less than three years and those who had been separated for longer (Weston, 1986). Average levels for repartnered women and men were, however, above their preseparation income. This study also looked at living standards using a measure of "income–needs difference" scores, based on equivalence scales which define the income required by different types of families to achieve the same standard of living. On this basis, lone-mother families were the least well off, receiving AUS$86 per week less than their assessed need, compared with lone-father families receiving AUS$69 *more* than their assessed need. Repartnered men and women with dependent children were just slightly below the level of their assessed need (by an average of $6 per week), while repartnered men without dependent children had average income levels $153 above their defined need levels.

Do lone-parent families recover from financial adversity over time? As we have indicated, any recovery is slight in the first few years (and even five years) after separation unless parents remarry, but few studies have considered longer periods. There may be some longer-term recovery, but perhaps not until ten years after divorce, and this may be a consequence of older children leaving the household (Holden & Smock, 1991).

In summary, there is remarkable consistency across countries in the socioeconomic circumstances of lone-parent families and, especially, the financial hardship endured by lone-mother families. Some of these differences arise because divorce is more likely for families of lower social-class origins, and a worsening in the economic fortunes of families may also lead to separation. The most significant aspect of financial disadvantage in postdivorce families, though, arises from the substantial decline in their

There is remarkable consistency across countries in the socioeconomic circumstances of lone-parent families and, especially, the financial hardship endured by lone-mother families. Some of these differences arise because divorce is more likely for families of lower social class, and worsening economic fortunes of families may also lead to separation. The most significant aspect of financial disadvantage in postdivorce families, though, arises from the substantial decline in their income at the time of separation and the limited recovery from this drop in subsequent years. Single-parent families do not require the same absolute level of income as two-parent families in order to achieve the same standard of living. However, because of economies of scale, the requirements of lone-parent families are not simply the equivalent of the relative number of people in the household. There are high cost overheads, such as housing, that are involved for all households regardless of the number of people involved.

income at the time of separation and the limited recovery from this drop in subsequent years. Single-parent families do not require the same absolute level of income as two-parent families in order to achieve the same standard of living. However, because of economies of scale, the requirements of lone-parent families are not simply reduced in proportion to the number of people in the household. There are high cost overheads, such as housing, that are involved for all households regardless of the number of people involved. Even when differences in the estimated need of different types of family are taken into account, lone-parent families are substantially disadvantaged, and this is, again, most apparent for lone-mother families. The increase in the number of lone-parent families in recent decades had had a substantial impact on the profile of poverty in English-speaking countries. In the United Kingdom, the proportion of children living in poverty (defined as half the average income) increased from 10.0 percent in 1968 to 32.9 percent in 1995–6 (Gregg et al., 1999). More than half of that increase can be attributed to the rise in numbers of children living in poor lone-parent families. By 1995–6, 42.5 percent of British children living in poverty were from lone-parent families.

Family Environment

Conflict

It might be assumed that higher rates of conflict exist between couples that subsequently divorce than those who stay together. However, a considerable proportion of divorces occurs in families where there has not been a high level of apparent conflict. In the United States many marriages end following a period of low overt conflict, and boredom may be a significant factor in precipitating separation (Amato & Booth, 1997; Booth & Amato, 2001). Couples may grow apart in their interests, or their affection for one another may gradually diminish (Wolcott & Hughes, 1999). Alternately, low levels of marital conflict may reflect an "emotional divorce" that takes place some time, even years, before parental separation (Hetherington, 1999). In such a situation, the atmosphere in a family may be contemptuous and withdrawn rather than openly hostile. At the other end of the spectrum are violent relationships marked by verbal, psychological, and physical abuse, sometimes involving abuse directed at the children, and not surprisingly such violence is associated with marital breakdown (Burns, 1980; Wolcott & Hughes, 1999). Between these extremes are relationships that may be relatively conflict free until particular circumstances, such as an extramarital affair, lead to a sharp increase in hostility. A similar acute phase of conflict may also occur between couples where one partner introduces the possibility of divorce and this is contrary to the wishes of the other. We know from general studies of the effects of conflict on child development that severity and, especially, chronicity of conflict and abuse are related to the degree of damage to children (Grych & Fincham, 1990; Cummings & Davies, 1994). Marital conflict is especially harmful for children if it happens in their presence, involves physical violence, is about the children themselves, or is unresolved. It is linked with behavior problems and conduct disorder especially, but also with anxiety and depression (Buchanan et al., 1991; Grych, 1998; Hetherington & Stanley-Hagan, 1999).

Families vary, then, in the presence and level of conflict leading up to separation, and there is further heterogeneity in the changes accompanying separation. For some families, separation may bring an end to a long period of conflict, and this can represent an escape route for children who have witnessed or been involved in such conflict. In other families, separation may signal the beginning of a period of anger and hostility between parents over such issues as property settlement, child support, residence

For some families, separation may bring an end to a long period of conflict, and this can represent an escape route for children who have witnessed or been involved in such conflict. In other families, separation may signal the beginning of a period of anger and hostility between parents over such issues as property settlement, child support, residence and contact with children – issues that often put the focus on children themselves ... Children can become both the weapons and the spoils in a war they have no wish to be involved in.

and contact with children (Maccoby & Mnookin, 1992) – issues that often put the focus on children themselves. Children are unlikely to remain ignorant of any dispute over residence or contact, and they are used all too often as intermediaries or messengers in such disputes (Buchanan et al., 1991). They face considerable difficulties in maintaining respect and affection for both their parents when these have been lost by the adults themselves. Children can become both the weapons and the spoils in a war they have no wish to be involved in. Furthermore, a small but fierce proportion of parents maintain high levels of dispute for some years after they separate. In the Stanford Study, for example, 34 percent of parents were engaged in conflicted relations one and a half years after divorce, and three and a half years later 26 percent were still engaged in conflict (Buchanan et al., 1991; Maccoby & Mnookin, 1992). It is, however, difficult to predict postdivorce levels of conflict from predivorce levels (Camara & Resnick, 1988; Booth & Amato, 2001) and, even long after separation, the repartnering of either parent may initiate or resurrect conflict between the child's parents or introduce new sources of conflict within stepfamilies (see chapter 6).

Parenting

Pivotal aspects of the family environment for children in all families are parenting and parent–child relationships. How are they affected by family transitions? The quality of parenting and of parent–child relationships diminishes possibly before, and certainly after, separation (Emery, 1982; Hetherington, 1989, 1993; Emery, 1994; Simons & Associates, 1996; Deater-Deckard & Dunn, 1999). Mothers in families that will subsequently divorce already display higher levels of negativity and lower levels of control toward their children than those in low-conflict nondivorcing families (Hetherington, 1999); and fathers in these families evidence less control than those in low-conflict nondivorcing families. After separation, mothers in the Iowa studies were more likely than those in distressed or happy marriages to show inept parenting (Simons & Associates, 1996). In another US study, 31 percent of lone-parent mothers said they left their children alone sometimes compared with 20 percent of mothers in original families (McLanahan & Sandefur, 1994); they were also less likely to set rules for TV watching (31.9 vs. 35.9 percent), to set bed times (8.7 vs. 8.8 percent), to help with schoolwork (85 vs. 90 percent), and to provide supervision for their children (75 vs. 84 percent). Separated parents are also more likely to display negativity than mothers in original and stepfamilies (Hetherington & Clingempeel, 1992; Deater-Deckard & Dunn, 1999) and less likely to show positivity (Hetherington & Clingempeel, 1992). Parenting styles, too, are different in lone-parent households; authoritative parenting (high support and monitoring) is found to be lower in lone-parent households (Avenevoli et al., 1999). However, not all studies report reduced parenting by lone parents; Scottish adolescents reported no differences by family structure in strictness, fights with parents, or relationships with parents (Sweeting & West, 1995a).

Parent–child interactions are, though, two-way streets. Just as the stress of conflict and hardship, and aspects of parents' personalities, affect adult behavior, so too do children's characteristics play their part. Temperamentally difficult, distressed, and badly behaved children make major contributions to the quality of parenting and to parent–child relations. The direction of effects between children and parents is by no means just adult to child, and in stepfamilies children may play a particularly significant role in determining the nature of interactions (Hetherington & Clingempeel, 1992).

The amount of time that has passed since a separation is an important consideration for parent–child relationships. Family transitions have an adverse impact on parent–child relationships at least in the short term (DeGarmo & Forgatch, 1999). However, in many instances, their quality improves over time and returns to levels similar to those in original families, although conflict between lone-parent mothers and children is inclined to persist (Hetherington & Clingempeel, 1992).

Abuse and neglect

Children of separated families are more likely to experience abuse and neglect than children who do not experience family transitions. The evidence for this comes predominantly from retrospective accounts because of the ethical and logistical problems of studying child abuse at the time.

Several studies of adults have collected information on a range of child-hood adversity, including psychological, physical, and sexual abuse, and have shown an association between parental separation and abuse. One community study of women in a Canadian city found a rate of around 16 percent for all forms of childhood sexual abuse for those women who did not experience parental separation, and about 35 percent for those that were separated from a parent (Bagley & Ramsey, 1985). A large survey in the South Island of New Zealand found higher levels of several forms of abuse reported by women whose parents had separated during their child-hood. Physical abuse was most likely to be associated with parental sepa-ration, followed by emotional, and then sexual abuse (Mullen et al., 1996).

From retrospective accounts, then, there emerges a significant link be-tween childhood abuse and marital breakdown. However, it is not usu-ally clear in studies whether the abuse occurred before or after separation or even whether birth parents or other adults (including stepparents) were the abusers (Jarvis et al., 1998; Gladstone et al., 1999). There is a good deal of controversy about the role of stepfathers in the abuse of children. Sociobiologists make strong claims about the danger stepfathers pose to children (Popenoe, 1994; Daly & Wilson, 1998); they argue that on the basis of nonbiological relationship children are at high levels of risk for abuse. Others dispute these claims (Coleman, 1994), citing research that suggests that although children living with biological parents are safest, those who do not are not preferentially abused by stepparents. It is prob-ably safe to conclude, with caution, that children in stepfamilies face higher levels of risk of abuse, but that it is not necessarily their stepfather who is the perpetrator. Nor is there good evidence on whether children abused in their original two-parent families are likely to escape from such abuse if the parents separate. At present, there is some concern that children re-main vulnerable to abuse after parental separation, especially from non-resident parents (Rhoades et al., 1999).

Parental Mental Health, Psychological Distress, and Substance Abuse

Psychiatric disorders

Professionals in psychiatric services and researchers have long recognized an association between divorce and problems with mental health and sub-stance abuse. Almost all forms of psychiatric illness are more common in divorced than in either married or never married people (Bloom et al., 1978; Robins & Regier, 1991). However, it is not clear to what extent divorce causes mental health problems or vice versa, whether certain common factors lead independently to both, or whether marital status is associated with different propensities to seek treatment (Bachrach, 1975; Gotlib & McCabe, 1990). Unmarried people are more likely to be admitted to psychiatric hospitals, while married patients are more likely to be treated as outpatients (Robertson, 1974), but associations between psychiatric disorders and marital status are also found in community surveys (Rodgers & Mann, 1986; Robins & Regier, 1991). The differential rates of seeking treatment by married and unmarried adults do not, therefore, explain the links between marital status and mental health. Some disorders have an impact on an individual's capacity to form and maintain relationships, and this is reflected in the reduced likelihood of marriage for those with substance abuse disorders and some severe psychiatric disorders, such as schizophrenia. For example, the earlier age of onset of schizophrenia in men compared with women (often in the late teenage years or early twenties), in combination with the tendency for women to marry at younger ages, leads to a much lower likelihood of men with this severe illness ever marrying (Häfner, 1992). However, severe mental illnesses such as schizophrenia and bipolar disorders are relatively uncommon, each affecting around 1 percent of the population (Helgason, 1964), and their significance cannot be great in the context of recent divorce rates in developed countries.

Paradoxically, many less severe psychiatric disorders (including substance use disorders) are associated with marrying at an *early* age (Forthofer et al., 1996). This, however, should not be taken to imply greater skill in romantic relationships, as an early age at marriage is consistently linked to the likelihood of divorce (White, 1990) and is associated with other adverse outcomes, including less financial security and poorer social support (Forthofer et al., 1996). The association between mental health problems and marital breakdown has been demonstrated in the US National Comorbidity Survey, which found that a first marriage was more likely to end in divorce for men and women with depressive, anxiety, or substance abuse disorders, and was especially likely for those with more than one psychiatric disorder (Kessler et al., 1998). This same study, making the assumption that these disorders were a causal factor in subsequent divorce, estimated that about 6 percent of all divorces in men and 10 percent in women are attributable to psychiatric disorders. The study, though, made no distinction between disorders that first occurred before marriage and those that began after marriage, and the authors point out that the associations could represent the influence of common risk factors for both divorce and disorder, such as childhood adversity.

High rates of marital breakdown are also seen in psychiatric patients. One follow-up study of depressed inpatients found that 20 percent had divorced or separated two years on average after discharge. This rate was 9 times greater than that expected in the population. Intriguingly, however, the large majority of these separations occurred in the patients whose spouse also suffered with a psychiatric illness (Merikangas, 1984).

Psychiatric disorder is, then, related to whether or not people marry in the first place and also to the likelihood that partnerships will last.

Psychological distress in divorced and separated people

Often, in studies of family transitions, researchers assess common symptoms of distress rather than specific psychiatric disorders. Typical scales include symptoms of depression and anxiety (often referred to collectively as *psychological distress*) that are frequently experienced by people in the general population. Higher scores on these scales are associated with diagnosed psychiatric disorder (especially depression and anxiety disorders), impairment of roles (for example, time off work or difficulty fulfilling family responsibilities), seeking professional help (from family doctors or specialist mental health services), and the likelihood of considering or attempting suicide (Lindelow et al., 1997; Rodgers et al., 1999). Community surveys are consistent in showing that divorced and separated people score higher on such scales than married or never married people, and this has been reported throughout English-speaking and other developed countries (Finlay-Jones & Burvill, 1977; Pearlin & Johnson, 1977; McGee et al., 1983; Cramer, 1993; Hope, Rodgers, & Power, 1999). These differences are often large, with divorced and separated adults having average scores that are considerably above those of married people. Correspondingly, measures of positive well-being show separated and divorced people are significantly worse off than the married and never married (Bradburn, 1967; Weingarten, 1985; Stack & Eshleman, 1998). These differences are considerably greater than those described in our summary of children's outcomes in different types of families (chapter 3). Are these differences a consequence of separation and its associated adversities, or does high psychological distress precede separation?

Psychological distress preceding separation

Several longitudinal studies have measured psychological distress on two or more occasions and so have been able to look at distress before and after marital transitions. Typically, these studies involve large samples selected from the general community, so that transitions such as first marriage, separation, and remarriage occur at the frequency expected in the general population. In an early study in Chicago, Menaghan (1985) compared the depression scores of married people who either remained married over the next four years or who subsequently divorced. At the start of the study, the 32 people who were to divorce over the next four years had very similar depression scores to those who were to remain married. Three further studies, two in the US (Doherty et al., 1989; Booth & Amato, 1991) and one in Norway (Mastekaasa, 1994), did find an association between initial psychological distress and later divorce, but this was only true when distress was measured within two or three years of the impending separation and not earlier. This suggests that there is an increase in psychological distress leading up to the time of separation, which is likely given that many marriages go through conflictual or turbulent phases in the years immediately before separation. Recent findings with young adults from the 1958 British Birth Cohort are consistent with this interpretation (Hope, Rodgers, & Power, 1999). Over 9,000 individuals were studied at ages 23 and 33, with their marital status and psychological distress scores obtained on both occasions. Distress in married people at age 23 predicted subsequent separation only in the two-year period following that first assessment, but was not related to separation after age 25.

Psychological distress following separation

As well as showing that psychological distress can precede separation by at least two years, studies have also shown increases in distress following marital separation. Four of the investigations already mentioned (Menaghan & Lieberman, 1986; Doherty et al., 1989; Booth & Amato, 1991; Hope, Rodgers, & Power, 1999) and one additional study in the US (Aseltine & Kessler, 1993) found that people had higher psychological distress scores after separation than before, and that these changes were significantly different from the average change seen in people who remained in intact marriages. Again, however, this basic picture is more complicated than it first seems. Distress rises at the time of separation and shortly after, but seems to abate in the longer term. Booth and Amato (1991) compared distress and unhappiness scores after divorce amongst those who had been separated for up to 2 years, for 2 to 4 years, and for longer than 4 years, and found there was a decline in moving from 2 to 4 years but not thereafter. A similar pattern was seen in divorced mothers studied in the Iowa Single parent Project (Lorenz et al., 1997), where depressive symptoms declined over time after separation, and eventually reached levels similar to those in comparable married mothers. An initial sharp rise in psychological distress followed by a fall in the years immediately following divorce was confirmed in the 1958 British Birth Cohort study (Hope, Rodgers, & Power, 1999). Men and women who were previously married (at age 23) and who then separated in the two years preceding their follow-up interview (at age 33) showed particularly marked increases in distress over the 10-year interval. However, in this study, even the men and women who had been separated for over 2 years, and possibly for as long as 10 years, still had significantly elevated distress scores compared to those who remained married throughout the 10-year period.

These studies have also helped to shed some light on what factors contribute to levels of distress following separation. Menaghan and Lieberman (1986) identified both deterioration in economic conditions and lack of social support as important factors contributing to the raised distress of the people who had divorced during the four years of their study in Chicago, although it is difficult to judge the importance of their findings given the small number in their sample who divorced in that time. Aseltine and Kessler (1993) concluded from their Detroit sample that financial pressures and role changes did not explain the impact of marital disruption on depressive symptoms. They did, however, find that marital disruption was associated with a *decrease* in depression for those who had prior marital problems (about 12 percent of their sample).

The contradictory findings for the importance of socioeconomic factors may be related to these holding a different significance for men and women after divorce. One cross-sectional study of psychological distress in divorced and separated people in northern California reported that material conditions contributed substantially to the greater distress of divorced women compared to those who were married, but was less important in explaining the heightened distress in divorced men (Gerstel et al., 1985). In the 1958 British Birth Cohort study, both economic circumstances and parental role were found to be important moderators of change in distress levels following separation for women, but not for men (Hope,

Rodgers, & Power, 1999). Divorced women who were upwardly mobile between the ages of 23 and 33 (as indicated by housing tenure) were similar to women who remained in intact marriages over that period, but other divorced women showed relative increases in their levels of distress. Furthermore, an increase in distress after separation was not seen in women who had no ongoing parental responsibilities (most of whom had no children at the time of their divorce). As expected, the mental well-being of women is particularly vulnerable to the impact of socioeconomic factors and the demands of childcare.

Financial hardship was found in the British sample to account for a considerable part of the elevated distress in lone mothers at age 33, even after adjustment for their distress levels 10 years earlier (Hope, Power, & Rodgers, 1999). However, it was not so much their income at that point in time which was important but their overall material circumstances, including arrears with rental or mortgage payments, other debts, lack of savings, living in rented accommodation, having problems with damp housing, having no access to a telephone, and having to share bathroom, kitchen, or washing facilities. It appears to be the state of accumulated resources (or lack of them), rather than current income level, that impacts on the mental health of adults, and this may explain why some studies with more limited measures fail to show the importance of economic factors (Aseltine & Kessler, 1993). These findings are reminiscent of research into the effects of unemployment on families, where long-term unemployment is seen to progressively erode material resources even when income (mainly from benefits) remains fairly constant (Fryer, 1990; Rodgers, 1991; Whelan et al., 1991).

Are there gender differences in distress following separation? Aseltine and Kessler (1993) reported greater increases in distress for women, but other studies have not found a sex difference (Gerstel et al., 1985; Booth & Amato, 1991; Hope, Rodgers, & Power, 1999). One possible reason for such variation is that women generally have higher scores on depression and psychological distress scales than do men and, indeed, have higher rates of diagnosed mood disorders and treatment for these (Weissman et al., 1993; Bebbington, 1996). This difference in base level makes it more likely that one will observe statistically significant changes over time for women, just as parallel changes in drinking levels are more easily demonstrated in men.

Another reason for different findings between studies may reflect the distinction between acute and chronic stress mentioned earlier. It has been suggested that divorcing men may be particularly vulnerable to the former

(Rodgers, 1995). Several studies have asked recently separated people to report their feelings of distress at the time of the separation and, sometimes, how they felt beforehand. Some have also inquired about consulting family doctors because of distress, taking medication, and having time off work. Men are indeed acutely distressed at the time of separation, and show surprisingly high rates of help-seeking, contact with health services, and use of medication (Burns, 1980; Ambrose et al., 1983; Jordan, 1985). They are also more likely than women to experience their first-ever period of depression at a clinically significant level (Bruce & Kim, 1992).

Further light has been shed on sex differences in the acute reaction to separation, by making the distinction between initiators and non-initiators of separation, since women are more likely than men to initiate separation. *Leaving* and *left* partners have been compared after separation, to investigate whether initiators would report more preseparation and less postseparation distress than the non-initiating partners (Pettit & Bloom, 1984). *Left* partners showed the strongest reaction to separation, regardless of gender, and it was this factor rather than gender itself that accounted for the greater acute distress of men (Weston, 1986). *Leaving* partners report their time of greatest distress as being before they initiated the separation, with relief often following their decision.

> Distress may change at the time of separation and subsequently, and factors that contribute to long-term distress in divorced parents include economic hardship for lone mothers. The chronic and acute effects of separation each have their own distinctive pattern and set of influences. Acute effects are common in men and seem to reflect their lower likelihood of initiating separation and their apparent failure to see it coming when initiated by their partner. However, women show the greater psychological distress in the longer term, and are more likely to be depressed at clinically significant levels, as is the case in the general population.

Overall, this area of research provides evidence that divorce and mental health each have an influence on the other. Psychiatric disorders of clinically significant levels are linked with very high rates of divorce and separation, but otherwise psychological distress does not seem to be a major factor causing divorce. Rather, it increases only during the period immediately before separation. Distress may change at the time of separation and subsequently, and factors that contribute to long-term distress in divorced parents include economic hardship for lone mothers. The chronic and acute effects of separation each have their own distinctive pattern and set of influences. Acute effects are common in men and seem to reflect their lower likelihood of initiating separation and their apparent failure to see it coming when initiated by their partner. However, women show the greater psychological distress in the longer term, and are more likely to be depressed at clinically significant levels, as is the case in the general population (Rodgers & Mann, 1986; Cramer, 1993).

Alcohol abuse and dependence in separated people

Generally speaking, divorced and separated men and women have higher rates of alcohol consumption and other substance abuse disorders than those who are married (Wilsnack et al., 1984; Helzer et al., 1991; Cramer, 1993; Joung et al., 1995; Hall et al., 1999). As with psychological distress, these differences are usually substantial. In the US Epidemiologic Catchment Area Study, the one-year prevalence of alcoholism was 4.2 percent for currently married adults and 9.9 percent for those currently separated or divorced (Helzer et al., 1991). Similarly, in Australia the prevalence of alcohol abuse/dependence in the National Survey of Mental Health and Well-being was found to be 4.5 percent in those currently married compared with 9.4 percent for currently separated or divorced people (Hall et al., 1999). Levels of consumption are also high in separated and divorced people. In the UK Health and Lifestyle Survey, divorced and separated men drank, on average, 50 percent more alcohol per week than married men, and separated and divorced women drank over one-third more than married women (Cramer, 1993). As a general rule, divorced and separated people have more than double the risk of heavy drinking or problems associated with drinking compared with married people, although some studies have indicated as much as a fourfold difference (Webb et al., 1990).

Alcohol abuse and dependence preceding separation

This raises the obvious question as to whether drinking problems contribute to marital separations or vice versa, or whether other factors are responsible for their association. The impression from personal accounts of reasons for divorce, given by couples involved, is that alcohol and other drug problems are seen as a major contributory factor (Gigy & Kelly, 1992; Wolcott & Hughes, 1999), especially in husbands (Kitson & Sussman, 1982; Burns, 1984; Cleek & Pearson, 1985). One estimate in Australia, prior to the Family Law Act 1975, suggested that 40 percent of all divorces were "associated with the problem of alcoholism" (Santamaria, 1972) and more recent evidence points to a very high rate of alcohol abuse in those with marital problems (Halford & Osgarby, 1993). As with psychological distress, problem drinking may increase during the course of difficult marriages, or it may be that chronic abuse or dependence contribute to eventual marital breakdown. Most longitudinal studies of separation have not included detailed measures of alcohol consumption or dependence as predictors, and this appears to be a relatively neglected area of research (White, 1990; Karney & Bradbury, 1995), although there are some reports that problems with alcohol or drug use are associated with an increased likelihood of subsequent separation (Amato & Rogers, 1997). As mentioned previously, the US National Comorbidity Survey (Kessler et al., 1998) found an association between substance use disorders and subsequent marital breakdown, but this was not as strong as that seen for depressive and anxiety disorders. The Chicago study of Doherty and colleagues (1989) and the much larger 1958 British Birth Cohort study both found little sign that heavy drinking preceded marital separation (Power et al., 1999).

Alcohol abuse and dependence following separation

Although the evidence that alcohol abuse leads to divorce is inconclusive, there have been many demonstrations that alcohol consumption increases after separation. One meta-analysis of 12 longitudinal studies found that "becoming unmarried" (i.e. separated, divorced, or widowed) was associated with increased consumption across all age–sex groups (Temple et al., 1991), and other studies have also shown such increases (Doherty et al., 1989; Romelsjo et al., 1991; Hajema & Knibbe, 1998). Does this represent a temporary increase in alcohol use as a response to the stress of separation (Bloom et al., 1978), or is it a reflection of a longer-term rise in consumption? The 1958 British Birth Cohort study was able to distinguish these acute and chronic changes by comparing findings for young adults who had been separated for up to 2 years with their peers who had been separated for 3 to 10 years, and looking at increases in consumption from the time they were married, 10 years earlier (Power et al., 1999). Although both groups drank more than those who remained married throughout, the risk of heavy drinking was much less in those who had been separated for more than 2 years (odds ratios around 1.5 to 2.0) than for the recently separated (odds ratios of 5.0 or more). In other words, there was a very dramatic increase in drinking associated with separation and these levels fell substantially thereafter, but still remained significantly above preseparation levels. This pattern was similar for men and women, although it has greater implications for men because of their generally higher levels of alcohol consumption.

Overall, the findings for alcohol consumption and abuse are similar to those seen for psychiatric disorders and psychological distress. Severe problems are associated with marital instability, but there is little evidence otherwise of high consumption leading to separation. There is not a notable increase in consumption in the years immediately preceding separation (as seen for psychological distress), but the increase at the time of separation is more dramatic. Although drinking levels decline substantially in the two years following separation, they remain higher than preseparation levels for both men and women.

Parental Antisocial Behavior

Antisocial behavior is a clinical diagnosis, defined as an antisocial personality within the DSM-III-R classification system, and as conduct disorder within the later DSM-IV classification. A study of the parents of a clinical sample of boys with conduct disorder found that at least one of their biological parents had a diagnosis of antisocial personality disorder in 62 percent of divorced families compared with just 5 percent of intact families (Lahey et al., 1988). In the US Epidemiologic Catchment Area Study, divorced people had a greater risk of antisocial personality disorder than never married people, and they in turn had a greater risk than married people. The respective rates of current disorder were 3.9, 2.8, and 1.6 percent for men and 0.9, 0.5, and 0.3 percent for women (Robins et al., 1991). One necessary caveat is that a history of multiple divorces is one of the criteria for applying the diagnosis of antisocial personality (although not sufficient in isolation). In the US National Comorbidity Survey, however, where it was possible to investigate the timing of disorders in relation to divorce, conduct disorder was not significantly associated with subsequent divorce, as had been found for depression, anxiety, and substance abuse (Kessler et al., 1998). This finding is not in agreement, however, with a broader literature relating such behavior traits to marital disruption. Simons and colleagues (1996) considered antisocial behavior to be far more important than depression or psychological distress in predisposing to divorce and contributing to differences between family types.

> Based on prior research, we believe that antisocial behavior trait is the personal characteristic that shows the most promise as an explanation for family structure differences in stress. . . . Antisocial behavior involves actions deemed risky, inappropriate, shortsighted, or insensitive by the majority of people in society. . . . Thus, individuals display an antisocial trait to the extent that they engaged in delinquent behavior during late childhood and early adolescence and continue as adults to participate in deviant actions such as interpersonal violence, substance abuse, sexual promiscuity, traffic violations, and the like. (Simons et al., 1996, p. 50)

They found that divorced people scored higher than married people on measures of delinquency as a child and deviant behavior in the past year (Simons et al., 1996). Other studies confirm this association, both for current and past behavior. In the US National Survey of Youth – Child Sample, delinquent behavior of future mothers, obtained when they were 15 to 22 years old, was found to be predictive of both nonmarital childbearing and divorce (Emery et al., 1999). Again, the size of differences by comparison with married mothers was considerable. Although the evidence seems strong regarding the link between divorce and present and past antisocial behavior, there appear to be no studies documenting changes in such behavior over periods of marital transition.

Stressful life events

Although the impact of stressful life events on children and adolescents has been widely studied, much of the work relating to family transitions has centered on events typically considered to be stressful for adults. Families after divorce are exposed to more stresses than intact two-parent families. In two studies in Oregon and Iowa, lone-mother families had higher levels of recent hassles and life events compared with two-parent families (Forgatch et al., 1988; Lorenz et al., 1997). Some of these differences come directly from their poorer socioeconomic circumstances (McLanahan, 1983; Simons et al., 1996), including problems with housing (Reeves et al., 1994), but they also involve other kinds of life events. There are, for example, large differences in the likelihood of such events as having a close friend move away, having a close friend with a marital problem, being physically attacked or sexually assaulted, and suffering injury or property damage (Simons et al., 1996). In this Iowa study, levels of stressful events fell over a two-year period of follow-up after divorce, but were still higher than in married families (Lorenz et al., 1997).

Social support

As with stressful life events, most of the research into social support and family transitions has concentrated on the social support of parents, especially lone residential parents, rather than on support provided to children, although the relationships children have with relatives both within and outside their immediate family have been considered. In adults, separated people have lower levels of social support than those who are married. An early study in Chicago (Pearlin & Johnson, 1977) reported that unmarried people generally (i.e. including never married, divorced, and separated) were more likely to be "considerably isolated" (29 percent) than married people (18 percent). Another study, in northern California, looked in detail at different facets of social support (Gerstel et al., 1985). Married people are more likely to say they have someone they can confide in (99 percent for women and 95 percent for men) compared with those who are separated and divorced (95 percent for women and 88 percent for men), and, as we might expect, many married people name their spouse as a confidant. Differences were also found on other dimensions of social support, including the size of social networks where divorced and separated people had smaller networks than did married people. Little difference was found, however, between the social support of married and divorced mothers in the Iowa studies (Simons et al., 1996).

For children, the Australian Living Standards Study found that adolescents in lone-mother families reported lower satisfaction with both the number of their close friends and with their relationships with other children in the household than did those in intact families, stepfamilies, and lone-father families (Weston & Hughes, 1999). An earlier Australian study, conducted by Amato (1987b), had also found that children in lone-parent families rated their sibling relationships less highly compared with children in intact families, although the size of the difference was smaller in young children than that seen in adolescents. Grandparents, though, are a significant source of support for children in lone-parent and stepfamilies, as we discussed in chapter 4. Children in these families may more likely to feel close to their grandparents than those in original families (Clingempeel et al., 1992; Kennedy & Kennedy, 1993) although findings are mixed in this regard (Lussier et al., submitted).

Children also turn to peers for social support. In the ALSPAC study friends were more likely to be named as people to whom children turned for intimate confiding at the time of separation than mothers or fathers; only grandparents and other relatives were named more frequently (Dunn et al., in press a). Although children were more likely to turn to mothers and relatives for minor confidences, friends were next most likely along with siblings.

Residential mobility and neighborhood resources

At the time of family separation many families move house, and often more than once. In a longitudinal study of Rhode Island adults, 50 percent moved house in the one-year period following divorce compared to 7 percent during one year for those who remained married (Speare & Goldscheider, 1987). Even after the initial movement, the future mobility rates of divorced and separated people are about one and a half times to double those of married people. Similar differences were found in the Panel Study of Income Dynamics and the High School and Beyond Study (McLanahan & Sandefur, 1994). As well as the disruption and stress of moving home, moves of lone-parent families are also likely to reflect downward mobility: people move to poorer houses in poorer neighborhoods. Further analyses from the Panel Study of Income Dynamics compared the mean incomes of areas from which families moved with those of the areas into which they moved (South et al., 1998). Lone-mother families were four times more likely and lone-father families five times more likely to move into a different census tract than original families. Lone-parent families moved to tracts that had average family incomes lower than the average for the areas they moved from, whereas original families tended to move to more affluent areas. Over time, such moves will have a cumulative effect on the characteristics of areas in which different family types reside. Lone-parent families live in census tracts with higher average poverty levels (11.0 versus 8.7 percent for white families and 26.0 versus 23.8 percent for black families), and there are similar differences for other measures of community resources (McLanahan & Sandefur, 1994).

Peer-group influences vary for children in different family structures. Young children from separated and divorced homes are more likely to be rejected by peers than those in original families (Patterson et al., 1992), and children in lone-parent families are more likely than others to have friends with negative attitudes and behavior problems such as creating problems for teachers (McLanahan & Sandefur, 1994). In turn, adolescents living in lone-parent families and stepfamilies are more susceptible to pressure from friends to engage in negative behavior than those in original families (Steinberg, 1987). Key factors having an impact on susceptibility to negative peer groups are likely to include living in areas and attending schools with high levels of deviancy; and lower levels of parental monitoring of their children's peer affiliations and activities.

Overview

In this chapter we have identified aspects of individuals, their families, and their contexts that are of consequence to the well-being of children in all families. We have noted, too, that the differences between families that separate and those that do not are large – considerably bigger, in fact, that the differences between outcomes for children in original and separated families.

Some factors predate family separation, such as parental antisocial behavior, while others emerge in the years leading up to separation, such as financial difficulties and parental psychological distress. A common feature of many of the adverse factors discussed is the sudden change around the time of family separation. For some of these factors, there is a subsequent drop over time in the years immediately following divorce, but some differences, especially between lone-parent families and intact families, remain substantial and significant. This suggests that although divorce may not be the cause of children's problems, some factors that contribute significantly to them are changed and often exacerbated at the time of separation.

Some factors predate family separation, such as parental antisocial behavior, while others emerge in the years leading up to separation, such as financial difficulties and parental psychological distress. A common feature of many of the adverse factors discussed is the sudden change around the time of family separation. For some of these factors, there is a subsequent restoration over time in the years immediately following divorce, but some differences, especially between lone-parent families and intact families, remain substantial and significant. This suggests that although divorce may not be the cause of children's problems, some factors that contribute significantly to them are changed and often exacerbated at the time of separation. The importance of change in risk factors is discussed further in chapter 9.

A particularly notable feature, looking across this wide body of research findings, is that there is considerable diversity within family forms and transitions as well as differences between family types. Not all families follow the same paths at the time of separation, and some encounter far more difficulties than others. Both the liberal and conservative perspectives fail to capture the complexity of families or the interrelationships between factors discussed here. We will return to many of these issues in chapter 8, where we consider the role that these several factors play in contributing to outcomes for children who experience family transitions.

6

Stepfamilies and Multiple Transitions

The modern stepchild . . . arrives by very diverse paths into a family form that is not merely inherently complicated and diverse in its sub-varieties, but also, at both a public and a popular level, suffers from a disputed model of how it ought to function.

Gorrell Barnes et al., 1998, p. 3

Introduction

Stepfamilies have always existed in communities, and are formed after the death of a parent or, more commonly now, as a consequence of the separation of children's biological parents. Children today do not usually live in a lone-parent household for long; the likelihood is that after their parents' separation or if their mothers have never partnered, they will eventually live in a stepfamily household. Stepfamily formation involves the rearrangement of households and has the potential to be remarkably complicated, since it involves the establishment of several new relationships as well as changes to existing ones. For children, these new relationships are not with people they themselves have chosen, and include those with stepparents and possibly with step- or halfsiblings. Figure 6.1 depicts a fairly typical assemblage of households formed after parental separation and repartnering.

In household 1 a lone mother lives with her three children who spend some of their time in household 2 with their father and his new partner. His new partner has two children from her former marriage who live predominantly with her, but visit their father in household 3. In household 3 her ex-partner lives with his new partner, and they have two children of their own. The most common stepfamily household is one where children live with their mothers and new partners as in household 2; the majority of stepfamilies are, then, stepfather families. Other children live with their stepmother and biological father in stepmother households,

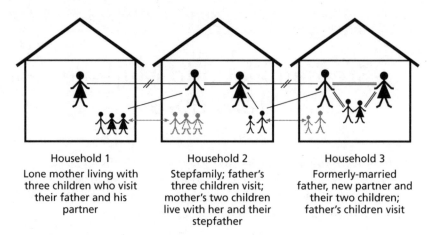

Household 1	Household 2	Household 3
Lone mother living with three children who visit their father and his partner	Stepfamily; father's three children visit; mother's two children live with her and their stepfather	Formerly-married father, new partner and their two children; father's children visit

Figure 6.1 Typical household structures after stepfamily formation

and still others with stepsiblings from the stepparent's original family (blended or complex stepfamilies). All of these (stepfather, stepmother, and complex) may include new biological siblings of their parent and stepparent.

Stepfamily households vary in their basic composition, and they also change from week to week. The numbers of children in household 2, for example, will vary from none when both sets of siblings are with their other parents, to five when the three from household 1 are visiting. Similarly, in household 3 there may be two or four children in residence. Children may also change residences of their own accord, especially in adolescence. In the AIFS Project 18 percent of children had moved residence 5 to 8 years after parental separation (Funder, 1996), and in the Stanford Custody Project one-third had moved residence in the 4 years since parental separation, 13 percent more than once (Buchanan & Maccoby, 1996). This movement between households calls for flexibility from family members at both practical and interpersonal levels. It is not surprising, then, that there is considerable variation in the relatedness, relationships, and experiences that children in stepfamilies have.

There is variation, too, in the paths by which children come to stepfamily living. Most typically, they will have moved from living with both biological parents to a lone-parent household and then to living with a parent and that parent's new partner. Other stepfamilies are formed when mothers who have never lived with a partner cohabit or marry; in most

European countries more than 70 percent of women who have a child while unpartnered, subsequently go into partnerships (Kiernan, 1999b). The Stepfamily Association in the UK has identified 72 different pathways to stepfamily living (De'Ath, 1992). In the US, over a third of children born to lone mothers in the National Survey of Family and Households sample lived in a stepfamily at some stage in their childhood (Aquilino, 1996). Children in these families will not, then, have experienced parental separation. For some, there is a direct transition from a household with both their biological parents to one in which they live with one biological and one stepparent, without a period of living with a lone parent. We know little about the experiences of children moving either from living with unpartnered mothers to stepfamily households or directly from original households to stepfamilies. In many stepfamily households, parents cohabit rather than marry, and later in the chapter some differences for children living in married and cohabiting stepfamilies will be discussed.

Although stepfamilies have always existed, fairytales and mythology have given them a bad press over the centuries; in particular stepmothers are maligned as "wicked." In recent times a conservative perspective on family change has emphasized the view that stepfamilies are not good for children. The comparative instability of stepfamilies, the risk to children of poor outcomes and of abuse, and reduced parenting resources, are cited as reasons why societies should be endeavoring to "halt the growth of stepfamilies" (Popenoe, 1994, p. 21).

The liberal view considers the restoration of two parents and adequate income levels to formerly lone-parent households as a positive aspect of stepfamilies. It sees stepfamilies as flexible and adaptive households, providing multiple interpersonal resources for children who, in turn, have considerable influence over family dynamics. Stepfamilies in this view are part of a continuum of transitions and influences that can and often do nurture children.

Several questions are addressed in this chapter. Are children at risk for poor outcomes in stepfamilies, in comparison with original and lone-parent families? What are stepfamily environments like in comparison with original two-parent households? What kinds of parenting do children experience in stepfamilies, and what are their roles? In this chapter we will consider children's lives in stepfamilies, the risks and benefits they experience, and address these questions. The majority of the discussion will focus on stepfather families, since most research includes only this family type. Later in the chapter we will consider stepmother families separately.

In a number of ways children in stepfamilies do not fare as well as those living with two biological parents and, as we discussed in chapter 3, are at similar levels of risk for adverse outcomes as those in lone-parent families. In particular, they are more likely to undertake adult roles early, such as entering the workforce, forming partnerships, and bearing children. What might it be about stepfamilies that puts children at risk, despite the restoration of household income that often occurs with repartnering and the presence of two potential parenting figures in the household?

Stepfamily Formation

Little is known about what predicts stepfamily formation. For the majority of families where stepfamily living is preceded by a previous partnership, however, there are some factors that we can identify that are associated with the risk for separation (see chapter 5). These include younger age at marriage, low educational levels, and socioeconomic disadvantage (Fergusson et al., 1986; Furstenberg, 1990; Hanson et al., 1998), and some may have a continuing influence on stepfamily formation. The experience of the separation itself may also have an ongoing impact since family breakdown is usually accompanied by elevated levels of conflict, parenting difficulties, lower household income especially for mothers, and higher levels of psychological distress in parents although not all children will have experienced separation if their mothers were not in partnerships before they entered stepfamilies. There may be, then, some earlier factors that accompany the establishment of stepfamilies: those adults who come to them are more likely to have been young when they first formed partnerships, to be relatively disadvantaged, and to have experienced the stresses associated with broken partnerships. Children, too, will typically have experienced their parents' separation and the changes in household income, parenting, and conflict associated with that transition. Overall, stepfamilies are likely to be formed by adults who have already experienced the stresses associated with separation and, at least in that regard, differ from adults in original families.

Relationships and Processes in Stepfather Families

It seems logical, in evaluating outcomes for children in stepfamilies, to compare them with those in lone-parent families since both groups will

have experienced parental separation (Kurdek, 1994). In considering relationships in families, however, original families are a more obvious comparison group since in both there are two adults in the household. They
also differ in several fundamental ways. The degree of biological relationship varies within the household, for example; and for children, relationships outside the household continue to be active and important. Family
systems theory (see chapter 2) has been widely used as a framework for
thinking about stepfamily relationships (Hetherington & Clingempeel,
1992; Hetherington & Jodl, 1994; Hetherington et al., 1999) as it offers
a means of conceptualizing the ways that relationships interact with each
other; and these aspects of stepfamily relationships suggest that the dynamics between relationships in stepfamilies might be somewhat different
compared with those in original families. In this section we will address
the family environment and individual relationships within it in stepfather families, and compare them primarily with similar relationships in
original families.

Family environment

The term "family environment" encompasses several aspects of involvement amongst family members. One aspect is cohesion, which includes feelings of closeness and emotional bonding (Olson et al., 1983). Cohesion is
lower in stepfamilies in comparison with original families (Bray, 1988; Visher
& Visher, 1990; Barber & Lyons, 1994), although some studies have found
no differences (Smith, 1992; Pruett et al., 1993). Differences in the time
since remarriage and the age of children in the family might explain these
contradictory findings, and these factors were taken into account in a longitudinal study in the US in which cohesion was compared in stepfamilies
who had been together for varying lengths of time and with children of
different ages (Bray & Berger, 1993a). Cohesion was assessed both by observation, and by reports from family members. Parents who were in the
early stages of stepfamily formation reported lower family cohesion than
original families; observers, though, rated both groups similarly when they
were interacting together. Stepfamilies who had been together for two and
a half years and had children aged 8 to 11, reported comparatively high
levels of cohesion, and at this time were observed to be more cohesive than
original families. Those who had early adolescents in the family and had
been together for 5 to 7 years reported similar levels of cohesion to birth-
parent families; however, they were observed to be less cohesive in comparison with original families with children the same age.

The presence of adolescents in any family can lower the levels of family cohesion; this decline, though, may be more precipitate in stepfamilies than in original families (Smith, 1992). In particular, if we take into account cohesion as perceived by adolescents as well as parents in families, then stepfamilies are less cohesive overall than first-marriage families. Young people in stepfamilies see their families as less emotionally close than those in first-marriage families, yet in one study (Smith) the majority also perceived their families as happy. From the perspectives of adolescents, then, stepfamilies may function optimally with lower levels of cohesion than original families.

There appears to be a progression whereby parents feel somewhat tentative at the beginning of stepfamily life, but become increasingly confident about being together. As children reach adolescence parents say they still feel the family is close, but their teenagers do not share those feelings. Observations of family interactions suggest that, indeed, stepfamilies with adolescents are less cohesive than original families with teenagers.

Another common measure of family environment is how much time family members spend being together: stepfamilies spend less family time with each other (Voydanoff et al., 1994; Sweeting et al., 1998) and do activities together less often than original families (Thomson et al., 1992). This seems to be particularly so for activities that take place outside the home; in the UK it was found that stepfather families spent as much time as original families having meals together, shopping, and spending evenings together, but not doing activities outside the house together that involved spending money (Ferri & Smith, 1998). The authors suggest this may reflect economic restraints in stepfamilies because of larger numbers of children in the home at times when outside activities are most likely to take place. It may also reflect the fact that children in stepfamilies spent part of the time with their other parent, especially at weekends. Another UK study noted no differences between stepfamilies and original families in time spent in joint activities (Dunn et al., in press a).

Marital conflict and satisfaction
In stepfamilies, children are potentially vulnerable to two sources of marital conflict – between partners within the household, and between their biological parent and his or her ex-spouse. In the US, the presence and levels of partner conflict in several stepfamily types have been compared with those in first marriages. When levels of conflict reported by 2,655 husbands and wives in first marriages, single remarriages (stepmother or stepfather), and double remarriages (both partners married previously)

compared, marital conflict levels were no higher for stepfamilies
for those in first-marriage families (McDonald & DeMaris, 1995).
since remarriage was important, however. Couples with stepchil-
ported lower levels of conflict in the early years than those with
al children, but by 6 years of marriage their levels were higher
se with biological children.

her set of comparisons using the same families, reported levels
of partner conflict in the household (intrahouse conflict) were compared
between stepfather households and first-marriage families; and levels of
conflict between ex-partners in separate households (interhousehold conflict) were compared between stepfather families and lone-parent households (Hanson et al., 1996). Stepfather families had no higher levels of
intrahouse conflict than two-birth-parent families, and reported *lower*
levels of interhouse conflict than lone-parent families. However, stepfather families experienced higher *overall* levels of parental conflict since
they experienced both intra- and inter-household conflict.

As well as reporting levels of marital conflict no higher than those in
original families, partners in stepfamilies also report high levels of relationship satisfaction. In the US remarried couples report at least as much
marital satisfaction as first-marriage couples (Vemer et al., 1989; Bray &
Berger, 1993a; Voydanoff et al., 1994), and in the first two years of marriage have been found to report higher levels of happiness (Hetherington,
1993). Their partnerships are described by them as more egalitarian, less
romantic, and more open (Bray, 1988). However, despite the fact that
parents in stepfamilies describe their relationship as comparatively harmonious, observations of their behavior suggest otherwise. They display
more negativity and less positivity toward each other than first-marriage
couples (Bray & Berger, 1993a; Hetherington et al., 1999). In the UK,
stepfamily members do not report levels of partnership satisfaction as
high as those in first-marriage families (Ferri & Smith, 1998). A common
source of conflict is disagreement over discipline, and this is more com-

Although adults in stepfamilies often say they are satisfied with their
partnership and that they do not argue very much in the first few years,
their behavior suggests otherwise. Over time, especially if adolescent
children are in the family, their relationships tend to deteriorate in comparison with those in first marriages. These differences, though, are not
large and are primarily between first-marriage and complex stepfamilies
... Given the particular stresses involved in establishing stepfamily relationships, this is not surprising.

mon between parents in stepfamilies than original families in the UK (Ferri & Smith, 1998) and in the US (Hetherington et al., 1999).

Time since remarriage is an important factor in evaluating stepfamily relationships. The studies of conflict using NSFH data showed that after 6 years of marriage, levels of conflict in stepfamilies were higher than those in original families. Many of the stepfamilies in Ferri & Smith's UK group were also well established, yet they too were less satisfied with their partnerships than those in first marriages (see table 6.1). Nevertheless, in their recent study of established stepfamilies Hetheringon and Henderson concluded that "the quality of marital relations in nondivorced families was found to be far more similar than different in this sample of nondivorced and long-established stepfamilies" (Hetherington et al., 1999, pp. 72–3).

These findings might be explained by differences in the expectations held for relationships between original and stepfamily parents. Parents may experience high levels of conflict yet feel satisfied with the relationship since they don't expect it to be as harmonious as a first marriage. There may also be high levels of optimism early in remarriage, so that negative aspects are less readily acknowledged. Some years later, however, a more realistic appraisal of the partnership might explain the increase in conflict and lower cohesion that is reported. Time often also means that children become adolescent and contribute to lowered family cohesion. Second marriages might just, too, be better than first ones for many people.

In sum, although adults in stepfamilies often say they are satisfied with their partnership and that they do not argue very much in the first few years, their behavior suggests otherwise. Over time, especially if adolescent children are in the family, their relationships tend to deteriorate in comparison with those in first marriages. These differences, though, are not large and are primarily between first-marriage and complex stepfamilies (Hetherington et al., 1999). Given the particular stresses involved in establishing stepfamily relationships, this is not surprising.

Psychological distress in parents

Psychological distress is comparatively prevalent in adults in stepfamilies. In Ferri and Smith's UK sample, many more women and men in stepfather and stepmother families were depressed than those in original families (see table 6.1), while in another English group of parents, both men and women in stepfamilies were more likely to be depressed and to have

Table 6.1 Percentages of women and men in stepfamilies and first-marriage families reporting levels of unhappy partnerships, life satisfaction, depression, and discipline agreement

Adult reporting	Unhappy partnership	Life satisfaction	Depression	Discipline agreement
Stepfather family, women	16	24	20	30
Stepfather family, men	14	19	12	25
Stepmother family, women	22	16	15	36
Stepmother family, men	28	9	9	36
Both stepparent, women	14	28	4	30
Both stepparent, men	11	10	0	30
First family, women	11	34	10	49
First family, men	8	24	5	52

Source: Ferri & Smith, 1998, by kind permission

experienced aggression in the partnership than those in intact families (Deater-Deckard et al., 1998). Depression levels were also comparatively high for spouses in remarried families in the Virginia Longitudinal Study in the US and in the NEAD study (Hetherington et al., 1999), and stepfamily couples reported higher levels of both positive and negative life events (Hetherington, 1993).

Biological parent–child relationships

Parent–child relationships are pivotal in all families; however, in stepfamilies they are subject to stresses that are not present in first-marriage families. Biological parents and their children have to renegotiate a relationship that has usually not, at least in the recent past, involved another adult. The typical path for families is that lone mothers and their children, after a period of disruption following separation, settle into patterns of interaction in which daughters and mothers are usually close and mothers and sons somewhat fraught (Hetherington & Jodl, 1994). The inclusion of a partner into the mother's life means that the family has to make adaptations that are not always welcomed by the children. Relationships between mothers and children often, therefore, deteriorate when a stepfamily is formed and observations of family interactions indicate that they oppose their children more frequently than mothers in first-marriage families (Vuchinich et al., 1991). Mothers in stepfamilies in the UK and USA are comparatively less positive and more negative with their children in early remarriage (Bray & Berger, 1993a; Dunn et al., 1998). Children, too, make a vital contribution to the quality of the relationships they have with their mothers: they show more negative behavior towards mothers in the early stages of remarriage (Vuchinich et al., 1991; Hetherington & Clingempeel, 1992; Bray & Berger, 1993a).

The age of children when their mothers repartner is also important. The Virginia Longitudinal Study of Divorce and Remarriage found that in families where children were young at the time of remarriage, although relationships improved over time they deteriorated again in early adolescence. (Hetherington, 1993). In families where children were 9 years or older at the time of marriage, relationships never became as close as those in the first-marriage group and, by the age of 15, one-third of boys and one-quarter of girls had disengaged from their families.

The Stanford Custody Project offers an interesting perspective on mother–child relationships (Buchanan & Maccoby, 1996). Adolescents in this group felt close to their mothers in stepfamilies so long as their mother and stepfather were legally married. Where mothers were dating (especially for girls), or cohabiting (especially for boys), feelings of closeness were low, and those whose mothers were legally remarried were the least likely to be disengaged from their families. There are several reasons why the parent–adolescent relationship in stepfamilies might be relatively strong if parents are married. For a girl, a strong parental relationship that is legally sanctioned may offer a buffer against the potential threat from a new stepfather to her developing sexuality (Hetherington, 1993). Adolescents too, especially those who are older, may be able to appreciate their parents' increased well-being with a new partner, and to see legal commitment as contributing to that. There is also some evidence that adolescents feel freed from the role of supporting their lone mother. Young people in the Stanford Custody Project were less likely to feel responsible for their mother if she had married, and were less likely to be put into the role of a confidant than if she remained alone (Buchanan & Maccoby, 1996).

Stepfather–stepchild relationships

The establishment of the stepparent–stepchild relationship is perhaps the most complex of all challenges faced by stepfamilies. It is a relationship that is different from the biological parent–child relationship in several key ways. First, it has not had the chance to develop through infancy and early childhood and so there has not been the opportunity for mutual growth and adaptation between adult and child. It has no shared history. Second, children usually have a biological parent of the same sex still involved in their lives. In stepfather families a stepfather typically faces the task of integrating himself into an existing family system of mother and children, a system with established attachments, rituals, and its own unique culture. Yet the stepfather–stepchild relationship is strongly linked to the quality of family life in stepfather families. Positive interactions between stepfathers and stepchildren have been found, for example, to be associated both with overall family closeness (Bray & Berger, 1993a) and with partnership quality (Fine & Kurdek, 1995).

Who determines the nature of the stepchild–stepparent relationship?

It is increasingly recognized that children hold a great deal of power, especially in adolescence, in influencing the nature of relationships in families. For example, one recent study examined effects in both directions – parent to child and child to parent – in predicting adolescent social competence (O'Connor et al., 1997). Adolescent-to-parent variables were equally predictive of competence as parent-to-adolescent variables, in both original and stepparent families. Direction of effects can also be examined by measuring behavior at several times, and using this method it has been found that the behavior of adolescents in stepfamilies, at least in the early years, is more likely to have a subsequent impact on stepparent behavior than vice versa (Hetherington & Clingempeel, 1992). The directional effect was not found in original or lone-parent families, nor was it apparent in long-established stepfamilies (Hetherington et al., 1999) indicating the distinctiveness of stepfamilies in their early years.

In many instances, then, what stepfathers do may reflect the reception they get from stepchildren who often respond with some ambivalence to an unrelated adult living in their family. They show less positivity and more negativity to stepfathers than to fathers (Hetherington & Clingempeel, 1992; Bray & Berger, 1993a), and girls in early adolescence show a pattern of behavior involving withdrawal, avoidance, resentment, and hostility (Vuchinich et al., 1991). Children themselves, however, do not necessarily *say* that they feel negative about stepfathers. In two studies that interviewed children and adolescents, comparatively high levels of acceptance and closeness toward stepfathers were reported (Buchanan & Maccoby, 1996; Funder, 1996). Seventy-four percent of the AIFS Australian sample of 8- to 22-year-olds felt they had a good relationship with their stepfather; and 56 percent reported high involvement with him. Only 10 percent of the Stanford adolescents in the US indicated they did not like their stepfather (Buchanan & Maccoby, 1996). Younger Australian children said they were more involved with their stepfathers, and younger adolescents in the Stanford study were more ready than older teenagers to accept their parents' new partner. The differences apparent between observed and reported findings reinforce the suggestion made earlier that stepfamily members may *want* closer relationships than they are in fact able to manage in the early years, and this was shown earlier in the differences between reported feelings and observed behavior found in regard to partner satisfaction.

The marital status of parents also differentiated feelings of closeness between stepfathers and stepchildren in the Stanford study. Those children whose parents were legally remarried reported higher levels of closeness and acceptance of stepparental authority in comparison with those

In many instances, then, what stepfathers do may reflect the reception they get from stepchildren who often respond with some ambivalence to an unrelated adult living in their family. They show less positivity and more negativity to stepfathers than to fathers . . . and girls in early adolescence show a pattern of behavior involving withdrawal, avoidance, resentment, and hostility. Children themselves, however, do not necessarily *say* that they feel negative about stepfathers. In two studies that interviewed children and adolescents, comparatively high levels of acceptance and closeness toward stepfathers were reported. Seventy-four percent of a sample of 8- to 22-year-olds felt they had a good relationship with their stepfather; and 56 percent reported high involvement with him . . . The differences apparent between observed and reported findings reinforce the suggestion . . . that stepfamily members may *want* closer relationships than they are in fact able to manage in the early years.

in cohabiting households. Overall, stepchildren say they like their step-fathers; for adolescents especially, though, acceptance of their authority seems to be more problematic.

Overall, adolescence is a time when to a considerable extent relation-ships with stepparents (and biological parents) are discretionary and some-what under children's control. One adolescent told her stepfather so:

> Although I liked him – not when he first moved in, but after a while when he was definitely permanent – I got so that when he told me what to do, or asked me to do something, I didn't want him to speak to me, it used to make my flesh creep. "You – this is not your place." (Gorrell Barnes et al., 1998, p. 78)

The pervasive drive at this age toward autonomy and independence makes it unlikely that teenagers will ease the establishment of a relationship with a stepparent. If the stepfamily is established when they are already adoles-cent, they may see little point in investing in a relationship that is likely to be comparatively short. The chances of a stepparent establishing a con-ventional parenting role with adolescents are therefore not particularly high.

Parenting in stepfamilies

In chapter 2 we described parenting styles that have been distinguished in family research. They include authoritative parenting, authoritarian parenting, permissive parenting, and neglecting or disengaged parenting. In general, authoritative parenting (high levels of support, monitoring, and encouragement of psychological autonomy) has been found to be optimal for children and adolescents. The nature of the stepfamily envi-ronment, though, especially in its early phases, suggests that authoritative parenting might be difficult to achieve for stepfathers. Monitoring, in particular, will be especially challenging as they endeavor to establish workable relationships with stepchildren. Not surprisingly, stepparents and even biological parents in stepfamilies are less likely than those in intact families to demonstrate authoritative parenting styles. Three of the four common typologies (authoritative, disengaged, and authoritar-ian) were identified in the Hetherington and Clingempeel study in the US, and mothers in stepfather families were more likely than those in first-marriage families to show a disengaged style with low levels of support and control, and were less likely to be authoritative, at all three waves of the study (Hetherington & Clingempeel, 1992). The differences between fathers and stepfathers was even more marked, with over half of stepfathers showing disengaged parenting early in the remarriage and 42 percent remaining so two years later.

Parenting by mothers in stepfather families

In the early stages of remarriage, mothers monitor their children less than those in original families and tend to be more negative (Amato, 1987c; Hetherington & Clingempeel, 1992; Bray & Berger, 1993a; Thomson et al., 1994; Hetherington et al., 1999). As time passes, although lower levels of monitoring continue for a time, parenting behavior returns to levels similar to that in first-marriage families and in stepfamilies, biological parent–child relationships are much the same as those in original families (Hetherington & Clingempeel, 1992). The age of children when their mothers repartner is, as we mentioned earlier, important. If children are early adolescents, then monitoring and control by mothers tends to remain low (Hetherington & Clingempeel, 1992).

Parenting by stepfathers

How do men behave toward children to whom they are not related biologically, but with whom they share day-to-day life? In the early phases of stepfamily formation, they are most likely to avoid moving into a conventional parenting role. They are comparatively uninvolved, with low levels of negative input and very little monitoring and control (Hetherington & Clingempeel, 1992; Bray & Berger, 1993a; Fine et al., 1993; Voydanoff et al., 1994; Hetherington et al., 1999). Findings are mixed about positive input: some report comparatively low levels, although one study found that compared with fathers in first marriages, stepfathers were less monitoring but more supportive of their children (Vuchinich et al., 1991).

Stepfathers, then, are generally tentative, low-key, and friendly toward stepchildren. One described his experience of integrating into a stepfamily as follows:

> With time, instead of coming in with authority, I said to [partner] "look, instead of me coming in with all this stuff because I feel they should or shouldn't do something, what say if I deal with just that stuff that directly affects me?" And since I have used that baseline things have been a lot better. (Fleming, 1999, p. 66)

Over time, these relationships do not become similar to those of fathers in first-marriage families; lower levels of monitoring and positive involvement remain (Hetherington & Clingempeel, 1992; Bray & Berger, 1993a; Hetherington et al., 1999). Their levels of involvement vary, however. Stepfathers of young children are seen by the children as providing less support than biological fathers in original families, but similar levels of control (Amato, 1987c). Adolescents perceive higher levels of support and lower levels of control than younger children do. Mothers and children in Australian stepfather families reported that stepfathers were involved in 45 percent of decisions related to guardianship (education, religion, and health), and had even higher involvement in day-to-day issues such as discipline, celebrations, discussion of problems, and holidays (Funder, 1996).

Adolescent perceptions of stepparents give us an idea of what might be optimal parenting styles from their perspective. Fifty-five percent of those in the Stanford Custody Project saw their parents' new partners as "a friend," and only one-quarter regarded them as parents. Half of these young people did not see the new partner as having a right to set rules in the family (Buchanan & Maccoby, 1996). As one young New Zealand woman put it, "We don't think of him as a step-dad, that's the difference. He's just a friend to us, he's just here" (Fleming, 1999, p. 118). A stepson in the UK recalled that his stepfather "has never told him off in 20 years of being married to my mum. My mum would say, 'They're not your kids'"(Gorrell Barnes et al., 1998, p. 80). Similarly, well-being in children in stepfamilies in the AIFS study was associated with high levels of closeness but low levels of involvement with stepfathers. This suggests that the permissive style of stepparenting (high support, low control) may be not only desirable from the child's point of view, but might also be optimal for children in stepfamilies. Most studies reporting that authoritative parenting by parents in stepfamilies is associated with well-being have not, though, included a permissive typology. One study that did, relabeled it as "supportive" (high support, low control) (Crosbie-Burnett & Giles-Sims, 1994). The four typologies were used to look at well-being in adolescents in relation to stepparenting styles. Biological parents' and adolescents' reports of well-being were obtained, as were adolescents' perceptions of support and control. It was found that family happiness and the quality of the stepparent–stepchild relationship were highest in families where the parenting style was supportive (high support and low control), and anxiety and discipline problems were lowest in these families with high support and low control on the part of stepparents. Other studies, too, reinforce the finding that adolescent well-being is lower with high levels of stepparental discipline and control (Bray, 1988; Fine et al., 1993), but is also lower where there are low levels of closeness (Funder, 1996).

Stepfather parenting may in some circumstances, then, provide an exception to the general conclusion that authoritative parenting is best for children. Not only do adolescents seem to prefer warm but also non-controlling parenting from stepfathers; their well-being and family happiness may flourish when this style of stepparenting is used. It might, however, be important that authoritative parenting with appropriate monitoring by biological mothers is needed to complement a more subdued style in stepfathers. This warm but low-key relationship with stepfathers may, too, not be so important for younger children, who are better able to accept discipline from stepparents since they have not spent so long in a household with their biological father, and are developmentally less likely to be striving for autonomy.

Are levels of stepfather involvement changing?

The low-key approach to parenting typically taken by men entering stepfamilies is congruent with the roles taken by fathers in many first-marriage families (Hetherington & Henderson, 1997; Hetherington et al., 1999), since men are usually not primary caregivers. Fathers perform childcare functions involving engagement, responsibility, and availability significantly less often than mothers (see chapter 7). However, like many fathers in original families, men who have become stepfathers in recent years may be more involved with their stepchildren than those in earlier decades. Using the NCDS cohort in the UK, Ferri and Smith compared levels of involvement of stepfathers in two generations (Ferri & Smith, 1998). They noted that levels had gone up considerably, and concluded that "Less than twenty years on, it seems that the behavior of stepfathers has undergone a considerable change" (p. 59). Many men both expect and are expected to take a greater share of childrearing tasks as gender roles change and both parents are increasingly likely to be in the workforce. Fathers who become resident members of a second family may indeed *want* higher levels of involvement with stepchildren than they have, especially if their relationships with their own biological children have been unsatisfactory or are diminishing. High levels of willingness to assume parenting roles are, for example, reported in the stepfathers in the AIFS study, who scored more than 4 on a 5-point scale of willingness to participate in parental responsibilities (Funder, 1996).

Stepfather parenting may in some circumstances provide an exception to the general conclusion that authoritative parenting is best for children. Not only do adolescents seem to prefer warm but also noncontrolling parenting from stepfathers; their well-being and family happiness may flourish when this style of stepparenting is used. It might, however, be important that authoritative parenting with appropriate monitoring by biological mothers is needed to complement a more subdued style in stepfathers. This warm but low-key relationship with stepfathers may, too, not be so important for younger children, who are better able to accept discipline from stepparents since they have not spent so long in a household with their biological father, and are developmentally less likely to be striving for autonomy.

Parental relationships and parent–child relationships

How closely is the quality of parent–child relationships linked with relationships between parents in stepfamilies? In first-marriage families they are related, and in remarried families too they reflect each other. Marital positivity is associated with parental warmth, and marital negativity with parental negativity (Anderson et al., 1992; Bray & Berger, 1993a; Fine & Kurdek, 1995). Positive interactions between parents and stepfathers' feelings of marital satisfaction are also linked with positive mother–child interactions, and negative interactions between parents are associated with negative stepfather–stepchild interactions (Bray & Berger, 1993a). However, parent–parent relations in stepfamilies are more sensitive to family problems such as conflict and child behavior problems. Not only do children exert considerable control on the nature of stepparent–stepchild relations, they also have more impact on parent–parent relations in stepfamilies than in original families.

Relationships with nonresidential parents

Although many children lose contact with their nonresident fathers, a significant number retain a relationship that continues when their mothers repartner and which includes spending a significant amount of time in their father's home. A variety of terms have been used to describe this situation from a child's perspective, including living in a binuclear family, having dual citizenship, and being part of a divorce or marriage "chain" (Bohannen, 1970). There may be a tension for stepchildren, however: how do they balance the relationships with nonresident fathers and resident stepfathers? The few studies that have considered that question find that there is either no association between closeness to fathers and closeness to stepfathers (Buchanan & Maccoby, 1996) or that there is a positive relationship between the two (Furstenberg & Nord, 1985; Funder, 1996). Nonresident fathers do not generally take a major disciplinary role with their children, and are most likely to act as companions (Gunnoe, 1993). As we have seen, stepfathers are usually low-key in relation to their stepchildren, so that for children, conflict between the relationships is unlikely. Children seem able to "add" a parent to their family group rather than replacing one. In the US, nonresident mothers are twice as likely as fathers to stay in contact with children (Gunnoe, 1993; Hetherington & Jodl, 1994). They are also more likely to want to take active roles in their lives. For children, then, there may be conflict between the relationships they have with their nonresident mothers and resident stepmothers, and this is discussed later in the chapter.

Sibling relationships

One aspect of stepfamily life that is particularly variable is the configuration of siblings within and outside a household. As figure 6.1 shows, relationships exist among biological brothers and sisters, stepbrothers and sisters, and halfbrothers and sisters. There can be wide variations in age differences, too, with stepsiblings of nearly identical age in a house and infants and adolescents co-existing as halfsiblings. Biological brothers and sisters may also live in separate households. Relationships between biological siblings in relatively recent stepfamilies are more negative and less positive than in intact families (Hetherington & Clingempeel, 1992), with boys, in particular, more likely to be aggressive, and less likely to receive positive support from their sisters (Hetherington, 1993). In well-established stepfamilies there are no differences, however, between full siblings in original and stepfamilies (Hetherington et al., 1999). Findings are mixed, though: one study reported that siblings in stepfamilies, but not in intact families, are providers of acceptance and autonomy on levels similar to fathers (Kurdek & Fine, 1995). In the UK, relationships amongst siblings in stepfamilies appear to be comparatively intense, either positively or negatively (Gorrell Barnes et al., 1998).

Relationships between stepsiblings are relatively benign (Gorrell Barnes et al., 1998). In comparison with biological siblings and halfsiblings, they are less negative and similarly positive, companionable, and empathetic

(Hetherington et al., 1999). A young man in the UK described the relationship:

> You don't class your stepbrother as your normal brother . . . I always relate to Simmie as my stepbrother, I wouldn't class him as blood brother. To me there's always that distinction, yeh. (Gorrell Barnes et al., 1998, p. 129)

In her New Zealand study, Fleming found that stepsibling relationships were most likely to be neutral and somewhat distant, although some were close. Those who had good relationships tended to be similar in age and came together on visits, rather than living together and having to share resources such as bedrooms, bathrooms, and parents (Fleming, 1999). One described her relationship with her stepsister as follows: "I like sharing [a bedroom] with Melissa – we're the same age basically, we actually think quite alike. Some days we do each other's hair, and other days we do silly things with makeup and stuff" (Fleming, 1999, p. 135). Those stepsiblings who were relatively disengaged from each other were likely to be very different in age. As one child put it:

> The two girls were incredibly older than me, and the two boys were about my age and younger, but what boys want to play with a girl at the age of eight and nine? And what thirteen-year-old girl wants to play with another girl at the age of eight or nine? (Fleming, 1999, p. 135)

Other researchers have noted that for the most part stepsibling relationships are most likely to be disengaged and to involve fewer positive and negative aspects than those of full siblings (Coleman & Ganong, 1994).

Relations between halfsiblings in stepfamilies are similar to those between full siblings (Hetherington et al., 1999). Younger half-siblings appear, in fact, to be appreciated, and this may reflect their being seen as blood relations, as well as symbols of the permanence of the parental relationship. As one woman put it, "I look upon them as my brothers. As far as I'm concerned, they are my brothers"(Gorrell Barnes et al., 1998, p. 128). An adolescent boy in Fleming's New Zealand study moved cities in order to live with his young halfsiblings:

> One of the reasons I decided to spend my sixth and seventh form with Dad . . . was 'cause I was sort of missing out on them . . . I don't have any strong preferences between Mum and Dad as people, but [my half-brother and sister] were one of the major factors. (Fleming, 1999, p. 136)

A difficulty in halfsibling relationships, however, is perceived unfairness when a stepparent treats a biological child differently from (and better than) a stepchild, and indeed positive parent–child relations are more likely between adults and their biological children than stepparents and children (Hetherington et al., 1999; Dunn et al., in press b). Similar tensions exist, too, in complex stepfamilies when biological parents are seen to treat their own children differentially in terms of discipline, presents, and attention (Fleming, 1999).

Stepmother Families

Stepmother families make up a small minority of stepfamilies, and have received comparatively little attention from researchers, yet there are some important differences between them that suggest that relationships in stepfather and stepmother families may be somewhat different. First, whereas 88 percent of stepfather families live together in the same house, 92 percent of stepmother families *do not*, both in the UK (Ferri & Smith, 1998) and in the USA (Nielsen, 1999). Most stepchildren, then, do not live with their stepmothers and the development of their relationships will occur outside the domain of day-to-day domestic living, in contrast with stepfather families where the stepparent usually lives with the stepchildren. It is probably easier to establish close and workable relationships when children and their stepparents live together; though on the other hand, a visiting relationship has the advantage of not having to adapt to continuous proximity.

One factor that sets the residential stepmother role apart from that of residential stepfather is the fact that after separation nonresidential mothers stay in regular phone and written contact with children more than nonresidential fathers do (Gunnoe & Hetherington, 1995; Thomson et al., 1994; Stewart, 1999). Nonresidential mothers are also more likely to take a direct and monitoring role with children (Hetherington & Henderson, 1997) and to maintain support and interest toward them (Gunnoe, 1993). This situation is a potentially difficult one for stepmothers who are taking day-to-day care of stepchildren. Contributing to this is the still-prevalent promotion of biological mothers as being uniquely important for children, in contrast to the "mythical malevolence" of stepmothers, depicted over centuries of folklore (Gorrell Barnes et al., 1998). The threat to a biological mother of being replaced in her children's lives by an unrelated woman has the potential to set up competition between two women for the loyalty of the children, who are more likely to find themselves caught in a conflict between mother and stepmother than between father and stepfather.

Another aspect of residential stepmothers is that many are childless when they come to the family (Ferri & Smith, 1998), so that they face the challenge of forging relationships with their partners' children from a basis of little experience of children and how they behave. This lack of experience, in combination with possible opposition from children and their biological mothers, may make the establishment of workable relationships in the household a formidable task.

Resident stepmothers take a major parenting role with their partners' children. In the NCDS sample in the UK, stepmothers were more likely than mothers in any other household to be solely responsible for teaching good behavior (Ferri & Smith, 1998). In the same group, more fathers in stepmother families than in first-marriage families worked full time, suggesting that they were not contributing substantively to childcare. Considerable responsibility for childrearing, then, falls to resident stepmothers, and this can lead them to feeling resentful toward their partners if they hold unrealistic expectations of them (Morrison & Thompson-Guppy, 1985).

For stepmothers a somewhat depressing picture emerges of a childless woman striving to build relationships with children who maintain frequent contact with their own mother and who may see her as a rival for the place of their mother and the affections of their father. Yet she is expected to take a central and specific parenting role in the household. Even greater complications are brought into a stepmother household if she has her own children, as is the case in complex families . . . Many of these dynamics are similar to those in stepfather families, but for stepmother families extra challenges lie in the likelihood that stepmothers will take on a direct parenting role with children who are not related to them. In contrast, stepfathers can often get by in a more passive role vis-à-vis stepchildren. That many stepmother families succeed in functioning happily is, then, a considerable tribute, and the conclusion . . . that stepmother families are the toughest to establish, is not surprising.

Serious sources of tension exist, potentially, in the configuration comprising stepmother, partner, biological mother, and children. A father may feel caught between the needs of his new partner and his children, and in turn his partner may resent the time and attention he gives to his children, especially if she also feels that she is taking undue responsibility for their rearing. Children, too, resent the intrusion of another adult into their relationship with their father and may feel protective of him. Gorrell Barnes has described the feelings of rivalry over their father felt by some step-daughters, and these include concerns over whether or not a new partner will care for him properly (Gorrell Barnes et al., 1998, p. 160). This was articulated by a New Zealand stepmother, who commented that

> His oldest girl took on the mother role in the family, and mothered the other kids, and Bart allowed her to be the Mummy and do the cooking. And then the big bad wolf, me, came on the scene and knocked her off her perch. (Fleming, 1999)

For stepmothers a somewhat depressing picture emerges of a childless woman striving to build relationships with children who maintain frequent contact with their own mother and who may see her as a rival for the place of their mother and the affections of their father. Yet the step-mother is expected to take a central and specific parenting role in the household. Even greater complications are brought into a stepmother household if she has her own children, as is the case in complex families. Loyalty debates and accusations of preferential treatment by both parents toward their biological children can result, and differences in approaches to childrearing and discipline exacerbate the disagreements (Coleman & Ganong, 1997).

Many of these dynamics are similar to those in stepfather families, but for stepmother families extra challenges lie in the likelihood that step-mothers will take on a direct parenting role with children who are not related to them. In contrast, stepfathers can often get by in a more passive role *vis-à-vis* stepchildren. That many stepmother families succeed in functioning happily is, then, a considerable tribute, and the conclusion from clinicians and researchers alike that stepmother families are the toughest to establish, is not surprising.

The family environment in stepmother families

The limited amount of research on resident stepmother families suggests a picture of the family environment that reflects the difficulties discussed above. One US study has reported that stepmother families are not less cohesive or more conflicted than other households are (Pruett et al., 1993). However, in the NCDS study in the UK, men and women in stepmother households reported levels of unhappy partnerships two to three times higher than those in other households, including stepfather families (Ferri & Smith, 1998) (see table 6.1). They also report low levels of life satisfaction, and high levels of depression. It is worth describing this English group of families in more detail in order to put these findings into context. The stepmother families were stable households; three-quarters had been married 8 years. They were very likely to contain stepchildren who were adolescent; in nearly half (44 percent) the youngest stepchild was 11 years or older (Ferri & Smith, 1998, p. 21). Most of these households also included preschool children; 70 percent had joint children, and of these 63 percent were under 5 years old. Many parents in stepmother families were therefore managing the needs of adolescent stepchildren alongside those of preschool children of their own. It is little wonder that partnerships, happiness, and mental health were under considerable stress. A further complication lies in the fact that in many cases these complicated stepmother households are formed when adolescents who are already troubled and in conflict with their mothers migrate to their fathers' homes (Buchanan & Maccoby, 1996). In those situations, stepmothers are faced with negotiating relationships with adolescents who bring their distress with them into the household.

Stepmother–stepchild relationships

How do stepmothers and their stepchildren get on? From the perspective of children, the answer is not particularly well. In comparison with young people in households with biological mothers, those in stepmother households report more conflict, less support, and a lower quality of relationships with their stepmother (Pruett et al., 1993). In turn, stepmothers report lower levels of both positive and negative responses to stepchildren in their households (Thomson et al., 1992) when compared with women in other family structures, indicating lower levels of engagement overall. This suggests a dilemma when put alongside the likelihood that stepmothers will be responsible for the majority of childcare. Stepmothers are not recognized as *bona fide* mothers, yet are evaluated as such. Children do not, though, express loyalty conflicts between two mothers (Ganong & Coleman, 1994), and no relationship has been found between closeness to biological mothers and acceptance of stepmothers (Buchanan & Maccoby, 1996). Children, overall, appear to be clear about the separate places of biological and stepparents in their lives, so stepmother–stepchild troubles cannot be attributed to divided loyalties.

Resident stepmothers are, overall, in an unenviable position. Despite this, most stepmother–stepchildren relationships are close rather than conflictual. "Successful" stepmothers are often not described as such; they are more likely to be seen as big sisters or friends. Parent–child relationships in stepmother families, overall, are qualitatively different from those in both original and stepfather households, where the biological parent is most likely also to be taking primary responsibility for childcare. Stepmothers face the challenge of establishing primary and workable parenting relationships with children who do not consider them as parents.

Children's perceptions of stepmothers provide further insight into these relationships. For example, children are least likely to say they feel close to stepmothers, in comparison with stepfathers and biological parents (Ganong & Coleman, 1994). Two-thirds of young people interviewed by Gorell Barnes in the UK actively disliked their stepmothers, compared with one-third who disliked their stepfathers (Gorrell Barnes et al., 1998). Children, too, are more likely to be satisfied with the degree of closeness to stepfathers than to stepmothers (69 percent compared with 48 percent: Funder, 1996). They are also more likely to say they would prefer a more distant relationship with stepmothers than with stepfathers (39 percent compared with 15 percent). Stepmothers are less likely than stepfathers to be seen by adolescents as having a right to set up rules in the household (Buchanan & Maccoby, 1996). Moreover, they do not see stepmothers as having a particular investment in their well-being. One young person in New Zealand commented, "like with my stepmum, it's like there is no connection there that makes me want to turn out really good, or wants her to be proud of me." Another, when asked about stepmothers' expectations, said "They don't really comment. They'll say, 'well done' if I do well in a test or something, but they won't say, 'I want you to do well'" (Fleming, 1999, p. 129).

Resident stepmothers are, overall, in an unenviable position. Despite this, most stepmother–stepchildren relationships are close rather than conflictual (Coleman & Ganong, 1994). "Successful" stepmothers are often not described as such; they are more likely to be seen as big sisters or friends (Gorrell Barnes et al., 1998). One New Zealand stepmother said "I don't want to be their mother, I've told them that. They've got a mother, a perfectly capable mother in my opinion. They don't need another one. I'm quite happy for them to have me as a friend" (Fleming, 1999, p. 61).

Parent–child relationships in stepmother families, overall, are qualitatively different from those in both original and stepfather households where the biological parent is most likely also to be taking primary responsibility for childcare. Stepmothers face the challenge of establishing primary and workable parenting relationships with children who do not consider them as parents. When one stepmother tried to impose rules, a stepson remembers that

> we started rebelling, because we were telling her where to go, saying "You're not our mother, you're not telling us what to do" etc., etc., so she used to say "Well go up to bed" and we used to say "We're not going . . . you're not our mother and that's it." (Gorrell Barnes et al., 1998, p. 86)

Nonresident stepmothers

Most stepmothers do not live full-time with stepchildren, but have them to visit on a regular basis. Many, it seems, anticipate this time with some dread (Coleman & Ganong, 1994). Their day-to-day routine is disrupted, their partner's attention is comprehensively diverted, and, because of the visiting nature of the relationship, there are reduced opportunities to establish mutually acceptable ways of being together. Women who have comparatively high standards for behavior and discipline, and who have had little experience with the ways of adolescents, find visits from stepchildren especially frustrating (Coleman & Ganong, 1997). In turn, children may see their father's partner as impossibly demanding and, indeed, filling the role of wicked stepmother. In many instances, nonresidential stepmothers never become significant people in their stepchildren's lives and achieve, at best, the status of their father's friend. Overall, the nonresidential stepmother–stepchild relationship seems either irrelevant to children's well-being (Amato & Rezac, 1994) or, in one case, has been found to be related to behavioral problems (Funder, 1996).

Taking everything into account, the role of stepmother seems to have little going for it. Residential stepmothers come to their role often with negligible support and experience, and expectations from themselves and others that they will mother children who are very likely not to want to be mothered by them. They simultaneously juggle the tasks of renegotiating relationships with their own children if they have them, and of establishing, fostering, and balancing often inimical relations among themselves and their partners, stepchildren, and nonresidential parents. Coleman and Ganong report that

> many [stepmothers] were dissatisfied enough with their role as residential
> or nonresidential stepmother that they would advise women against marry-
> ing men who have children from previous relationships. Although they in-
> dicated that they loved their husbands, several were unsure that the
> remarriage was worth the stress. (Coleman & Ganong, 1997 pp. 112–13)

Nonetheless, many stepmother families flourish, and find ways to over-
come the challenges described here. One important contribution to success is the way in which a stepparent is introduced into a family (Gorrell
Barnes et al., 1998). Men, it seems, are not so good at introducing stepmothers gradually, but are likely to bring them in somewhat abruptly and
to expect them to take over childrearing roles without adequate time for
adapting, unlike stepfather families, where stepfathers are inducted more
gradually into a parenting role. One daughter was told by her father that
"If you don't like it, well she's going to be my wife, so you could go and
live with grandma. It's up to you" (Gorrell Barnes et al., 1998, p. 81).

Research that examines the unique and variable issues for stepmother
families is sparse. A focus on those that succeed might help to identify
factors that confer resilience for this family form which, although it has
minority status, is bound to become more common as more men become
residential parents to their children.

Multiple Transitions

So far, a comparatively small volume of research has looked explicitly
beyond second transitions of children into stepfamilies, to examine subsequent changes in their households. The findings of the few studies we do
have are clear: multiple transitions are associated with significantly increased levels of risk for children when compared with those in original,
lone-parent, and (usually) stepfamilies, and these have been discussed in
chapter 3. In order to understand why these children are so vulnerable,
some researchers have started to consider family processes in families where
parents have undergone several partnership transitions. Again, the evidence combines to suggest that parenting and parent–child relationships
in general suffer in these families. Parenting involvement, encompassing
monitoring and parent–child activities, is negatively associated with the
number of transitions a mother has had (Capaldi & Patterson, 1991), and
adolescents in families who had gone through three or more transitions
saw their parents as providing less supervision, promoting less autonomy,

providing lower levels of acceptance, and being more conflicted than those in families with no or few transitions (Kurdek et al., 1995). By following a group of children and their mothers in the US, a short longitudinal study also demonstrated that transitions occurring during the two years of the study were associated with a decline in parent–child relations including problem-solving, and levels of mother-initiated conflict bouts (DeGarmo & Forgatch, 1999).

In the UK, children whose families had been redisrupted after stepfamily formation were more likely than those in other family structures to say they were unhappy, to fight with their mothers, and to have a low social self-image (Cockett & Tripp, 1994). The number of transitions that parents have been through is also linked with the quality of the relationships both they and their partners have with their children (Dunn et al., in press b). Positive relationships between mothers and fathers and children are more likely in families where both parents have had few partnership transitions, and negativity in father–child relationships is higher where the fathers have been through more transitions. Children whose mothers have had a number of relationships are, too, less likely to feel close to maternal grandparents (Lussier et al., submitted).

From all we know so far, then, parenting and more generally family processes appear to be diminished in families where parents have had several transitions. There is evidence, too, that one transition is predictive of subsequent ones (Capaldi & Patterson, 1991; DeGarmo & Forgatch, 1999; O'Connor et al., 1999a). In DeGarmo and Forgatch's sample, 34 percent of multiple-transition families underwent further transitions during the two years of the study, compared with 20 percent of stepfamilies, 33 percent of single mothers, and 11 percent of original families. Maternal risk factors for transitions were also identified in this group. They were depression, number of arrests, young age at first partnership, and low socioeconomic status. In turn, Capaldi and Patterson identified maternal antisocial behavior as a mediator between the number of family transitions and parenting behavior, and noted that "with each transition antisocial parents with poor parenting skills represent an increasing proportion of the parent group" (Capaldi & Patterson, 1991, p. 501). It may be, then, that the particularly high risks for children in multiple-transition families represent a propensity in parents both for poor parenting and frequent partnership changes. Alternatively, the transitions in themselves with their associated stresses and relationship changes may act cumulatively to endanger the chances of children avoiding behavioral, educational, and psychological adversity.

Overview

There is little that is straightforward about stepfamilies. They are complex, diverse, flexible, and increasingly ubiquitous. This does not mean, as we have seen, that they fail their members; the majority of adults and children in stepfamilies thrive. It does mean, though, that they face particular challenges and risks that are not present in original families, and their ubiquity suggests that understanding and overcoming these challenges is important.

A particularly significant difference between stepfamilies and original families is the variation in biological relatedness between parents and children. There is no doubt that they both experience more positive relationships with those to whom they are biologically related (Hetherington et al., 1999; Dunn et al., in press). Nonbiological stepkin relations are comparatively fragile, and in many cases do not achieve the depth and stability of biological ties. Conservative proponents in the family change debate regard stepfamilies as "inherently problematic" for this reason, and use evolutionary biology as a basis for arguing that "Stepfamily problems, in short, may be so intractable that the best strategy for dealing with them is to do everything to minimize their occurrence" (Popenoe, 1994, p. 19). A further, logical extension of this argument is that divorced parents should remain single rather than subject their children to the further risks of stepfamily living.

Much of the evidence considered in this chapter supports the view of stepfamilies as difficult to establish, and of relations within them requiring negotiation and definition rather than fitting an assumed template. Over 20 years ago, Cherlin described stepfamilies as incomplete institutions (Cherlin, 1978). Since then they have not become more "complete"; rather they continue to become more diverse, as do families in general.

Children, too, are at the same level of risk for outcomes such as distress, poor academic performance, early home and school leaving, partnerships, and parenthood, as those growing up in lone-parent families. Neither an increase in household income nor two potentially parenting adults in the home ensures good outcomes for children in stepfamilies.

While the significance of biological relationship, or "ownness," is apparent in the well-established differences between biological and non-biological relationships, the explanations for these are debated. Stepkin do not share genes; neither, commonly, do they share the child's infancy and early childhood when the fundamentals of close parent–child relationships are established. Not only are the positive building blocks of parent–child relationships laid down then; so, too, are the crucial inhibitors of negative aspects such as neglect and abuse. The intricacies of biological and social relationships and their intersections are obvious, although their manifestations in the nature of stepfamily relationships are becoming better understood.

How might those taking a liberal perspective interpret the research we have discussed here? First, they might argue that children are not, overall, worse off in stepfamilies than they are in lone-parent families. It would be noted that stepfamilies offer to children interpersonal resources they might not otherwise have, especially as they do not lose the relationship with their biological parent by gaining one with a stepparent. The diversity that exists among stepfamily households offers options for children that they do not get in original families, although it is not always apparent how these options should be exercised.

Kurdek emphasizes a pragmatic point, that stepfamilies are probably unstoppable:

> Like it or not, women are no longer economically dependent on their husbands. Like it or not, women no longer need to define themselves in terms of their social roles as wives and mothers. Like it or not, women benefit from participating in roles other than or in addition to that of mother. Like it or not, men and women are going to renege on vows of lifetime commitments to one person because life with that one person sometimes reaches intolerable limits that could not be foreseen at the time of marriage. Finally, like it or not, as a result of these economic, social, cultural, and psychological dimensions of contemporary life, many children will experience the stresses associated with parenting transitions. In sum, rather than being de-institutionalized, it seems to me that marriage is being re-institutionalized to adapt to a new set of economic, social, cultural and psychological conditions. (Kurdek, 1994, p. 42)

To minimize the occurrence of stepfamilies, then, is a difficult call, although few would argue with the aim of promoting happy and stable original families. Furthermore the alternative to stepfamilies is not, usually, to remain in an original family but to stay in a lone-parent household; in which case comparisons of the welfare of children should lie between these two family structures. If, as a result of biology, the situation in stepfamilies is intractable and the problems inherent, then the outlook is pessimistic. If, however, difficult relationships in stepfamilies are a result of factors associated with previous transitions, and of the challenges of establishing good enough parent–child relationships between nonrelated stepkin, then there is some hope that the diversity in stepfamily households may in itself be an advantage in overcoming the hurdles faced by those who are trying to adapt their lives to their current circumstances.

7

Fathers and Families

*Although sometimes admiring the family man as nurturer, protec-
tor, mentor, adviser, role model, authority figure, romantic partner,
or big pal, popular culture has more often depicted such men in
much more negative ways – as aloof and distant, inept and ineffec-
tual, philandering or violent, neglectful and irresponsible, self-
absorbed and emotionally insensitive, or simply superfluous.*

Mintz, 1998, p. 3

Introduction

Relationships between fathers and their children have become one of the
most contested issues in debates about families, and it is when parents
separate and stepfamilies are formed that these issues come into particularly sharp relief. The heat of the debate is reflected in emotionally laden
terms such as "fatherless families," with father absence being seen by
some as almost single-handedly responsible for children's problems. Others see fathers' involvement with children as properly being at the discre-
tion of mothers and argue that in situations where conflict or violence is
involved, involvement should not happen at all. A simplistic version of
these views is that fathers are either all good or all bad. The first position
is represented most vehemently by fathers' rights groups who argue that
men are deeply disadvantaged by separation and court processes and pro-
pose, for example, that shared joint physical custody should be a legal
presumption. A milder version of this is reflected in the Children Act 1989
in the UK, with its emphasis on joint parental responsibility after divorce.
More generally, a conservative view is that families and children need
fathers as providers of guidance and discipline and income. Conversely, a
liberal perspective ranges from the view that children simply do not need
their fathers at all and that women do a perfectly adequate job of raising
them, to the notion that men can, under some circumstances, be a positive
influence for children.

Fatherless homes are not new, although at the beginning of the twenty-first century a significant proportion of children is growing up living in homes without their fathers. A major difference now, in comparison with earlier times, is that men are usually still alive and potentially accessible, whereas death was a more likely cause of father absence in the past. Many men want to continue involvement with their children; for some women, however, the ongoing contact with ex-partners that is involved is troubling, since it prolongs a relationship that is a source of distress for them. The need to make decisions about living arrangements for children after separation has, then, highlighted questions about men's competence, rights, and their willingness to be active parents in their children's lives.

Children may want their fathers in their lives, but parental separation raises a fundamental question of whether children *need* fathers in order to develop optimally. Many children grow up in households where men are absent, and go to schools where women predominate as teachers, yet these children develop into well-functioning adults. However, there are widely held concerns about father-absence, particularly for boys. One of the main questions in this regard is whether boys can develop appropriate gender roles in the absence of male models. On the other hand, the stress that mothers may experience through continuing contact with ex-partners may mean that advantages to their children of continuing contact with fathers are outweighed by the reduced quality of parenting that might result.

In this chapter we attempt to answer some of the questions raised by these issues. Do children unequivocally need fathers in their lives, or are men largely irrelevant to them? Under what circumstances might children benefit from contact with their fathers after parents separate? Before looking at the place of separated fathers in the lives of their children, we will first examine the roles of men in families in general, and try to identify the myths and realities that accompany much of the rhetoric surrounding men as fathers. We will start by looking at the recent history of men's roles in families, and men's places in original families.

Changes in Fathers' Roles in Original Families

How much have men's roles in families changed over the last century? Some writers see the industrial revolution as a critical transition for families and especially for men, removing them from the center of the family and leading them to occupy a role as economic provider with little involvement in the nurturing of children (Popenoe, 1993). The provider role was most apparent in nuclear families, where men were breadwinners, and women were economically dependent. The nostalgia for this "traditional" family form is evident in much of the agonizing over family decline that is apparent in the writing of many current commentators (Blankenhorn, 1995), despite the fact that for many families the nuclear family form has never been a possibility because of the economic necessity for both parents to work.

In reality, men's roles in families have always been diverse (Mintz, 1998), and that diversity is particularly evident now at the beginning of the twenty-first century. An informative illustration of this is in an analysis of popular magazines published in USA between 1900 and 1989, showing that the depiction of the father's role alternated over this period between that of nurturer and of provider, with the predominant focus on men as nurturers since the 1940s (Atkinson & Blackwelder, 1993). The major increase in popular interest has been in parenting that is nonspecific in regard to gender. Over the same period, interest in *mothering* specifically has declined. Fathers were more likely to be depicted as providers at times when fertility rates were high and families had more children to support, and the provider role became less prominent as families became smaller and men were portrayed as appropriately involved in parenting their children. Their parenting involvement, however, is seen not specifically as fathering, but as co-parenting. Mothers and fathers are depicted as a team, despite the fact that men have not taken on parenting roles to the extent that women have moved into full-time employment. Why have men not moved into the home to the same degree that women have entered the workforce?

Polarization of men's roles

Two historical developments occurred last century that have produced a dilemma for men and women in families (Mintz, 1998). The first is the move from an economy based on provision of a family wage that enabled a household to live on the income brought in by a father, to an individual wage economy where temporary employment and part-time work have become more common. This change has led to a decline in men's real wages and has given women increasing amounts of economic independence, at the same time as increasing the need for both parents to be in the workforce in order to support the family. The shift in emphasis from men's identity being based on being the main provider toward that of being a nurturer which might have been propelled by this economic change, has been confounded, however, by the second development identified by

Mintz: the emphasis on the fundamental importance of the mother–child relationship, underscored by the writings of Freud and Bowlby, and advocated by childrearing experts such as Benjamin Spock in the United States. Freud was quite explicit in this regard, when he described the mother–child relationship as "unique, without parallel, established unalterably for a whole lifetime as the first and strongest love-object and as the prototype of all later love relations – for both sexes" (Freud, 1940). Women, then, found themselves expected to maintain primary nurturing roles as well as working outside the home, and men who might have moved toward more balanced work/family roles were not encouraged to do so. There has been a continuum of responses to this tension between the impetus for fathers to take up more nurturing, propelled by women entering the workforce, and the impediment to doing so emanating from the high value placed on mothers *vis-à-vis* children. Fathers' responses range from withdrawal from their children's lives, to total involvement and primary parenting. Increasing numbers of men are involved with the day-to-day care and nurturing of children in both original and separated families, yet many are physically absent as a result of long hours and work pressures, or through parental separation. This polarization of roles is reflected in popular depictions of fathers as either nurturing, new-age men, or totally absent from their children's lives. On the one hand, for example, images of sports heroes holding their babies are prominent; on the other, there is widespread media concern about absent fathers and lone-parent families.

These issues are particularly apparent in relation to separation and divorce. Dilemmas are reflected in questions about the involvement of fathers in their sons' and daughters' lives after separation. If mothers provide all or most of what children need, then contact with fathers after separation might be both unnecessary and complicated. If children do gain specific benefits from having a relationship with their fathers, then what

Increasing numbers of men are involved with the day-to-day care and nurturing of children in both original and separated families, yet many are physically absent as a result of long hours and work pressures, or through parental separation. This polarization of roles is reflected in popular depictions of fathers as either nurturing, new-age men, or totally absent from their children's lives. On the one hand, for example, images of sports heroes holding their babies are prominent; on the other, there is widespread media concern about absent fathers and lone-parent families.

are the optimal arrangements? Fathers increasingly apply for, and often gain, sole custody of their children. How adequate can they be as primary parents? Finally, do fathers need children for their own well-being?

Fathers and children in original families

The question of whether or not fathers matter at all for children's well-being has been addressed by studies of father-absence through either divorce or death. Not surprisingly, it is found that in general children who grow up being parented by a lone mother are more likely to suffer a variety of adverse outcomes (Biller, 1993). However, factors such as the absence of a second parent to share childcare responsibilities, and the emotional and economic stress experienced by lone mothers, are as likely to explain the outcomes as father absence *per se*. Studies of father absence do not make a distinction between the absence of a father in particular and the absence of a second parent, and often do not distinguish between total absence and variations in levels and types of contact. They do not, then, address the question of the *specific* importance of men for children. In order to understand the particular role of fathers, the foci in more recent investigations have been upon their role in the family context, and upon the unique contributions their involvement might make to children's well-being.

How much time do fathers spend with children?
Fathers' involvement with children remains lower than mothers' even in dual-income families (Lamb, 1995; Pleck, 1997). Lamb has reported, for example, that the time fathers spend in direct interaction with their children in single-earner families is between 20 and 25 percent of the time that mothers spend, and in dual-earner families is about 33 percent of mothers' time. A quantitative measure of involvement based simply on the number of hours spent together misses more subtle aspects of father–child relationships, however. A more sophisticated approach has led to the identification of three major aspects of involvement: availability to children, engagement with them, and responsibility for their care (Pleck, 1997). Findings across studies in the 1980s and 1990s show that the proportion of time fathers spend engaged with children in relation to mothers is about 44 percent of the time that mothers do (Pleck, 1997). The equivalent proportion they spend being available to children is nearly 66 percent. In terms of time, these figures translate to 2 hours per day of engagement on weekdays and 6.5 hours of engagement on Sundays. For

availability, the comparable figures are between 3 and 5 hours per day on weekdays, and 10 hours on Sundays. However, fathers are comparatively rarely involved in areas of responsibility such as organizing childcare, decision-making, and being available for sick children. Fathers, too, tend to be more and more consistently involved with sons, and with younger children (Pleck, 1997).

Workplace factors
Active parenting, however, requires ready accessibility both to and for children. Most employers are slow to respond to the needs of parents for flexibility in working schedules, despite demonstrable benefits to them in terms of employee productivity and loyalty (Edgar, 1997). Men are doubly disadvantaged in this regard since they are more likely than women to be in full-time employment, and attitudes to men as involved parents are not yet as positive as they are toward women. Involved fathers are also likely to encounter workplace hostility (Russell, 1986; Bolger et al., 1989). Men's work role orientation is also related to their parenting. The still-pervasive view of men primarily and properly as providers for their families exerts pressure to perform highly at work, and creates both internal and external tensions between the demands of work and parenting. Men who work long hours are less available to their children (Pleck, 1985) and read less and share fewer leisure activities with them (Marsiglio, 1991). Those who are highly occupationally satisfied by and psychologically heavily invested in their work are also less accessible to their children (Grossman et al., 1988).

How important is father–child interaction for children?

The fact that many men are not particularly available and accessible to their children may not, of course, matter. However, in families where fathers are involved parents, children show high levels of well-being in a variety of ways including cognitive competence, empathy, and internal locus of control (Radin & Sagi, 1992). Positive benefits exist particularly in family contexts where both parents welcome fathers' involvement in childcare; if men are forced into high levels of involvement through, for example, unemployment, the effects on the children tend to be negative. A father's motivation in caring for children may be, then, more important than the amount of time he spends with them. Motivation is not the only important factor, though; the nature of fathers' parenting also matters. Monitoring, support, and nurturance are linked with positive child adjustment (Barnes, 1984; Conger & Elder, 1994). More specifically, fathers are important in fostering children's abilities to regulate their emotions (Gottman, 1998). This happens in the context of physical play, where fathers stimulate their children to thresholds of fear and excitement. To the extent that fathers are sensitive to their children's limits of tolerance for stimulation, they help them to acquire effective ways of regulating their emotions. Benefits are apparent, too, beyond childhood: in adolescents, perception of fathers as caring is positively related to good family functioning, and negatively to depression, especially for girls, in all kinds of families (McFarlane et al., 1995). In adults, levels of empathetic concern are predicted by high levels of paternal care in their childhood, even when dimensions of both their mothers' and fathers' behavior are taken into account (Koestner et al., 1990). The mere presence of fathers, then, and their more traditional behavior of disciplining are not the most crucial components of father–child relationships. Involvement in care, the provision of nurturing, and generally engaged parenting behavior are the aspects of fathering that are important for children, just as they are for parenting in general.

> The mere presence of fathers, then, and their more traditional behavior of disciplining are not the most crucial components of father–child relationships. Involvement in care, the provision of nurturing, and generally engaged parenting behavior are the aspects of fathering that are important for children, just as they are for parenting in general.

Indirect influences

Although there are direct links between father–child relationships and children's well-being, some of the impact fathers have on children is indirect, via mothers (Furstenberg et al., 1987). In the majority of original families, a large proportion of father–child interaction takes place in the presence of mothers, and the amount of time fathers spend with children is closely associated with the amount that mothers spend (Cooksey & Fondell, 1996). Fathers in two-parent households very often act as part of a couple (de Singly, 1993). When combined parenting is taken into account, weaker but nonetheless significant links between father–child relationships and outcomes for children are found, including social competence (Amato, 1989) and academic achievement (Forehand et al., 1986). Amato has identified the separate contributions of mothers and fathers, and noted the particular salience of fathers for educational achievement and levels of distress, and of mothers for kin ties and friendships (Amato, 1998). There is, though, a large contribution to children's outcomes made by joint parenting in which the paternal and maternal components cannot be disentangled from one another. Generally, then, strong links between positive interactions with fathers and a wide range of optimal outcomes for children aged between 5 and 18 years are found, even after taking into account the effects of mothers' involvement and co-parenting.

As well as their participation in joint parenting, the importance of fathers for children is indirect in other ways; their behavior in the relationship with their partners has a bearing on children's well-being. For example, unsupportive behavior by men toward partners is associated with harsh discipline by mothers (Conger & Elder, 1994). Conversely, where fathers show affection toward their partners, children have been found to be popular with peers (Boyum & Parke, 1995). Fathers' life experiences are also important. The number of cohabiting relationships men have had earlier are linked with the quality of both father–child and mother–child relationships (Dunn et al., in press b); parent–child relationships are more positive and less negative if fathers have had fewer relationship transitions. Similarly, father–child relationships are linked with their mothers' life events. Fathers and their partners tend to have similar levels of lifecourse events such as numerous cohabiting relationships, so that children's relations with their parents are affected in similar ways from two sources – their mothers' and their fathers' past life events.

In practice, then, fathers in original families have an influence on their children in at least four ways: through their behavior in interaction with mothers in the spousal relationship; through joint parenting as a parenting team; as a result of previous life events; and in direct interactions with children independent of mothers' behavior.

Fathers have an important contribution to make to their children's well-being, and their involvement has the capacity to foster development. So their absence can be a potential loss for children. However, ambivalence and tensions in the social definitions of their roles mean that there is wide variation in men's behavior (Gottman, 1998), and their potential for contributing to psychopathology in children has been emphasized (Phares, 1996). Indeed, men can be forces for good or ill in their children's lives. Fathers' absence can be a loss if their influence is potentially positive or an advantage if their presence would have a negative impact.

Fathers and Children after Separation

When parents separate, children continue to live with their mothers in the overwhelming number of cases, and the percentage who do so is remarkably consistent across countries and decades regardless of legal agreements about custody (see chapter 1). There is, however, some increase in the prevalence of joint residential custody arrangements. In the UK joint custody arrangements doubled from 13 to 26 percent between 1985 and 1991 (Simpson et al., 1995). More generally, a belief that children should continue to have a relationship with their nonresidential parent after separation is widespread amongst lawyers, the judiciary, and professionals working with families. In this section we will examine the evidence relating to this belief.

Do children want to see their fathers after separation?

Most children say they want continuing contact with their fathers after parental separation (Walczak & Burns, 1984; Mitchell, 1985). Loss of regular contact with their fathers is sometimes cited by them as the worst aspect of parental separation (Kurdek & Siesky, 1980). They are more likely than not to see their nonresidential fathers as a part of their families: for example, 91 percent of Australian children from separated homes, who constructed family sculptures, included their nonresidential fathers as members of the family group (Funder, 1996). One-quarter indicated that they wished for closer relationships with them than they had. The picture, as always, is somewhat varied. In one US study, nonresidential fathers have been found to be less likely than fathers who lived with their children to be named as important or as someone upon whom to call for help (Munsch et al., 1995). However, those who did nominate their nonresidential fathers as important in their lives considered that they received the same, or in some cases higher, levels of support than children who named their residential fathers as important. Overall, children want continuing contact with their fathers and see them as important and significant in their lives.

Mothers and fathers, after separation, face the tasks of negotiating or renegotiating relationships they have with their children and their ex-partners. In very few instances is this straightforward. Women, in the main, continue in residential parenting roles at the same time as assuming extra responsibilities formerly taken by their children's father. Men's challenges are somewhat different. Continued parenting means overcoming several significant obstacles. The most apparent of these is that they no longer live in the same house and, often, live some distance from their children's home (Gibson, 1992). They face, too, the task of developing and assuming roles in relation to their children that they may not have had in the original family household. It is sometimes believed that men's involvement with children before separation predicts their postseparation involvement; there are, however, mixed findings about this. A negative relationship between pre- and postseparation involvement by fathers has been found in one study (Kruk, 1991). Fathers who were disengaged from their children after separation were found to have had particularly powerful attachments to their children before the separation; it appeared that their withdrawal from contact arose from their intense psychological response to the loss of the earlier relationship with them. In contrast, though, it has also been found that men who do not want contact with children after separation report being less involved with them when living with them (Grief, 1995). Fathers' involvement preseparation has been found in a recent meta-analysis to be positively related to both frequency of father–child contact and the quality of the father–child relationship (Whiteside & Becker, 2000). In practice, there is no straightforward way of predicting the nature of fathers' ongoing involvement with children from the kinds of relationships they had before separation. The structures of parenting that are in place before parents separate are not necessarily optimal for children after separation, when parents are living apart. Factors occurring during and after separation may be more important in determining how men and their children develop their postdivorce relationships (Lamb, 1999).

Fathers and domestic violence

When parents separate as a result of severe conflict and domestic violence, the question arises whether or not children should have contact with their fathers (who are usually but not always the perpetrators of the violence). There is no doubt that being victims themselves of violence, and witnessing violence between their parents, both have damaging consequences for children. Far less clear, though, are the possible risks and benefits of children maintaining contact with a father who has abused their mother. The tension lies between children's rights to protection from psychological and emotional harm, and their right to have relationships with both parents fostered. What are the risks associated with continued, physically safe involvement with an abusive father? Does the benefit of contact outweigh some of the risks that might be involved?

We have almost no evidence upon which to rely in answering these questions. In chapter 4 we noted that children have mixed but generally positive responses to contact with fathers who have been abusive (Chetwin et al., 1998). Some react with relief when a violent father leaves home. One in Gorell Barnes' UK study said:

> A lot of children may say that losing their father, for whatever reason, was not good for them, but from my point of view it wasn't a bad day at all because things were actually easier ... Life became better ... I was not sorry to see him disappear over the horizon, frankly. (Gorrell Barnes et al., 1998, p. 121)

Another said that "If he had come back in the past ten years, I would have beat him up really, for all the times he beat my Mum up" (Gorrell Barnes et al., 1998, p. 92). Some, though, who resumed contact with their fathers when they were older, revised their views of their fathers when they realized that there had been "mutual goading" in their parents' relationship.

One approach to this question is to distinguish the kinds of violence that occur in relation to the separation. One distinction that has been made is that between control-initiated and conflict-initiated violence (Ellis & Stuckless, 1996). Violence associated with control is likely to have other attributes such as being an ongoing chronic pattern of behavior, with physical abuse being not the only or even the main means of control. Children whose fathers exhibit this kind of behavior may be subject to emotional manipulation, and contact might need to be monitored carefully. Conflict-initiated violence, on the other hand, may be acute and specific to a particular relationship. Janet Johnston suggests that "The case of separation and postdivorce violence, where one or two violent incidents occur only around the time of traumatic separation or stressful divorce, and where there is no history of violence or any evidence of ongoing control in the relationship, can be and should be clearly distinguished from other forms of abuse" (Johnston, 1999, p. 425). If this distinction can be made, then to deny children contact with a father who has demonstrated conflict-initiated violence might be to deny them a safe and nurturing relationship with their father, especially if he accepts responsibility for the abuse and is open to ways of addressing the problems.

What happens when children have no contact with an abusive father? Again, we have little research upon which to call. Gorrell Barnes noted, though, that children who did not see their fathers either idealized them or demonized them. A third possibility is that children may blame themselves for their fathers' absence unless parents give them clear and understandable explanations.

Overall, the topic is a vexed one and the priority is to keep children safe. It is probably never justified to insist that children have contact with their fathers if they are adamant that they do not want to do so. Conversely, a child's desire to see a parent should be taken seriously and, where possible, safe and appropriate arrangements made to maintain contact.

Levels of contact

To what extent do nonresidential fathers remain involved in their children's lives? Until recently, the answer has been comparatively little. In the US, several reports have indicated that over half of children whose parents separate lost contact with their fathers completely 10 years after separation (Furstenberg & Nord, 1985; Seltzer, 1991). Others find that 1 in 5 nonresidential fathers see their children weekly (Thompson, 1986). There is, though, some indication that children and fathers may be seeing each other more frequently. In one recent UK sample only 39 percent saw their fathers less than monthly 5 years after separation (Simpson et al., 1995), and another study of parenting found that only 5 percent of nonresident parents did not have contact with their children (Maclean & Eekelaar, 1997). In Australia, a 1992 report of men 2 to 3 years after separation found that 64 percent of them were seeing their children at least once every 2 weeks (Gibson, 1992). The Australian Bureau of Statistics reports that in 1997 only 42 percent of children saw their fathers at least once a week, and 36 percent saw them once a year or less (Australian Bureau of Statistics, 1999), although this report did not indicate how long after separation their data were collected. A 1998 study of New Zealand adolescents found that only 52 percent had seen their fathers in the last year (Anyan, 1998). Older children, though, are less likely to stay in regular contact with nonresidential parents than those who are younger (Australian Bureau of Statistics, 1999), because their lifestyles as adolescents make regular visitation less easy, and because father–child contact attenuates over time after separation. It is difficult to make accurate comparisons between studies, since follow-up is done at varying times and with different samples of fathers and children. These figures tentatively support, though, a general impression of fathers and children being more likely now to maintain relationships after parental separation than in the past.

Two changes in legislation that have occurred in most English-speaking countries may have contributed to an increase in involvement. The first is the institutionalization of child support payments. There is strong evidence that payment of child support is linked with father–child contact (Seltzer, 1991; Arditti, 1992). Similarly, joint custodial arrangements (both legal and residential) in the USA are associated with higher levels of involvement between nonresidential parents and their children (Pearson & Thoennes, 1985; Seltzer, 1991; Arditti, 1992). It may be that parents who enter joint custody arrangements might also be those who are more likely to foster close father–child links because they have more cooperative relationships after separation. It has been noted in the US, however, that fathers in joint legal custodial arrangements with their children's mothers have more contact with their children than those in sole custody arrangements, even after taking into account the quality of the parents' relationship (Seltzer, 1998a).

Father–child contact and fathers' well-being

Continuing contact with children is of benefit to fathers. Men who have frequent contact with their children have been found to feel more competent, to have better self-esteem (D'Andrea, 1983), and to feel happier with family relationships (Guttman, 1993). Men who have custody of their children are, too, less likely than those who are noncustodial parents to experience adjustment difficulties after separation (Stewart et al., 1986). In terms of well-being it is in the interests of men, then, to stay in contact with their children, yet many do not. Before considering the question of whether or not it is beneficial for children to have contact with their fathers, we will look more closely at why some fathers do not maintain relationships with their children.

What predicts fathers' involvement with children after separation?

As we have seen, there is wide variation in the amount of contact children have with their fathers after separation, and the ways in which contact is defined and measured also vary. Aspects of contact include frequency and regularity of visits, as well as the length of time spent together, and levels of telephone, written, and email contact. Levels of contact vary with the source of information (Arditti, 1994; Seltzer, 1994); mothers' estimates of contact are typically lower than those of fathers' (Seltzer, 1994; Funder, 1996). Despite these variations, similar factors emerge from studies as being important for determining levels and quality of contact. In this section we draw on two US studies (Seltzer, 1991; Cooksey & Craig, 1998), two Australian studies (Gibson, 1992; Funder, 1996), and two UK studies (Simpson et al., 1995; Gorrell Barnes et al., 1998), all of which reached similar conclusions.

Relationships with former partners
The extent to which parents cooperate after separation, and the attitude of the residential parent, are key factors in determining father–child contact (Gibson, 1992; Funder et al., 1993; Simpson et al., 1995; Arditti & Bickley, 1996; Gorrell Barnes et al., 1998). Communication, cooperation, and support between former spouses are especially associated with the frequency of visitation, and with the nature of the involvement of fathers with children. In the AIFS study, mothers' accounts of frequency of overnight stays by their children with fathers were positively related to their attachment and warmth toward their ex-spouse, and to positive views of him as a parent (Funder et al., 1993). Given these findings, we might expect that there would be lower levels of father–child contact if conflict is high between ex-partners, but this association is less often found. The AIFS study found that for men anger, hurt, blame, and revenge were strongly predictive of whether they saw their children at all; however, other studies report no associations between conflict and contact (Gibson, 1992; Simpson et al., 1995).

Distance between houses and socioeconomic factors
Geographical distance between parental homes is an important determinant of father–child contact. Frequency of visitation and levels of phone contact are lower when parents live further apart (Cooksey & Craig, 1998); children who have regular contact with their fathers are, though, more likely to stay overnight when the distance between households is significant (Simpson et al., 1995). Employment status and education level are also predictive of contact, with unemployed men less likely to have their children to stay (Simpson et al., 1995), and more highly educated men more likely to visit their children (Cooksey & Craig, 1998).

Child support
Payment of child support is found to be associated with father–child contact in the United States (Furstenberg et al., 1983; Seltzer, 1991; Arditti &

Keith, 1993). In the AIFS study, however, payment of child support was not connected with father–child contact. Australian parents reported that if they had *bargained* at the time of separation over access and child support then the children were less likely to have any contact with their fathers, or to stay overnight or through holidays with them (Funder et al., 1993). Bargaining involved threatening the withdrawal of access or child support if the other was not forthcoming. It was relatively infrequent in this study, with only 13 percent of men and 9 percent of women saying it had been an aspect of their separation.

Children's gender

Findings are mixed with regard to the gender of children and contact. In one UK study of men, fathers were three times more likely to stay involved with boys than with girls (Simpson et al., 1995). (See figure 7.1.) Most US studies report no gender differences, though, and one found a slight tendency for fathers to see daughters more than sons (Seltzer, 1991). Generally it is found that fathers spend less time with children in families where all the children are girls or mixed, than in all-boy households (Cooksey & Fondell, 1996). Fathers possibly feel that sons need them

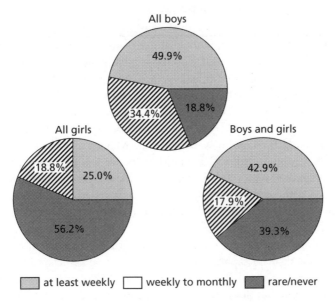

Figure 7.1   Fathers' contact with children after separation
Source: Simpson, McCarthy, & Walker, 1995

more than daughters, or may be more comfortable interacting on their own with boys. On the other hand, sons may seek contact with fathers more readily than daughters.

The motivation of the child to seek, maintain, or renew contact is also an important influence on father–child contact (Gorrell Barnes et al., 1998). If children resist seeing their fathers then contact is difficult to maintain; if they want to then it is easier. Some seek their fathers out after some time, even years, of no contact and reestablish the relationship.

Child's age at time of separation

Children who are older when their parents separate are more likely to remain in contact with their nonresidential parents than those who are younger (Maclean & Eekelaar, 1997), and, the authors suggest, this may explain why divorced fathers are more likely to stay in contact than formerly cohabiting fathers, since marriages last longer than cohabitations. "Sharing a home," they concluded, "seemed to create a relationship which could survive high levels of conflict between the two biological parents around the time of the divorce, which sometimes interrupted the meetings but did not end them" (MacLean & Richards, 1999, p. 266).

Marital status and living arrangements

Fathers who were not residing with the child's mother at the time of birth have a comparatively low likelihood of maintaining contact, probably because they have not established close relationships with their children by living in the same household (Cooksey & Craig, 1998). Mothers of these children, too, may feel that the father has no right of access. Levels of contact for fathers who were cohabiting with the mother at the time of birth fall in between those who were not living with the mother at the time of the child's birth and those who were married (Maclean & Eekelaar, 1997; Cooksey & Craig, 1998). Cohabiting fathers are less likely than married fathers to visit their children after separating from their mothers (McHenry et al., 1996), although they are just as likely as married fathers to maintain phone and written contact. This suggests the possibility of a sense of entitlement or commitment to children being weaker or stronger according to the commitment made to the relationship with their children's mother. Living arrangements *after* separation, too, appear to be associated with visiting; remarried men are likely to maintain high levels of contact even if they have stepchildren, but not if they have new biological children (Cooksey & Craig, 1998). Cohabiting men and those who are single are less likely to maintain contact postseparation than those who have remarried.

If fathers are to remain or become increasingly involved with their children after separation, they face the challenge of redefining their roles as workers and parents. A key factor in determining contact is the nature of the relationship they have with the children's mother after separation. Distances, employment status, payment of child support, children's motivations, marital status at the time of their child's birth and after separation, are also important. Some men . . . lose contact completely with their children after separation; given the possible benefits for children and fathers if contact is maintained, it is important to understand more about this group of "absent" fathers.

In summary, if fathers are to remain or become increasingly involved with their children after separation, they face the challenge of redefining their roles as workers and parents. A key factor in determining contact is the nature of the relationship they have with the children's mother after separation. Distances, employment status, payment of child support, children's motivations, marital status at the time of their child's birth and after separation are also important. Some men, as we have seen, lose contact completely with their children after separation; given the possible benefits for children and fathers if contact is maintained, it is important to understand more about this group of "absent" fathers.

Fathers who do not see their children

What is known about fathers who lose contact with their children after separation? There is a common perception of these men as having knowingly abandoned contact with, and responsibility for, their children, hence the epithet "deadbeat dads." Interestingly, the 1998 United States Congress Child Support Bill was called the Deadbeat Parents' Punishment Act. When men who do not see their children have been asked, many say they want contact but that they feel discouraged by several factors. These include the involvement of the judicial system, opposition by their children's mothers, their own issues and problems, and distance (Dudley, 1991; Grief, 1995). A few men are, though, content with lack of contact. These fathers are more likely than those who want to see their children to report domestic violence in their partnerships, and to have had low levels of involvement with their children when they lived with them. They are also more likely to feel indifferent about their children, to assume that their children feel indifferent towards them, and to be satisfied with the lack of relationship with them. One suggestion is that these men who are comfortable with a lack of contact with their children interpret harassment and negativity from their ex-partners and children during separation as rejection, rather than seeing it as part of the usual separation process (Grief, 1995). Some, too, feel inadequate as parents and may see it as in their children's best interests to remain uninvolved, and this is likely to have been the case most often in the years when divorce was seen to be best as a "clean break." Men who become stepparents to new partners' children may go through "child swapping" (Furstenberg & Nord, 1985), transferring their parental investment to a subsequent set of children in their current household. It is clear that no one explanation applies to all situations, however.

Quantity and quality of father–child contact

So far we have established that, in the main, contact with children is good for men and often desired by them, and that children say they want to see their fathers. It is a different question to ask, however, whether it is important for children's well-being that they maintain a relationship with their fathers, especially as so many grow up apparently unscathed by the absence of a father in their day-to-day lives. The view is now widely held that frequency and regularity of father–child contact after separation is associated with children's psychological well-being, unless abuse or psychopathology is present. Although positive contact is in itself a good outcome for children who usually want it, the assumption that contact per se is measurably good for children does not stand up to close scrutiny. Several studies have found that there is no direct or simple relationship between levels of nonresidential father–child contact and child well-being (King, 1994a), while others have reported both positive and negative relationships (Amato, 1993). This does not mean that contact with fathers is unimportant for children, and these mixed findings suggest several explanations. First, contact between fathers and children is not necessarily a positive experience for children if the child does not want it or if the relationship is negative. Separation, too, sometimes increases interparental conflict, and father–child contact in situations of high parental conflict can be negatively related to well-being, especially for boys (Amato & Rezac, 1994).

Since children usually want to see their fathers, contact with them is good in its own right. In the US, a curvilinear relationship has been found for levels of father–child contact and distress (Laumann-Billings & Emery, 2000). Young people who saw their fathers one to three times a month – which approximates every other weekend, the default position in many countries – reported higher levels of distress than those who saw fathers either weekly or only a few times a year. It may be that those who rarely saw their father adapted to not having him around, and those who had regular contact did not feel his absence keenly. Those in the middle, however, were less able to resolve their feelings about their fathers.

Because frequency by itself does not have a consistent link with children's well-being, attention has more recently been given to the *quality* of the father–child relationship. In particular, feelings of closeness have been examined as a potentially important factor related to well-being in children. Again, findings are somewhat mixed, with some investigators finding no relationship (Furstenberg & Teitler, 1994) and others reporting positive associations between feelings of closeness and psychological well-being (Buchanan & Maccoby, 1996; Salem et al., 1998). Feelings of closeness between fathers and children are also linked positively with academic success and negatively with anxiety (Amato & Rivera, 1999). From what we have discussed earlier about men in original families it is apparent that, apart from economic provision, fathers' contributions to their children's lives depend on more than their mere presence. To the extent that men remain involved in parenting after separation, or assume parenting practices they have not done before, they have a positive influence on their children's well-being. As in original families, the most effective ways in which they can parent are by providing support and monitoring, or authoritative parenting (see chapter 2 above). In both original and separated families it is these aspects of parenting encompassing monitoring, encouragement, love, and warmth, that are consistently linked with child and adolescent well-being (Young et al., 1995; Amato, 1998). Positive and involved relationships with fathers after separation, then, are good for children in a number of measurable ways.

For many children, support from their nonresidential fathers is not focused on parenting activities, but rather on entertainment and the provision of gifts; they are taken to movies and given presents since these activities are less demanding and often easier in comparison with the active involvement that is associated with more involved parenting. In two-parent families, active parenting by fathers predicts life satisfaction in adolescents far better than feelings of closeness and material provision; and in separated families active parenting from fathers is linked with lower levels of externalizing behavior . . . Fathers' involvement in their children's lives as active parents, then, is more important for their well-being than frequency of visiting or even feelings of closeness.

For many children, support from their nonresidential fathers is not focused on parenting activities, but rather on entertainment and the provision of gifts: they are taken to movies and given presents since these activities are less demanding and often easier in comparison with the kind of behavior that is associated with more involved parenting. In two-parent families, active parenting by fathers predicts life satisfaction in adolescents far better than feelings of closeness and material provision; and in separated families active parenting from fathers is linked with lower levels of externalizing behavior (Simons et al., 1994). Fathers' involvement in their children's lives as active parents, then, is more important for their well-being than frequency of visiting or even feelings of closeness. As Buchanan and colleagues have observed,

> As difficult as such responsive parenting might be, our data indicate that it is one of the most important facilitators of adolescent adjustment after divorce; parents' efforts in this area should have high pay-offs. (Buchanan & Maccoby, 1996, p. 261)

Provision of support and monitoring is difficult for fathers who are not in daily contact with their children. Staying overnight in their fathers' homes facilitates the establishment of involved parenting, especially for younger children, because it calls for involvement at levels not needed with visiting, or telephone and written contact. These include providing meals, preparing children for bed, and being involved in comforting and monitoring by setting limits and disciplining them. For school-aged children, overnight staying means that fathers have to ensure that they are dressed, prepared, and delivered to school. For some separated fathers, these are tasks they have not undertaken by themselves during marriage, and this single-handed provision of parenting fosters a very different and often closer father–child relationship than they had before separation. This kind of relationship is difficult to establish if visits are just in the daytime and encompass mainly entertainment. Children in the US in the early 1980s were unlikely to stay overnight, even in the first two years after separation (Furstenberg & Nord, 1985); 80 percent reported they had never stayed with their fathers. It is notable in Gibson's Australian study of separated men that where access included overnight stays, levels of contact were sustained over the two years of the study, whereas daytime access levels diminished by half over that period. Closeness between fathers and their children, then, is fostered and sustained when men are involved in caretaking activities such as those called on when their children stay the night with them.

Fathers face several challenges in continuing or assuming effective parenting roles after separation. The opportunity for doing so is reduced because of lack of day-to-day contact. Many men have not been closely involved with their young children's upbringing, and lack experience in caretaking. If contact is brief or infrequent, men may be reluctant to exert control and discipline in the short time they have with their children, for fear of alienating them. There is, too, a continuing "mother mystique" that suggests that women can care for children better than men. In many situations, then, it is easier for men to provide entertainment and gifts than it is to be involved parents. Opportunities for involved parenting are more readily available when children are in shared custody arrangements or stay overnight with their fathers. We know little about how men's parenting practices change after separation; there is some evidence from Australia that, by their own accounts, their levels of responsiveness and control remain very similar (Gibson, 1992). As shared residence arrangements and involvement of fathers in their children's lives are increasing, a more detailed examination of the links between men's parenting before and after separation and their children's well-being is needed.

Fathers face several challenges in continuing or assuming effective parenting roles after separation. The opportunity for doing so is reduced because of lack of day-to-day contact. Many men have not been closely involved with their young children's upbringing, and lack experience in caretaking. If contact is brief or infrequent, men may be reluctant to exert control and discipline in the short time they have with their children, for fear of alienating them. There is, too, a continuing "mother mystique" that suggests that women can care for children better than men. In many situations, then, it is easier for men to provide entertainment and gifts than it is to be involved parents. Opportunities for involved parenting are more readily available when children are in shared custody arrangements or stay overnight with their fathers.

Men as Single Fathers

Although the majority of children continue to live with their mothers after separation, a proportion live predominantly with their fathers (see chapter 1). For example, 1 in 6 single-parent households in the United States are lone-father homes, and between 10 and 15 percent of divorcing fathers are awarded sole custody (Hetherington & Henderson, 1997;

Cancian & Meyer, 1998). There continue to be strong social pressures for children to live with their mothers, and indeed when parents make uncontested decisions about living arrangements – which happens in 80 percent of cases in the US (Maccoby & Mnookin, 1992) – mothers usually take the main caregiving role. It is sometimes in unusual situations, then, that children (especially girls) go into the primary care of their fathers. These can include maternal mental illness, relocation, vexed mother–child relationships, financial problems, the need to "find themselves," and difficulties in relationships with mothers' new partners (Herrerias, 1995). Father custody is more likely to be the arrangement for boys and for older children (Maccoby & Mnookin, 1992; Fox & Kelly, 1995; Cancian & Meyer, 1998; Australian Bureau of Statistics, 1999). It is less likely with higher total income, or as the mother's share of total income rises (Cancian & Meyer, 1998), suggesting that in some cases there may be economic reasons for children living with their fathers.

Just as single mothers assume some aspects of the roles fathers usually take in original families, such as involvement in children's sporting activities, so single fathers find themselves taking on childcare tasks more usually performed by women. For some, lone parenting is challenging, with about one-quarter of men indicating that they feel uncomfortable in the role (Nieto, 1990; DeMaris & Greif, 1997). Nonetheless, lone fathers have better relations with children and fewer problems than lone mothers after separation (Furstenberg, 1988), although they also find it difficult to monitor their children's health, behavior, and schoolwork (Maccoby & Mnookin, 1992). Levels of well-being after separation are similar for lone mothers and lone fathers (Cohen, 1995). Men who are parenting alone have the advantage of being more likely to have more economic resources at their disposal (Downey, 1994); on the other hand, women receive more social support (Cohen, 1995) and possess more interpersonal resources than men (Downey, 1994).

What is lone parenting like for men? In probably the only study to address this question, 1,132 men who were lone parents responded to a survey in a single parents' magazine (DeMaris & Greif, 1997). Successful parenting experiences were more likely if the men had been involved parents before separation; if they experienced high levels of social support from friends, employers, and co-workers; if they had contested custody; and if they had a satisfying social life. Conversely, fathers' experiences with children were less successful if they were fathering children who were all the same sex, had three or more children, had continuing conflict with their ex-wives, or were dating frequently.

Children's well-being in single father households

There is little research that has examined well-being for children living primarily with their fathers. Adolescents in the Stanford Custody Project who lived with their fathers were less well adjusted than those with their mothers (Buchanan & Maccoby, 1996); they were in the main, though, troubled young people who had moved to their father's house because of disruption in their mother's. In comparison with mothers, too, fathers have fewer interpersonal resources such as helping with homework, knowing children's friends and their parents, attending school meetings, and setting household rules (Downey, 1994). We have insufficient evidence to conclude, though, that children are either better or worse off living with lone fathers.

Same-sex Custody

The belief that children do better if they live with a parent of the same sex has been widely held in the past, although there has been little evidence to support or refute it. The well-being of children who live with their same-sex parent has been compared with those who do not (Downey et al., 1998). Deviance and behavior in school, self-concept, relationships with others, and cognitive skills were assessed. Single mothers are disadvantaged in comparison with single fathers in a number of ways, including levels of income, education, and occupational status, but when these factors are taken into account there are no differences in the levels of well-being of young people living with parents of the same or the opposite sex.

Overall, men and women cope equally well as lone parents. They both face the tasks of at least partially fulfilling the roles of both parents on a day-to-day basis, and ... children fare similarly in both kinds of households. For a number of reasons, father-headed households are likely to become more common as women increasingly take on demanding careers, and as the belief that children need their mothers as primary caregivers recedes. . . . Optimal outcomes for children will be linked with parenting behaviors which encompass warmth, support, and monitoring; involvement in school activities and time spent with children; and social and community support for men who are in roles more usually accepted as appropriate for women.

Overall, men and women cope equally well as lone parents. They both face the tasks of at least partially fulfilling the roles of both parents on a day-to-day basis, and the evidence we have suggests that children fare similarly in both kinds of households. For a number of reasons, father-headed households are likely to become more common as women increasingly take on demanding careers, and as the belief that children need their mothers as primary caregivers recedes. We do not have a good understanding of the factors that are linked with competent and satisfying fathering for men, and with optimal outcomes for children. Findings discussed here suggest, however, that they will include parenting behaviors which encompass warmth, support, and monitoring; involvement in school activities and time spent with children; and social and community support for men who are in roles more usually accepted as appropriate for women.

Overview

The roles of men in families are in a remarkable state of flux. Polarization of views and the diversity of ways in which men, women, and children adapt their lives to each other make it impossible to be definitive. Mintz suggests that "400 years of history of [American] men in families end not with a bang, but a whimper, an outcome particularly appropriate to the postmodernist age: fragmentation and splintering into diverse, indeed highly polarized adaptations" (Mintz, 1998, p. 27). However, there are some patterns to be discerned in this changing picture. With few exceptions, children want their fathers around, and the loss of them from their lives can be an ongoing source of pain (Laumann-Billings & Emery, 2000). In situations of total absence, children are likely either to idealize their fathers or reject them as totally bad. The mere presence of fathers, though, is not enough. Children benefit from having them in their lives when the relationship is positive, supportive, and involved, and this is true whether parents are together or apart. Conversely, negative, intrusive, and abusive father–child relations are not good for children, regardless of family structure.

This picture fits neither the conservative nor the liberal perspectives in the debate. Children want their fathers around, but not unconditionally. Presence is not enough to ensure that their involvement is beneficial. Fathers' rights groups exaggerate the damage done by father absence, since structure is not the crucial issue. On the other hand fathers are or can be positive elements in their children's lives, and their absence causes distress for children who are better off without them only when their presence would be negative. The emphasis is on the *quality* of the relationship, and not on quantity or household structure. Moreover, fathers can be as effective in lone-parenting roles as mothers. For children who experience separation and stepfamily living, then, the answer is neither that they must have contact with their fathers nor that they are better off without them. Rather, to the extent that the relationship is positive and involved, they flourish.

8

Explaining Outcomes for Children and Young People

Perhaps what is most insensitive and unjust is to arrive at conclusions about divorce and its effects on children without carefully considering what we know, not just what we believe.

Emery, 1999, p. 1

Two of the most striking aspects of families and family change that we have discussed so far are complexity and diversity. Given these, it is hardly surprising that no one factor or model accounts for the range of outcomes seen in children who go through family transitions. Separation, for example, or reduced household income, do not by themselves explain the processes through which children whose parents divorce are at risk for troubled behavior. Instead, there is a wide spectrum of factors that, in combination, contribute to the risks faced by individual children. In this chapter, we return to the explanatory frameworks outlined in chapter 2 and attempt to evaluate each of these in terms of how well they account for the large body of research evidence available. Are some explanatory frameworks better than others in accounting for findings overall? Are some more useful than others in relation to particular outcomes for children (such as their educational achievement)? We have documented, in chapter 3, the areas of disadvantage for children who experience parental separation and stepfamily formation, in comparison with children who are brought up in original two-parent families. Children who have experienced transitions not only show short- and medium-term distress but are also at risk for long-term difficulties over many domains of development and achievement. These disadvantages are remarkably similar over geographical locations and over time, even though divorce rates have varied considerably between countries and have been much higher towards the end of the twentieth century in comparison with just a few decades earlier. One important point, however, needs to be reiterated. Although children from lone-parent families and stepfamilies are significantly more likely to experience problems and to have lower achievement compared to those brought up in original two-parent families, the majority of these children do not experience the adverse outcomes we have considered. There is substantial overlap between these groups of children, in their development and adjustment. How is it that different children who ostensibly experience the same risk factors, i.e. parental separation or repartnering, come through these with very different degrees of success?

Trauma Theories: Loss and Abandonment

There are several predictions made by trauma theories that can be tested using existing research findings. The importance of the loss of a parent figure can be assessed by: (1) considering the significance of parental death for children by comparison to parental divorce; (2) comparing outcomes for children after separation with those before separation; (3) evaluating outcomes when families "stay together for the sake of the children"; (4) seeing to what extent contact with nonresident parents influences children's outcomes; and (5) considering outcomes for children who lose contact with a parent who initiates separation or where children perceive the parent as abandoning them at the time. The last four of these issues are also relevant to the notion of abandonment, as is the question of whether the lost parent is the one who made a choice to live apart from the child(ren) or who initiated the separation. More specific predictions within the trauma framework are (6) that loss earlier in childhood, especially in the first 5 or 6 years of life, is associated with poorer outcomes more than is loss at later ages, and (7) that maternal loss is more important than paternal loss. We will address each of these predictions in turn.

1   Loss of a parent through death

If the loss of a parent is the most significant factor in explaining the poor outcomes for children from separated families, then we would expect similar outcomes in children who lose a parent through death. There is little doubt that parental death is a very distressing event for children, as well as for the surviving spouse, and that children show emotional and behavioral signs of such distress appropriate to their age at the time (Marris, 1958). Do they, though, also show the range of long-term disadvantages we identified in chapter 3? The broad conclusion from research is that losing a parent by death does not confer the same degree of risk as parental separation. By carrying out a meta-analysis, Amato (1991b) pulled together the findings of a wide range of studies that addressed outcomes for children. He showed that children who lost a parent by death had lower levels of well-being than those from intact two-parent families but also higher levels of well-being than children from divorced families. His subsequent review (Amato, 1993), covering a larger number of studies, concluded that "most studies show that well-being is lowest in divorced families, intermediate in bereaved families, and highest in intact families." Our own review of research in the United Kingdom reached a similar conclusion:

> Overall the findings on outcomes for children who have experienced the death of a parent suggest that children are adversely affected, but this does not apply to the same range of poor outcomes as shown by children from separated families. In particular, parental death does not carry the same implications for poorer educational attainment, later socio-economic disadvantage, and mental health difficulties. (Rodgers & Pryor, 1998, p. 34)

More recent studies based on large representative samples have reinforced these views. McLanahan and Sandefur's (1994) analyses of the US National Survey of Families and Households found that 21 percent of young women of widowed single-mother families became teenage mothers themselves, compared with 33 percent of those from families disrupted by divorce or separation and 11 percent of those from nondisrupted families. Again, the bereaved group was intermediate between those from divorced families and nondisrupted families. However, for high school dropout, the percentages for young men and women in those same three groups were 15 percent, 31 percent, and 13 percent respectively, putting the children from families disrupted by death much closer to the nondisrupted families than to the families disrupted by divorce or separation. Few differences between adults from original families and those who lost a parent by death were found in another large US sample (Biblarz & Gottainer, 2000). Educational attainment, occupational status, and psychological well-being were similar in adults from original and widowed households, and significantly lower in lone-parent households formed by separation.

In the 1970 British Birth Cohort study (Ely et al., 2000), educational qualifications obtained up to the age of 17 years were significantly poorer in children from divorced or separated families compared with children from intact original families. The findings for those who lost a parent by death varied for the level of qualifications considered. For the relatively small proportion of children who obtained no qualifications at all, parental death was also a risk factor, although not quite such a disadvantage as parental separation (odds ratios of 1.7 and 2.3). The disadvantage associated with bereavement was linked to the poor socioeconomic status of the families concerned. For higher levels of qualifications, however, only the children from divorced or separated families were disadvantaged, being more than twice as likely not to achieve levels typically required for post-16 education courses. In the same sample, parental separation and divorce were also associated with cigarette smoking (again approximately doubling the risk), but smoking was not associated with losing a parent through death.

Given the emphasis of psychoanalytic and object relations theory on the issue of loss, long-term mental health and other adult outcomes are particularly relevant in considering the significance of childhood bereavement. Early reviewers of the literature on parental death and adult mental health reached conflicting conclusions as to whether it was a significant risk factor (Crook & Eliot, 1980; Lloyd, 1980; Tennant et al., 1980); however, later commentators arrived at more of a consensus that any increase in the likelihood of long-term mental disorders or psychological distress was small (Tennant, 1988; Parker, 1992). Furthermore, this small increase in risk was not attributed to the loss *per se* but to such factors as the strain of a chronic illness preceding parental death or problems in providing good-quality care for children following their bereavement (Harris et al., 1986). An early study conducted in Scotland examined a broader range of adult outcomes for women who had experienced parental death or separation during childhood (Illsley & Thompson, 1961). Those women, whose fathers had died, were much more like their peers from intact families than those from separated families, in terms of their socioeconomic status in adulthood and their likelihood of having a teenage birth or conceiving a child outside of marriage. If they lost a mother by death, however, they were intermediate between women from intact families and those from separated families in terms of the risk of poor outcomes.

Recent large-scale studies of adult outcomes are consistent with this pattern. Findings from the 1946 and 1958 British Birth Cohort studies have shown only a minor association between loss of a parent by death and depressive symptoms in early to mid adult life, whereas the children from divorced and separated families had significantly poorer adult mental health than those from bereaved families (Rodgers, 1990a, 1994; Rodgers et al., 1997). Similarly, Amato's (1991) study of adult depression using the US National Survey of Families of Households found an insignificant link with parental death in comparison to parental divorce in the sample as a whole. However, there was a significant association in the African American subsample and, indeed, this was a stronger relationship than that found for parental divorce.

The 1958 British Birth Cohort study also provided information on alcohol consumption and problems with use in early adulthood in relation to type of parental loss, and there was a different pattern for men and women (Hope et al., 1998). The findings for men at age 33 showed those from bereaved families to be intermediate between men from divorced and intact families. The women who had lost a parent by death, however, showed no increased risk of heavy drinking or problem drinking, unlike those from divorced and separated families who were almost twice as likely to be heavy drinkers or problem drinkers compared with women from intact original families.

> The overall picture indicates that parental death is not such an important risk factor for childhood and adult outcomes as parental separation, yet it should also be acknowledged that bereaved children *on average* do not fare so well as children brought up in original two-parent families. It remains possible, therefore that bereavement may have some small effect or even an appreciable effect on a subset of children. Such differences, though, may not be due to the loss itself, but could arise from the factors already mentioned that are associated with parental death, including the economic consequences of subsequently living in a lone-parent family.

The overall picture indicates that parental death is not such an important risk factor for childhood and adult outcomes as parental separation, yet it should also be acknowledged that bereaved children *on average* do not fare so well as children brought up in original two-parent families. It remains possible, therefore that bereavement may have some small effect or even an appreciable effect on a subset of children. Such differences, though, may not be due to the loss itself, but could arise from the factors already mentioned that are associated with parental death, including the economic consequences of subsequently living in a lone-parent family.

2   Outcomes for children before and after separation

If the loss of a parent from children's lives is a major predictor of poor well-being, then it is logical to expect that problems would be apparent after separation but not before. Several longitudinal studies have followed children from before the time of their parents' separation until some time afterwards, and found that children were as disadvantaged before separation as afterwards (Elliott & Richards, 1991a). For example, the apparent impact of divorce on boys' behavior problems and achievement is considerably reduced by taking into account the levels of these factors before divorce (Cherlin et al., 1991). In fact problems in families that subsequently separate can be apparent as much as 8 to 12 years before divorce (Amato & Booth, 1996), although with very young children (3 years or less) few differences are detectable between those whose parents stay together and those who later divorce (Clarke-Stewart et al., 2000). This test of loss as an explanatory factor, then, suggests that the loss of a parent in itself does not account for educational, psychological, or behavioral outcomes in children.

3   Staying together for the sake of the children

Although we cannot know for sure whether or not parents are staying together for the sake of their children, some longitudinal studies are able to examine the outcomes for children whose parents do stay together throughout their childhood but then subsequently divorce. Some of these families may have been happy and harmonious during those earlier years and only faced problems after the children had left home. Other parents may have had little desire to separate even though things were not going well, so not all of these families would have been "staying together" in a deliberate sense. However, the expectation from the viewpoint of loss would still be that children from these families would do well compared with those whose parents separated while they were children. Children from the families that "stayed together" are in fact disadvantaged in many ways and are more similar to children whose parents separated earlier than to those whose parents do not separate at all. This has been found in the 1946 and 1958 British Birth Cohort studies, looking at psychological distress and depression in early to mid adulthood (Rodgers, 1994; Rodgers et al., 1997). The 1958 cohort study also examined heavy alcohol use and problems associated with drinking, and the children whose parents stayed together were intermediate between those whose parents divorced early and those whose parents did not separate (Hope et al., 1998).

Using the same sample, Kiernan considered a range of early-adult demographic outcomes in relation to parental divorce occurring in the age ranges 0–16 years, 17–20 years, and 21–33 years. The outcomes included early parenthood and own partnership breakdown, and socioeconomic outcomes such as educational qualifications, unemployment, and living in social housing. For men, disadvantages in demographic outcomes were less severe for those whose parents divorced when they were older (21–33 years) rather than during childhood, but the disadvantages in socioeconomic terms appeared as great or greater for the later divorcing families. The opposite pattern was seen in the young women, with similar demographic disadvantages associated with early and late parental divorce, but less severe socioeconomic difficulties linked with later divorce (Furstenberg & Kiernan, in press).

The general pattern, then, for families that "stay together for the sake of the children" and separate later, is that the children do not fare well in their own adult lives. One interpretation of this is that parental separation is a disturbing and influential event for young adults even when it happens beyond childhood. However, many of the poorer outcomes described in these several studies were present *before* the separation of the parents occurred, and are obviously not a consequence of the event in itself. A more likely explanation is that the poor outcomes derive from the preseparation experiences of the children and families concerned. However, there is also some direct effect of later parental divorce. Some evidence for this was provided by the 1958 British Birth Cohort study, in that those whose parents divorced when they were between the ages of 23 and 33 years showed an increase in psychological distress over that 10-year period, whereas those whose parents had divorced before they were 23 had a relative reduction in distress over that time (Rodgers et al., 1997).

Those adults whose parents separate after staying together until they are grown up also suffer considerable distress at the time of separation (Pryor, 1999). Parents call on them heavily for support, they experience strong loyalty conflicts, and they find themselves having to reevaluate, in the light of their parents' separation, a family and childhood they had assumed was stable if not happy.

4   Contact with nonresident parents after separation

If loss of a parent were the most significant damaging feature of separation then we would anticipate that its consequences would be most apparent when loss was total and permanent. We know from the previous chapter that there is considerable variation in the extent to which nonresident parents maintain contact with their children after separation and that a significant proportion of children lose contact altogether with fathers. However, the evidence (Amato, 1993; King, 1994b) does not support the assumption that frequency of contact with nonresidential parents is associated with outcomes. The *quality* of the relationship after separation is important, however (Salem et al., 1998; Amato & Gilbreth, 1999), and this suggests again the greater relevance of factors such as parenting for children's well-being.

5   Loss of a parent who chooses to leave or who initiates separation

This issue is particularly appropriate to the consideration of abandonment as distinct from more general ideas of loss. Unfortunately, there appears to have been no specific investigation of the importance of the distinction between "leaver" and "left" in relation to children's outcomes, unlike the research on adult adjustment covered in chapter 5. Similarly, children's perceptions of feeling abandoned at the time of separation have not been systematically studied in relation to their long-term outcomes.

6   Separation in early childhood

Theories of loss predict that separation in early childhood leads to poorer long-term outcomes than separation at later ages. There are mixed findings on the consequence of parental separation in the early childhood years. Amato's (1993) review of childhood outcomes found 8 studies supporting the hypothesis that children experience more problems when parental separation occurs at an early rather than a later age, and 18 studies that did not support this hypothesis. In fact, he pointed out that a few studies reported later separation to be more problematic for children. This may, in part, be due to the inevitable association of time since separation with age at separation, given that children are likely to show some adverse responses in the immediate aftermath of family transitions.

Studies of longer-term outcomes in the late teenage years and adulthood have failed to support the hypothesis that separations at a very young age are particularly harmful. Kiernan's analyses of the 1958 British Birth Cohort showed similar risks for those whose parents separated when they were aged 0–6 years as those whose parents separated later in their childhood, across a wide range of educational, socioeconomic, and demographic outcomes extending into early adulthood (Kiernan, 1997). She drew attention to one notable exception to this – the experience of homelessness in adulthood, and pointed out that children whose parents separate earlier are more likely to be brought up in a stepfamily and, in turn, leave home because of conflict in the family. This could well explain why homelessness is particularly related to early separation, with a doubling of the risk in comparison with later separations, and it also highlights the general issue that many studies fail to disentangle the factor of early separation from the experience of subsequent (and possibly multiple) transitions. Other studies based on the British longitudinal cohorts have produced inconclusive findings regarding age at separation. It has variously been reported from the 1946 British Birth Cohort that girls were more than twice as likely to give birth outside marriage if their parents separated when they were under 7 years old than if the separation was later (Douglas, 1970), that delinquency was similarly more likely in boys if separations were in the first 4 years of life (Wadsworth, 1979), and that adult psychiatric disorders were twice as common for girls if they experienced parental separation before age 5 (Rodgers, 1990a). However, none of these differences was statistically significant with the numbers of children available.

In a subsequent follow-up of the 1946 British Birth Cohort, where mental health was again assessed, and in a similar study of the 1958 British Birth Cohort, where a substantially greater number of children experienced parental divorce, there were no differences in outcomes for children who experienced separation at different ages (Rodgers, 1994; Rodgers et al., 1997). In the United States, McLanahan and Sandefur (1994) found relatively small and nonsignificant differences in rates of high school dropout and risk of teen births according to age at family disruption, using data from the National Survey of Families and Households. Amato and Booth (1991) reported a range of findings from their national sample from the Study of Marital Instability Over the Life Course, identifying adults who experienced parental separation at ages 1–6 years, 7–12 years, and 13–18 years. Only one of 17 measures in the areas of adult psychological, socioeconomic, social, and family outcomes showed a significant difference. The proportions of those in these three age groups at the time of parental separation who had been themselves divorced were 35 percent, 27 percent, and 16 percent respectively. For other outcomes, the small differences between groups were as likely as not to favor those whose parents separated when they were younger, and this one significant and detrimental difference may have arisen by chance.

In summary, there is little support for the idea that early separation is particularly harmful for children. Furthermore, those studies that do support the hypothesis have failed to take account of the occurrence of multiple transitions when assessing the apparent importance of early separations.

7   Maternal loss and paternal loss

There are three particular difficulties in assessing the prediction that maternal loss causes more serious disadvantages than paternal loss. First, the numbers of children who live with their fathers after separation is relatively small. Second, children who do remain with their fathers retain more frequent contact with their nonresident parents than those who live with their mothers. Third, there are more often extenuating circumstances when children continue to reside with their fathers, such as mental health problems in their mothers. Nonetheless, we do have some evidence to address this question. Young people in the NSFH in the US were found to be no more likely in father-headed than in mother-headed households to drop out of school or to become adolescent parents (McLanahan & Sandefur, 1994). On the other hand, young people in the Stanford study who lived with their fathers were more likely to report deviant and troubled behavior than those living with mothers. However, most adolescents living with their fathers had moved to their homes because of conflict in their mothers' homes, with mothers or stepfathers. These young people had moved from house to house several times, and were generally a troubled group before moving to their fathers' care (Buchanan & Maccoby, 1996).

Despite father-headed households having, on average, more economic resources than mother-headed homes (Meyer & Garasky, 1993; Downey, 1994), the academic performance of children in both household types has been found to be the same and somewhat lower than those in original homes (Downey, 1994). There is, overall, little evidence to support the prediction that children suffer more from maternal than paternal loss.

Summary of findings on loss and abandonment

Taken together, these findings indicate that theories of loss and abandonment do not explain medium- or long-term outcomes for children of separated families. Nonetheless, there are often short-term consequences of losing a parent. Children may be disturbed for some time after separation, and this relatively short-term distress may lead to difficulties if, for example, they have school examinations or other educational milestones during this time. It may be fruitful to examine the sense of loss and abandonment in children, since they may not experience the objective absence of parents from their lives as a loss. Subjective experiences may be more important than the simple absence or loss of parents.

Life-course Theory

In chapter 2 we contrasted loss and absence, noting that, conceptually, absence fits within a life-course framework. Nonetheless, findings from the first six areas considered for loss apply also to parental absence. Findings related to the amount of time spent in a lone-parent family also address absence. For example, children in the NSFH sample who spent longer periods of time in a lone-parent family were no more likely than those who spent shorter periods to drop out of high school or (for girls) to have a teenage birth (McLanahan & Sandefur, 1994). Evidence does not, then, support an absence framework. In this section we will evaluate outcomes within the broader frameworks offered by life-course theory.

Historical time and place

An evaluation of the principle of time and place requires research that addresses factors across communities and cultures, and that spans significant periods of time. One prediction with regard to time is that as transitions have become more commonplace, the stigma of coming from a "broken family" may have diminished. Legal and policy changes, too, aimed at reducing the trauma for families going through separation, might be expected to reduce the risks for children. Indeed, there is some evidence to suggest that the magnitude of risk in studies in the 1980s was less for children whose parents have separated than the magnitude in older studies (Amato & Keith, 1991a, 1991b). However, a comparison of the three main birth cohort studies in the UK found that the relative risk for having no educational qualifications increased over time, despite the overall rise in proportions of those having five O-level qualifications (Ely et al., 1999). Studies of delinquency were also pooled and a meta-analysis used to determine their overall findings, and no major historical change was found in the significance of family structure (Wells & Rankin, 1991). Despite changes in the social and legal climate in the last decades of the twentieth century, then, levels of risk at least for some outcomes have not changed. It may be, though, that psychological outcomes are more likely than educational outcomes to have been improved by changes, such as mediation, that are designed to make the process of divorce less harsh for families. So far, though, there is no evidence that mediation increases psychological well-being for children (Pearson & Thoennes, 1985; Kelly, 1991; Emery et al., 1994), although a 12-year follow-up of families that were randomly assigned to litigation or mediation found that nonresidential parents were more involved with their children if they had mediated their divorce than those who had litigated (Emery et al., in press). In fact, studies measuring a wider range of outcomes in the 1990s suggest that differences in levels of risk between children from intact and divorced families have increased slightly (Amato, 2000). The evidence suggests, overall, that over half a century risks for children whose parents separate have not lessened and, indeed, may have increased, although the reasons for this are not clear.

The importance of *where* families live can be considered by examining possible differences in the levels of risk for children from separated families across countries with different legal systems and varying attitudes to divorce and lone-parent families. Again, studies that make direct comparisons are hard to find; however, it seems that the "rule of thumb" that there is roughly a doubling of risk for adverse outcomes for children from separated families applies at least across the UK (Rodgers & Pryor, 1998), Australia (Rodgers, 1996b), and the United States (McLanahan & Sandefur, 1994; Simons & Associates, 1996). In New Zealand, the risk may be somewhat higher (Rodgers, 1998), although there are relatively few New Zealand-based studies that address outcomes for children directly. Adult distress in separated adults across several countries is higher than in those who are married (Mastekaasa, 1994; Stack & Eshleman, 1998); given the associations between parental distress and children's outcomes, this suggests that there may be similarities for children too.

Overall, there is insufficient evidence to reach conclusions about the importance of time and place for children's well-being, and indeed it is hard to know how we might find evidence. What little we do know suggests that there are surprisingly few differences across decades and countries.

Timing within lives

Timing of family transitions might be of consequence for children in two ways. The first is their age at which parents' separation and stepfamily formation occurs: does it matter whether children are younger or older, for example, when they enter a stepfamily? The second is the age at which their own transitions take place. Leaving school, the formation of partnerships, and becoming parents are all milestones that may happen comparatively early or late in a young person's life.

Age at the time of family transitions
Earlier in this chapter we noted that findings are mixed regarding the comparative risks for children whose parents separate early in their life. A major difficulty in considering age at the time of separation is its confounding with the time since separation. Children who are young when parents separate are more likely than those who are older to spend long periods of time in a lone-parent family. They are more likely to undergo a second transition into a stepfamily household and indeed to experience further subsequent transitions, since early transitions predict later ones (DeGarmo & Forgatch, 1999). So parental separation at a young age may be an early phase of an ongoing cumulative process, rather than a risk factor by itself. That findings are inconsistent is not, then, surprising. An early study by Allison & Furstenberg (1989) noted that children who were younger than 6 at the age of separation were at higher levels of risk for problem behavior and distress than those who were older, although differences that were significant were few. Conversely, younger children have been reported to be at less risk for poor outcomes than those who are older (Amato & Keith, 1991b; Fergusson et al., 1994). A child's age at the time of a family transition is, however, more clearly associated with their immediate responses to separation. Age, for example, gives a guide to predicting the reactions children are likely to have at the time of separation (see chapter 4). Similarly, age is a factor in children's adjustment to stepfamily living (see chapter 6), particularly in regard to the kind of relationship they establish with their stepparent. But age has an ambiguous relationship with behavior and well-being some time after a transition has occurred.

Timing of young people's own transitions
In order to evaluate the significance of the timing of young people's own life transitions, we need to look for associations between early (or late) assumption of adult roles and outcomes. The links between family change and life transitions are well established; those who have experienced parental separation and stepfamily living are likely, in comparison with those living in original households, to undertake at an earlier age transitions such as leaving home, forming partnerships, and becoming parents (Kiernan, 1992; Sweeting & West, 1994; Kiernan & Hobcraft, 1997) (see chapter 3). In turn, early transitions pose risks for young people, includ-

ing their own partnership breakdown, delinquency, drug abuse, and psychopathology (Fergusson et al., 1984; Newcomb, 1986). The timing of such important passages forms a link, then, between family changes and long-term outcomes.

One aspect of timing in children's lives is the early adoption of roles that are more usually taken by parents or other adults, involving the blurring of child/adult boundaries. They can be distinguished as two domains: *instrumental* roles refer to such things as caring for siblings and taking household responsibilities, and *emotional* roles involve being a confidant and supporter for a parent. In both cases, such "parentification" refers to the premature adoption of adult responsibility in regard to parents.

Is the premature adoption of adult responsibility linked to children's outcomes? As we might expect, findings are mixed (Hetherington, 1999). Very high levels of emotional and instrumental responsibility are associated with depression and anxiety in daughters, but not in sons. On the other hand, moderate levels of emotional responsibility for fathers, and of instrumental responsibility for both parents, are associated with high levels of adult social responsibility in sons. Sons and daughters who take emotional responsibility for mothers also show greater social responsibility in adulthood. Girls in divorced families are likely to be "competent at a cost" in young adulthood: they show high levels of social and cognitive ability and social responsibility, but also low self-worth and depression (Hetherington, 1999).

> Timing within lives is clearly of consequence in explaining outcomes for children. Its importance lies particularly in the likelihood that transitions early in children's lives make them vulnerable to further risk factors such as poverty and subsequent family transitions, and to early transitions in their own lives that make them vulnerable to adult adversity such as low socioeconomic status and partnership breakdown. Early adoption of adult instrumental and emotional roles, in moderation, can lead to feelings of competence and well-being, although high levels of responsibility for parents predicts depression, anxiety, and (in men) irresponsibility in adulthood.

In sum, timing within lives is clearly of consequence in explaining outcomes for children. Its importance lies particularly in the likelihood that transitions early in children's lives make them vulnerable to further risk factors such as poverty and subsequent family transitions, and to early transitions in their own lives that further make them vulnerable to adult adversity such as low socioeconomic status and partnership breakdown. Early adoption of adult instrumental and emotional roles, in moderation, can lead to feelings of competence and well-being, although high levels of responsibility for parents predicts depression, anxiety, and (in men) irresponsibility in adulthood.

Human Agency and Individual Differences

The part that children play in determining their own life paths is being increasingly acknowledged, although it is remarkably difficult to measure. A major problem in trying to assess the contribution of children's individual differences to outcomes is that we are seldom able to measure individual characteristics before a family transition occurs. It is difficult, then, to know whether a factor existing before a transition has a moderating effect on the relationship between transition-related stresses and outcomes, or whether it arises from these stresses and mediates the links between stressful events and outcomes. For example, a child's level of self-esteem before separation may buffer its impact so that she is less affected than if her self-esteem was low (a moderating effect). Alternatively, separation may lower self-esteem so that negative outcomes are more likely (a mediating effect). One study addressed this question by obtaining measures of children's temperament both at the time of separation and retrospectively, from mothers, fathers, and nurses' ratings during well-baby visits in the first year of life (Hetherington, 1991). Children with difficult temperaments had parents who were more likely to divorce. As the authors pointed out, however, children's temperament might have been influenced by the stresses in families *preceding* separation. In the Christchurch Health and Development Study in New Zealand, children whose parents subsequently separated were already exhibiting comparatively high levels of behavior problems at the age of 3 (Woodward et al., 2000). However, parental psychological distress and unhappiness usually increase some years before separation (Kitson et al., 1985; Booth & Amato, 1991; Mastekaasa, 1994), and these parent factors are likely to influence children's behavior both directly and through their parenting.

The Hetherington study suggests some impact of individual factors (in this case temperament) on outcomes, but as the authors conclude, "the effects of personal vulnerabilities such as difficult temperament are moderated by their interactions with other risk and protective factors" (Hetherington, 1991, p. 190).

Locus of control

Children whose parents have separated have higher levels of psychological distress if they believe that control over events lies outside themselves (external locus of control) (Kurdek et al., 1981). Attributions of control to external factors in children have been found to encompass two dimensions: belief in powerful others as causing things to happen, and attribution of control to unknown causes (Connell, 1985). Children often simply do not know what makes things happen to them. In turn, children whose parents have separated and who attribute what happens to unknown sources of control show high levels of distress (depression, anxiety, and conduct problems) (Kim et al., 1997). If attributions of control are stable and exist before separation, then this has obvious relevance to the ways in which children are told, or not, about what is happening at the time of separation. If they have no idea why the separation is happening, then they will cope less well.

Establishing and sustaining relationships

The skills that children and young adults bring to relationship formation become particularly significant as they form and establish their own partnerships, and the fact that parental separation increases the risk for dissolution of partnerships in adulthood suggests that these skills may be jeopardized by the experience of divorce. Indeed, interpersonal skills mediate a large share of the relationship between parental separation and one's own divorce (Amato, 1996). Similarly, links between parental divorce and adult depression are strong in women whose own partnerships run into problems, but not in those who remain in stable partnerships (Rodgers, 1994). This interaction between parental separation and their own divorce in predicting depression suggests that difficulties in establishing or sustaining intimate relationships mediate the links between experiencing parental divorce in childhood, and depression in adulthood. The finding that adults who experience one transition are then more likely to go through others (DeGarmo & Forgatch, 1999) indicates the likelihood that relationship skill is an individual difference that is relatively stable, and contributes to well-being in later life.

Gender

It is generally found that boys are more adversely affected immediately after separation than girls are (Zaslow, 1988, 1989; Allison & Furstenberg, 1989). This is not the case, though, for long-term outcomes. In the US and

New Zealand, no consistent gender differences in long-term outcomes are found (Amato, 1993; Fergusson et al., 1994; Woodward et al., 2000), and several studies indicate that women are at *higher* risk than men in adulthood. For example, women but not men whose parents had separated had higher depression scores than those from original families in one US and one UK study (Rodgers, 1994; McLeod & Shanahan, 1996). Similarly, early transitions to adulthood, adverse economic conditions, and the likelihood of their own partnership dissolution were higher for women than men (Kiernan, 1997). Some writers have suggested that there is a "sleeper effect" whereby some girls who initially cope well with family transitions experience a significant reversal in adjustment (Wallerstein & Corbin, 1989). This was not, though, detected in an Australian longitudinal study of children (Dunlop & Burns, 1995).

Initial adjustment to stepfamily formation also differs by gender, with boys finding it easier to form close relationships with stepfathers. In well-established stepfamilies, though, there are no gender differences in young people's adjustment (Hetherington et al., 1999). Some studies have suggested that girls in stepfamilies are at greater risk than boys for stress and behavior problems (Bray, 1988; Lee & Burkham, 1994). In many cases, however, especially those involving adolescents, inconsistent or no gender differences are found in outcomes for children in stepfamilies (Amato & Keith, 1991b; Hetherington & Clingempeel, 1992; Thomson et al., 1994; Henry & Lovelace, 1995; Nicholson, 1999). Gender differences in response to stepfamily living, where they exist, seem to be most apparent in younger children, with differences disappearing in adolescence (Hetherington, 1993; Hetherington & Jodl, 1994). An exception to this is in early transitions to adulthood, where the risks for young women of entering partnerships and parenting early are somewhat higher than for men (Kiernan, 1992).

The power of gender to explain well-being is, then, not straightforward. There are no simple processes by which girls or boys weather family transitions better. Rather, a child's gender interacts with several other factors including sex of parent, socioeconomic circumstances, and other family relationships and may be important for some outcomes but not others (Clarke-Stewart et al., 2000).

Overall, a great deal more work needs to be done to illuminate the contribution that child-based individual differences make to their outcomes. Children's impact on family dynamics and the importance of individual differences to their well-being have only recently begun to be addressed by researchers, and this has been an unfortunate omission since both common sense and the little evidence we do have points to their significance. As they become adult, the control individuals have over their lives and environments increases, and changes of trajectories and levels of well-being are often brought about by the choices made of partners and career paths.

Linked lives

In chapter 2 we introduced the idea of linked lives as a framework for understanding family transitions. Here we consider factors within families, including conflict, parent-child relations and parenting, sibling relationships, and grandparents. Other family factors such as parental aspirations and monitoring will also be discussed. Conceptually these are components both of Bronfenbrenner's theory – specifically the microsystem – and aspects of family social capital.

Conflict

Conflict has consistently been identified as a major contender in explaining links between family transitions and distress in children. There are two obvious reasons for this. First, a large body of literature has documented the pervasive effects of family and interparental conflict on children in all families (Emery, 1982; Grych & Fincham, 1990; Cummings & Davies, 1994; Grych, 1998; Emery, 1999). Second, it is rare for parental separation to occur without some level of conflict preceding, accompanying, or following the transition. Conflict is a frequent precursor of separation, both as a symptom and a cause, and separation is sometimes seen as a way of removing children from war zones. Unfortunately, separation can bring about an escalation of fighting and, often, turns its focus onto children as decisions are faced about their living arrangements.

In 1993, Amato concluded that parental conflict held the most explanatory power for the risk of poor outcomes for children whose parents separate (Amato, 1993). By the last decade of the twentieth century, it was also generally accepted that it was worse for children to stay in high-conflict families than to experience parental separation (Amato & Booth, 1997; Jekielek, 1998; Hanson, 1999; Morrison & Coiro, 1999). However, the picture proves not to be so simple. Although conflict is clearly demonstrated to be important, it by no means explains all the variance in children's outcomes, although it is sometimes presented in direct competition with divorce as an explanatory factor for poor outcomes for children. In young children, especially, conflict does not appear to be such a powerful predictor as parenting and demographic factors (Clarke-Stewart et al., 2000). One reason for varied findings is that the measurement of conflict is imprecise in many studies; in particular, the extent to which the child is *aware* of interparental disagreement is often not considered. A further measurement problem is that in earlier studies preseparation conflict was often not delineated from conflict accompanying separation, nor from postseparation conflict.

A second reason for varied findings is that children respond in different ways to parental conflict: their temperaments and their cognitive appraisal of their parents' fights influence their responses (Grych, 1998; Emery, 1999). Adolescents in separated families may, too, be somewhat invulnerable to the impact of conflict in comparison with children in original families (Aseltine, 1996). They appear to distance themselves from what is going on, although it is not clear what other costs might be incurred by such an apparently protective mechanism.

Longitudinal studies have confirmed that children in high-conflict families are generally better off if their parents separate in terms of behavior problems, school performance, anxiety, depression, self-esteem, and close kin and friendship networks (Amato & Booth, 1997; Jekielek, 1998; Hanson, 1999; Hetherington, 1999; Morrison & Coiro, 1999). In turn, young people from families where levels of conflict were low before separation may be worse off afterward in a number of ways (Amato & Booth, 1997; Jekielek, 1998). Booth (1999) has suggested that children who are particularly affected by the dissolution of a low-conflict marriage may themselves have characteristics, such as excessive dependence on both parents or low self-esteem, that render them vulnerable to the separation. Alternatively, or perhaps as well, the explanation may lie with parents who are overly focused on their own problems to the exclusion of the needs of their children. Hetherington (Hetherington, 1999) has noted that in many cases an emotional divorce has occurred long before the actual separation, so that interparental relations are characterized by distance, withdrawal, and "contemptuous disengagement" with low levels of overt conflict. The emotional tone of relationships can seep through to children, despite parents' efforts to contain it (Grych & Fincham, 1990). Measured low preseparation conflict may therefore be present not only in marriages in which partners have become dissatisfied and bored but do not fight, but also others where the style of interaction is such that disagreement and unhappiness are manifest in covert rather than overt ways. There are, then, two mechanisms that might explain these findings. Low reported levels of conflict may conceal what is a toxic, emotionally neglectful environment for children; or the unanticipated separation of parents may be more distressing for children than one they had seen coming. In some families, both explanations may apply.

The ways in which preseparation conflict is expressed are important, and so are the ways in which children appraise it. Of equal importance is postseparation conflict. In Booth and Amato's studies (Booth & Amato, 2001) there was a negative although nonsignificant association between pre- and postseparation levels, a finding also reported earlier (Camara & Resnick, 1988). Children whose parents continue to fight after separation have low self-esteem (Cockett & Tripp, 1994; Amato & Booth, 1997) and clinically significant levels of psychological distress (Hetherington, 1999), which become particularly apparent more than two years after separation if postseparation family conflict continues at high levels. Hetherington has concluded that "If conflict is going to continue, it is better for children to remain in an acrimonious two-parent household than to divorce. If there is a shift to a more harmonious household a divorce is advantageous both to boys and girls" (Hetherington, 1999, pp. 101–2).

The potential for conflict in stepfamilies exceeds that in original families or lone-parent families because the range and variation in relationships is wider. In stepfamilies, "family conflict" can encompass interparental, parent–child, and parent–ex-spousal disagreement. In chapter 6 we discussed the existence of two potential sources of parental conflict in stepfamilies – interhouse conflict between ex-spouses; and intrahouse conflict between parents in the same household (McDonald & DeMaris, 1995; Hanson et al., 1996). Although when both kinds of conflict were combined, children in stepfamilies experienced more overall conflict than those in either lone-parent or original households, neither kind of conflict was linked with adverse outcomes.

In the ALSPAC sample, negativity between partners was associated with parent–child and sibling relationships in non-stepfamilies but not in stepfamilies (Dunn et al., 1999). In the Virginia Longitudinal Study of Remarriage, however, negativity between parents contributed to levels of behavior problems in both stepfamilies and original families (Anderson et al., 1999), although in a paradoxical way. For daughters in stepfamilies, a close marital relationship was associated with negative behavior, whereas for boys it was associated with positive behavior (Hetherington, 1993). Negative relations with former spouses in stepfamilies also went some way toward explaining differences in behavior problems between young people in original and stepfamily households (Anderson et al.,

1999). Bray and colleagues have also found links between family conflict in stepfamilies and children's levels of distress and internalizing problems, although not with social competence and externalizing problems (Bray, 1999).

Interparental conflict undoubtedly puts children at considerable risk for lowered well-being. Several pathways by which conflict can affect children have been suggested (Grych & Fincham, 1990; Emery, 1999). First, conflict is a direct stress for children who experience it, and children as young as 18 months show distress in the presence of parental conflict. Second, children may directly model their parents' aggressive behavior. Third, children whose separated parents are fighting are often in loyalty traps, where they are pressured to take sides by one parent or the other. Ways in which parental conflict and children's outcomes are linked include the disruption of parenting caused by the distress of feuding parents, and inconsistent discipline between parents arising, for example, from a desire by one parent to undermine the control of another. The conflict preceding, surrounding, and following parental separation works in similar ways, and to the extent that separation removes children from the arena of parental disputes they are advantaged. However, conflict does not so readily explain the risk of poor outcomes for children, especially adolescents, in stepfamilies, and it may be that the increased risk relates to exposure and involvement at the time of separation, so that conflict that might accompany stepfamily living does not in itself add to children's risk for distress (Anderson et al., 1999). Yet, young people who leave home early in stepfamilies are most likely to give conflicted family relationships as the reason for leaving (Kiernan, 1992). We know too little about the very complicated dynamics of relationships and conflict in stepfamilies to come to firm conclusions about how they affect children.

Parent–child relationships

Within the framework of linked lives, the most significant aspect for children resides in the relationships they have with their parents. The nature of family transitions is such that perturbations in parent-child relationships are almost inevitable, and in chapter 5 we noted that when parents separate, and possibly before they do, the quality of parent-child relationships diminishes (Hetherington, 1989; Amato & Keith, 1991b; Emery, 1994; Simons & Associates, 1996). Family transitions, then, are usually accompanied by reduced quality of parenting (DeGarmo & Forgatch, 1999). In many cases, but not all, these relationships improve over time and return to levels similar to those in original families, although conflict between lone-parent mothers and children is inclined to persist (Hetherington & Clingempeel, 1992; Hetherington et al., 1999). The nature of these relationships, from the perspectives of both parents and their children, is consistently associated with outcomes in lone-parent and stepparent families, as well as original families (Buchanan & Maccoby, 1996; Simons & Associates, 1996; Dunn et al., 1998; DeGarmo & Forgatch, 1999; Hetherington et al., 1999). For example, negativity from mothers toward their children is linked with behavior problems in 4-year-olds (Dunn et al., 1998) and externalizing behavior in adolescents (Hetherington et al., 1999); and aversive discipline (smacking and coercing) with behavior problems in 4-year-olds (Deater-Deckard & Dunn, 1999) and antisocial behavior in boys (DeGarmo & Forgatch, 1999). For the adolescents in the Iowa studies mentioned above, mothers' inept parenting was directly associated with behavior problems and depression in children (Simons & Associates, 1996). Maternal warmth, on the other hand, is associated with high levels of social competence and low levels of externalizing behavior in all family structures (Hetherington & Clingempeel, 1992). The links between affective relations and outcomes extends into young adulthood, with feelings of closeness to parents being associated with subjective well-being (Amato, 1999). Parental warmth and control are also associated with depression in adulthood. Adults in the NSHD sample in the UK had higher levels of depression at ages 36 and 43 if parents had shown higher levels of control or low levels of care on the Parental Bonding Instrument (PBI) (Rodgers, 1996a). The risk for depression was especially high if, as children, they experienced both high levels of control and low levels of care.

In general, then, very similar patterns of associations between parenting and outcomes are found in original, lone-parent, and stepfamilies. Parenting and parent-child relationships also mediate associations between outcomes for children and associated with family change, such as household income, parental distress, and conflict (Forehand et al., 1990; Forgatch et al., 1996; Simons & Associates, 1996; Deater-Deckard & Dunn, 1999).

Patterns of parenting, or parenting styles, change with family transitions. In particular, authoritative parenting involving high levels of support and monitoring is lower in lone-parent households and in stepfamily households. Authoritative parenting is consistently associated with lower levels of distress, delinquency, and externalizing problems and with higher levels of self-esteem (Hetherington & Clingempeel, 1992; Avenevoli et al., 1999). Permissive parenting (high support and low monitoring) is, in some contexts, also associated with beneficial outcomes for some children, especially with less psychological distress and high self-esteem (Avenevoli et al., 1999). In chapter 6 we noted that a permissive typology has not been systematically examined in stepfamily households, but that there is some evidence to suggest it might be an especially adaptive pattern for stepfathers and their adolescent stepchildren (Crosbie-Burnett & Giles-Sims, 1994).

Authoritarian (low support, high control) and neglectful (low support, low control) parenting patterns are consistently associated with negative outcomes for children (Avenevoli et al., 1999), and an increase over time in authoritarian parenting by mothers and stepfathers is associated with behavioral problems in children (Bray, 1999).

Father–child relationships following separation are usually constrained by the fact that contact is sporadic, making consistent parenting behavior difficult. In the Iowa studies, for example, dysfunctional parenting by fathers was 2 to 3 times as prevalent in separated fathers as those even in distressed marriages (Simons & Associates, 1996). Yet relationships with fathers are potentially of benefit to children; feelings of closeness between fathers and children and, in particular, authoritative parenting behavior by fathers, are associated positively with academic performance and negatively with externalizing and internalizing behavior in children in lone-parent households (Amato & Gilbreth, 1999).

Relations with nonresident fathers in stepfamilies are somewhat more complex, because children may be juggling relationships with two fathering figures. Early in stepfamily formation, relations with nonresidential fathers are associated with behavioral adjustment; four to five years later, though, there is no association between the quality or frequency of contact and children's behavior (Bray & Berger, 1993b). Instead, relationships with stepfathers become more important. There are difficulties involved in establishing close stepfather–child relationships, yet they matter for children's well-being. Their importance depends somewhat on children's ages, with young children being more vulnerable to the quality of the relationship. Steppaternal behaviors of support and warmth are associated positively with outcomes such as academic performance and social competence, and negatively with externalizing behavior (Hetherington & Clingempeel, 1992; Thomson et al., 1994). In turn, children's reported feelings of closeness and acceptance toward stepfathers is related positively with happiness in the family home (Funder & Smyth, 1996) and compromise in solving problems (Buchanan & Maccoby, 1996), and negatively with deviance, behavior problems, and levels of unstructured time (Buchanan & Maccoby, 1996).

In sum, the central role of parent–child relationships cannot be over-emphasized. Their quality reflects the impact of other important stress factors, such as conflict and economic hardship, and in turn predicts a wide range of outcomes in childhood and adolescence, and extending into adulthood.

Sibling relationships

Brothers and sisters are potential sources of both support and distress for children, yet relationships between siblings have not been widely studied in relation to family transitions, despite their centrality to children's lives and the likelihood that they will be affected by change. The presence or absence of siblings for children in themselves may be an important moderating factor: in one study adolescents in separated families who had either older or younger siblings showed lower levels of behavior problems than those who had no sibling (Kempton et al., 1991). There were, though, no differences for levels of internalizing behavior or depression. Studies of siblings generally show that negative relations between them are associated with externalizing behavior and poor peer relationships (Dunn, 1992; Hetherington & Clingempeel, 1992), while positive sibling relations are protective especially in adverse situations (Jenkins, 1992; Caya & Liem, 1998).

> In sum, the central role of parent-child relationships cannot be overem-phasized. Their quality reflects the impact of other important stress fac-tors such as conflict and economic hardship, and in turn predicts a wide range of outcomes in childhood and adolescence, and extending into adulthood.

How do sibling relationships vary by family structure? Siblings in lone-parent families are more negative (Dunn et al., 1999) and less positive toward each other than those in original families (Hetherington & Clingempeel, 1992; Simons & Associates, 1996). In stepfamilies there are mixed findings; some are more distant (Dunn et al., 1999) while others show particularly high levels of negativity and low levels of positivity (Hetherington & Clingempeel, 1992). Girls show higher levels of positivity than boys, and across time siblings tend to disengage from each other earlier in lone-parent and stepfamilies than in original families. The quality of sibling relations is linked to other family relationships, and to individual behavior.

In the Iowa samples in the US, sibling hostility and warmth were directly predicted by maternal parenting and, to a lesser extent, by fathers' parenting (Simons & Associates, 1996). In the UK, the quality of sibling relationships were predicted by the quality of parental relationships and by parent–child relationships (Dunn et al., 1999). Positive sibling relationships, in turn, are associated with high social competence and low levels of behavior problems, while negative sibling relationships predict low social competence and high levels of behavior problems (Hetherington & Clingempeel, 1992). Overall, siblings have the capacity to buffer children through family transitions if relationships are good. Separation and stepfamily formation seem to put stresses on sibling relationships, however, that result in their reduced quality in lone-parent families and stepfamilies. The inconsistent findings across studies and countries suggest that more research is needed in order to understand the roles played by sibling relationships in relation to family transitions.

Relationships with grandparents

As with other family relations, child–grandparent relationships may be vulnerable to change when family transitions occur. Yet if grandparents are able to provide support and monitoring for children then they may be able to buffer the impact of transitions and poor outcomes. What is the nature of changes (if any) in child–grandparent relationships associated with family transitions? And, are there links between these relationships and outcomes for children?

When parents separate children are more likely to maintain contact with maternal than paternal grandparents, since in most cases they live with their mothers, and grandparent involvement is associated with the grandparent's adult child having custody (Kruk & Hall, 1995; Hilton & Macari, 1997). Contact with paternal grandparents tends to diminish (Kruk & Hall, 1995), especially if children experience several family transitions (Creasey, 1993; Cockett & Tripp, 1994). Young people also feel closer to their grandparents if their parents are separated than do those in original families (Kennedy & Kennedy, 1993; Cogswell & Henry, 1995), although in the UK children in separated families were not so close to grandparents (Lussier et al., submitted). Clingempeel and colleagues combined measures of frequency of contact and feelings of closeness to derive a child–maternal grandparent involvement score, and found that children in lone-mother families were significantly more highly involved with grandparents than those in original or stepfamilies. Children felt particularly close to grandfathers in this sample: between 60 and 65 percent of children in lone-mother families said they felt close to grandfathers, compared with 55 percent of those who felt close to grandmothers. In original families, between 46 and 48 percent said they felt very close to grandfathers, compared with 42 percent who felt close to grandmothers (Clingempeel et al., 1992). Children in stepfamilies were similar to those in original families in their feelings; however, in a group of college students young people in stepfamilies were closer to grandparents than others in lone-parent or original families (Kennedy & Kennedy, 1993).

Grandparents, then, become increasingly involved in their grandchildren's lives when parents separate. Cherlin and Furstenberg have earlier described the latent function of grandparents as "volunteer firefighters" at times of stress in their adult children's families (Cherlin & Furstenberg, 1986), providing support as babysitters and, for younger lone mothers especially, being *in loco parentis*. There is little research that examines their involvement in relation to outcomes for children, however, and findings are mixed. McLanahan & Sandefur (McLanahan & Sandefur, 1994) noted that 16-year-olds living in households with mothers and grandmothers were at a higher risk of dropping out of school than those living just with their single mother, although those living with both were less likely to be left unsupervised. In the Iowa studies, a close relationship with a grandmother mediated the association between mother's antisocial behavior and daughter's delinquency and association with deviant peers (Simons & Associates, 1996). In the ALSPAC study in the UK, closeness to both maternal grandmothers and grandfathers was associated with lower levels of externalizing behavior in children in original families in early and middle childhood (Lussier et al., submitted). In stepfather families, closeness to maternal grandparents was linked with lower levels of internalizing behavior, and closeness to paternal stepparents with lower levels of externalizing behavior. In lone-mother families, closeness to maternal grandparents was weakly linked with decreased externalizing behavior, while closeness to paternal grandfathers *increased* the likelihood of behavior problems. In general, closeness to maternal grandparents made a unique contribution to behavior problems, suggesting that grandparents can be a significant buffer for children following parents' divorce.

Whether or not the contribution of grandparents to the well-being of their grandchildren is positive will depend on several factors, including the nature of the relationship between grandparents and their adult children, the readiness of the grandparent to assume the role, the ages of children, and whether or not the grandparents' involvement compromises the relationship the children have with their own parents (Lavers &

Sonuga-Barke, 1997). Overall, contact and closeness between children and grandparents appear to be important where children have experienced parental separation although the few studies we have, and the number of factors associated with grandparenting, make it difficult to be conclusive about the benefits of these relationships to young people.

Monitoring, aspirations, and supervision

The social capital framework predicts that children in lone-parent families will be disadvantaged by the day-to-day absence of one parent, which leaves the burden of time and investment with one, often stressed, residential parent. Similarly, it can be predicted that in stepfamilies these resources are to a large extent restored by the presence of two parenting figures in the household. Results from three US studies indicate that mothers in lone-parent families share fewer meals, supervise and talk with their children less, help less with school work, and have lower aspirations for their children than mothers in original families (McLanahan et al., 1991). Stepfamily mothers, too, share fewer meals, talk less, and have lower aspirations (see also Ferri in the UK (Ferri, 1984)), and are less likely to help with schoolwork than mothers in original families. Families in lone-parent and stepfamily households spend less time together than those in original families (Thomson et al., 1994; Voydanoff et al., 1994; Sweeting et al., 1998).

Do these lower levels of family involvement and aspirations matter? In lone-parent families the answer is yes, at least in regard to the risk of dropping out of high school. The difference in the level of risk between original and lone-parent families is halved when parenting involvement, supervision, and aspirations are taken into account (McLanahan & Sandefur, 1994). The comparative risk for children from stepfamilies is not, however, reduced. Parenting involvement, supervision, and aspirations do not account for their higher risk for dropping out of high school, birth during adolescence, or idleness in young men.

Community resources

Family transitions lead to a drop in the quality of neighborhoods and schools, and a decline in the connections between families and neighborhoods, and these factors are associated with poor outcomes for children. Community resources are, indeed, not in good supply for lone-parent or stepfamilies. McLanahan and her colleagues (1991) compared school climates for young people in lone-parent, stepparent, and original families and found that those in lone-parent and stepfamilies were more likely than original families to attend schools with high dropout rates. Their peers, too, were more likely to have low academic aspirations than those of original families.

Do these factors matter as far as outcomes for young people are concerned? Furstenberg and Hughes (1995) examined the contribution of some aspects of social capital to a range of outcomes for young people, including academic achievement, employment, stability of economic status, mental health, and avoidance of criminal activity and early parenthood. After controlling for mothers' education and the socioeconomic position of the family, factors that were found to be important included intergenerational support in the family (between mothers and grandmothers), help with homework, and the number of friends their mothers knew. Community factors included the presence of a strong help network and regular contact with friends for mothers, change of schools for children, quality of school, and peers' educational expectations. As well as these being in comparatively short supply for young people in lone-parent and stepfamilies there is, too, another dimension of disadvantage. They are more likely than those in original families to *move* from one community to another, so that their connections with community resources, peers, and neighbors are more tenuous and temporary. Indeed, community factors, specifically school quality and residential changes, account for 40 percent of the difference between original and stepfamilies in high school drop-out rates (McLanahan & Sandefur, 1994). Amato & Booth (1997) also noted in their longitudinal study that residential moves after separation are associated with poor psychological well-being in young adults.

A consideration of community resources widens the focus from the immediate family to neighborhood and community factors and to the connections families have with them. In all family structures, the contribution of resources from within the family and community to educational achievement and psychological well-being is clear.

Economic resources
The socioeconomic circumstances of separated families are, by any measure and in all countries, lower than those of either original families or stepfamilies. In the UK, on a range of indicators lone-parent families are worse off (for a summary see Rodgers & Pryor, 1998). In the US, mother-only families are four times as likely to live below the poverty line as two-parent families, and similar comparisons apply in Australasian countries (see chapter 5). Obvious factors that affect economic resources for families after separation are economies of scale: the cost of running two households include not just economic support for the same number of people as

in the previous household, but also baseline costs of running a house such as rent and insurance. Parents with low levels of household income are stressed by having to cope with little money and with changes of houses and neighborhoods (usually to poorer areas).

How important are economic resources for children's well-being after divorce? Links with academic outcomes are the most common, with household income explaining about half of the risk for low school attainment in the US (McLanahan & Sandefur, 1994) and a lesser amount of risk for behavioral problems. There is, too, a tendency for living in a lone parent family in childhood to be linked with economic indicators in adulthood such as unemployment or low employment status (Rodgers & Pryor, 1998). Several issues complicate research in this area, however. One is the possible influence of economic well-being before separation, since the rate of divorce is higher in low-income families. However, some studies that have controlled for preseparation socioeconomic status have found that differences in outcomes remain even when it is taken into account. Another is that household income *per se* may not be as important as its relativity to economic needs (Simons & Associates, 1996); or that relative decline in household income as a result of separation may be as important as absolute levels. One study, though, that contrasted groups of children where household income had fallen after separation with those where it had not changed, found no differences in rates of delinquency or emotional well-being in the two groups (Wadsworth & Maclean, 1986).

The processes by which income is related to children's outcomes are not well understood. It is usually assumed that the stresses of coping with little money affect parenting and parent–child relationships by raising levels of maternal distress. Moves to poorer neighborhoods and fights between parents about money might also contribute to children's lesser well-being. It is notable that economic support through child support payments from nonresident parents is more strongly linked with children's outcomes than money from other sources (Seltzer, 1998b). This suggests that the father–child relationship is an important aspect of the relationship between income and outcomes, since payment of child support is linked with levels of father–child contact. More specifically, it is probably linked through the *quality* of father–child relationships (Simons et al., 1994): fathers who have good relationships with their children are also more likely to pay child support. Overall, although there is no doubt that economic hardship is a potent factor in children's well-being (especially in relation to educational outcomes), it is most likely to operate through its impact on family processes and, in particular, parent–child relationships.

Family Systems

The main implication of family systems theory is that outcomes for children are best understood by considering the arrangement and rearrangement of the network of interdependent relations in families. In original families, the interparental relationship is the founding relationship, and usually precedes others such as parent–child and sibling relations. Family members, too, are usually related biologically to each other. In these families, it is well established that the parental relationship is closely associated with the nature of parent–child relationships and sibling relationships, with, in the main, hostile or negative parental relationships being linked with poor parent–child relations and, in turn, negative parent–child relationships predicting hostile sibling relations (Hetherington & Clingempeel, 1992; Simons & Associates, 1996; Dunn et al., 1999; Hetherington et al., 1999). Overall, the pattern of interrelationships appears to be similar across family types, despite their rearrangement following family transitions. There are, however, a few notable differences between original families and stepfamilies that are both quantitative and qualitative. For example, the associations between relationships are weaker in stepfamilies than in original families (O'Connor et al., 1997). In particular, mothers' positivity in their partnerships is found to be correlated with postivity toward their children in original but not stepfamilies. A similar lack of association between the marital dyad and parent–child relationships was noted in the ALSPAC study in the UK (Dunn et al., 1999). Mother–partner hostility in stepfamilies was not related to parent–child negativity, or to sibling hostility, whereas it was in non-stepfamilies. *Qualitative* differences include the nature of the association between relationships, and directionality. In Hetherington's studies, positive relations between parents in stepfamilies have been found to be *negatively* related to parent–child relations, whereas this association is almost always positive in non-stepfamilies. In this regard, Hetherington suggests that a strong parent–stepparent bond disrupts the formerly close relationships between lone mothers and their children.

The direction of influence in relationships can also differ. One example is Hetherington's (1999) finding that in stepfamilies but not other families adolescent externalizing behavior at one time predicts stepfather negativity at a later time. One reason why interrelationships might be weaker in stepfamilies is that family members are not all equally biologically related, and Hetherington and her colleagues have demonstrated that "ownness" predicts closeness of parent–child relationships better, overall, than family structure. Genetic relatedness is an important factor, as demonstrated by these studies and others that have compared adoptive and biological children in families after separation (O'Connor et al., 2000); this has been emphasized by sociobiologists such as Daly and Wilson (1998). So, too, may be co-residence. The period of infancy and early childhood when adults and children live together is when close adult–child relationships are most easily established and become an integral part of the self-definition of both adults and children. Weaker interrelationships in stepfamilies may be related to the lack of opportunity to establish these close early relationships as well as to genetic relatedness. In this regard, Buchanan and colleagues (1996), have found that there are more similarities between relationships within households than between relations with biological residential and nonresidential parents

Stresses and Resources

There is another way of looking at the interplay of factors that we have discussed in this chapter, and that is to consider the balance between positive and negative factors, or stresses and resources, that exist for children. A key feature of stress in families is parental distress, since psychological well-being is closely linked with other stress factors such as economic hardship, conflict, and children's behavior problems. In chapters 5 and 6 we noted that mental health, psychological distress, and substance abuse is particularly common in adults in lone-parent families and stepfamilies. In turn, parental well-being is a significant resource for children that can both buffer the impact of other stresses and, where well-being is affected by divorce, mediate the potential effects of other factors.

In chapter 2 we noted that the three major sources of influence on stresses and resources are individual, sociocultural, and family factors. It is clear from most of the research that we have considered that the pivotal point for all of these in relation to children's outcomes is parenting and parent–child relationships. More than any other, these two factors mediate the influence of others. Individual characteristics of children and parents, economic and life stresses and neighborhood influences, and family environment factors work through parent–child relationships to regulate outcomes for children.

Overview

When we use the lens of these various frameworks to view the research on outcomes for children whose lives encompass family transitions, it becomes clear that although no one theory fits perfectly, some explain children's well-being better than others. Trauma theories, incorporating the causal impact of a single event, do not, for example, stand up to scrutiny overall, although the impact of the loss of a parent in the short term is undeniable.

Several aspects of life-course theories are useful in explaining outcomes. In particular, the timing in a young person's life when their own transitions occur are both outcomes of separation and stepfamily living, and themselves predict later events such as the dissolution of their own partnerships. Individual differences in children such as temperament and attribution of control are also important, and act in concert with influences outside the child. These include conflict and other family and community factors such as household income, parental aspirations, and the school environment. Finally, parenting and parent–child relations emerge as key mediators of the impact of other major risk factors for children.

Together, life-course and ecological theories provide useful ways of assessing the cumulative processes and the interplay amongst risk factors and outcomes. They are also helpful in identifying dynamics that are not so generally understood. For example, it is apparent for both adults and children that risk factors are present before parents separate. Behavioral problems and distress in children, psychological distress and conflict in parents, and reduction in household income, have all been identified at elevated levels some time and even some years before separation occurs. What is not well understood, however, is whether these problems "cause" transitions, or are a "result" of the impending separation, and it is most likely that both situations occur.

It has also been established that separation often, although not always, exacerbates existing risk factors. Household income may fall, behavioral problems in children may increase (or decrease), parenting may diminish, parental psychological distress may increase, and conflict may be increased or reduced at the time of separation. Neighborhood changes, too, may be for better or worse. Conflict is a good example of the complexities inherent in understanding these changes. "Low conflict," as reported by parents, may in fact represent disengaged, quietly contemptuous parents who, when separation does occur, escalate their conflict and focus it on

Table 8.1 Areas of debate about families from three perspectives

Topic of debate	Conservative perspective	Liberal perspective	Emergent perspective
Consequences of divorce for children	Children inevitably damaged	Divorce does not harm children who are better off if unhappy parents separate	There is a range of outcomes for children, with some benefiting and some being harmed by divorce. Many harbor painful feelings into adulthood
Frameworks for explanation: divorce as process or event	Divorce is an event with direct causal impact on children's outcomes. Damage to children caused by a single factor such as loss, trauma, or abandonment	Divorce or separation is part of a process starting some years before, and continuing after parents separate. The main cause of risk for children is conflict, although outcomes are caused by multiple factors	Parental separation and divorce are part of a cumulative process for children. Single-factor explanations do not work. Children contribute to their own outcomes in measurable ways
Mothers	Mothers are the key to the well-being of children, and should put childrearing before a career.	Mothers can be adequate parents while working full- or part-time. Lone mothers can be and usually are competent parents	Children benefit most when mothers make choices about careers and families that suit them, and are supported by others
Fathers	Fathers should be present in families as economic providers and heads of the household	Fathers can be positive or negative influences for their children. If other factors are positive, children can thrive without fathers	Economic provision and presence not sufficient. Children want their fathers in their lives, and thrive in supportive, involved relationships

Children	Children are dependent and vulnerable, should be protected and treated as "children"	Children are resilient and agentic, and should have equal say with adults in decisions regarding their lives	Children do not see themselves as vulnerable, and want involvement in decisions but not responsibility for them
Marriage	Parents' marriage should be legal and binding, and divorce actively discouraged	Divorce should be allowed without judgment	Children thrive best with *happily* married parents; where this is unachievable they may be better in a supportive lone-parent household
Stepfamilies	Stepfamilies are weak family forms, violating biological imperatives; children are imperiled by living in stepfamilies	Stepfamilies are adaptive family forms that are diverse and potentially functional	Children in stepfamilies are at the same level of risk as those in lone-parent families. Stepfamilies are difficult but work more often than not
Diversity	Family diversity is bad for children and society	Diversity of family forms allows individuals to adapt to current social and economic circumstances	Diversity in itself is not bad, but instability is. Family relationships regardless of family structure are central to children's well-being

their children. High preseparation conflict may be followed by continuing high levels of disagreement after separation, or may diminish dramatically when one parent leaves the household.

There is no one model that fully explains children's vulnerability and well-being. It is apparent, however, that most risk factors are linked with outcomes primarily through parenting. Economic adversity, conflict, and parental distress all contribute to adverse outcomes through the parent-child relationships and parenting behavior that children experience. These predominantly family-based factors exist alongside neighborhood and community factors, such as schools and peer groups, as major contributors to outcomes for children. Again, parents, in their interactions with schools and knowledge of peer groups, are often the mediators between children and neighborhoods. In turn, parenting takes place in the context of those other factors that have been shown to be important for children's well-being, including characteristics of children themselves.

In sum, although some of the frameworks we have discussed work better than others in explaining outcomes for children, there is no one model that fully explains children's vulnerability and well-being. It is apparent, however, that most risk factors are linked with outcomes primarily through parenting. Economic adversity, conflict, and parental distress all contribute to adverse outcomes through the parent–child relationships and parenting behavior that children experience. These predominantly family-based factors exist alongside neighborhood and community factors, such as schools and peer groups, as major contributors to outcomes for children. Again, parents, in their interactions with schools and knowledge of peer groups, are often the mediators between children and neighborhoods. In turn, parenting takes place in the context of those other factors that have been shown to be important for children's well-being, including characteristics of children themselves.

How do these conclusions inform our original debate between conservative and liberal perspectives? Table 8.1 shows the topics identified in table 1.1, together with an emergent perspective reflecting the conclusions we have arrived at in this book.

An emergent perspective

Children whose parents separate are, as a group, vulnerable to problems later in their lives. There is, however, wide variation in how they fare, with some being harmed by their parents' divorce and others benefiting. The majority are sufficiently resilient through their own coping skills, and the circumstances surrounding and following the separation, to emerge unscathed – although many continue to hold painful feelings, a "permanent ache."

Whether or not the risks for children associated with divorce are actually realized is determined not by the separation itself, but by the complex interplay of other factors that are present before, during, and after the separation. Many of these, such as conflict, operate through their impact on parenting and parent–child relationships. The contribution of children's individual differences to their own outcomes is also important, and not well understood.

Children have the best chance of thriving within *happy*, two-parent families. In turn, the legal status of their parents' partnership may be less important than the level of commitment they have to their relationship. Where families are unhappy and in conflict, the least risky alternative for children may be separation, where they are better off living with one parent and not exposed to conflict. Within two-parent families the roles of women and men are diverse, and the traditional home-maker/provider divisions are often no longer either possible or relevant. The negotiation of these and other roles is increasingly common in families, rather than conforming to social blueprints. The key to children's well-being both within and without original families is the quality of relationships with parents, and this is of particular consequence for children's relationships with their nonresident parents after separation.

Just as women's and men's roles have changed, so have children's within families. They are likely to be as well or better educated than their parents, and to have impressive economic power. These factors, and the recognition of children's legal rights, mean that children hold and articulate views about family life and family change. There is a developmental sequence to their understanding of families and change that reflects their age and their experiences. To acknowledge and work with this is to empower rather than to "objectify" children. They do not, though, want to take responsibility for decisions made; rather, they see themselves as participants in decision-making processes.

The formation of stepfamilies is common, and challenging for family members. They pose risks, not least because they are less stable than original families, so that there is the chance of future and multiple transitions for children. The associated instability of family membership, community links, and relationships probably contribute to the increased vulnerability of children who experience multiple transitions, as does the possibility that adults who have a series of relationships have high levels of psychological distress. The majority of stepfamilies, though, function well, and involve family dynamics that are different but not necessarily better or worse than original families. As with separation, the transition to stepfamily living brings with it risks for some and benefits for others, with most having a mix of both.

Finally, the diversity of families brings with it both risks and opportunities for children. It is doubtful that the shape of families and households matters for children's welfare. Far more important is the nature of the relationships within them, and the extent to which they remain stable.

Three major themes emerge from these conclusions. First, children's understandings and views are remarkably accurate and sophisticated. Their preferred form of families is essentially conservative; they want to live with both parents in a family that is happy and supportive. Where this is not their situation, or it changes, they are both pragmatic and resilient in adapting to family change and incorporating altered family structures into their understanding of families. They suffer ongoing distress when they are not told what is happening, and when adults do not take their feelings and views into account. Their views about how relationships should be in, for example, stepfamilies, largely accords with what research suggests works best for them.

Second, changes in the ways in which relationships in families are established and sustained are profound. No longer are kinship and its obligations taken for granted; instead, relations are negotiated on an individual basis. The significant disadvantage of these changes is that many people no longer form partnerships with the expectation that they are lifetime commitments, so that family transitions are often an unfortunate accompaniment to the changing nature of relationships. Changes are also apparent in the kinds of relations that children have with parents, especially stepparents. They are often more akin to friendships than to traditional parent-child relationships (Gorrell Barnes et al., 1998). The lack of uniformity and consensus about kin and nonkin relations leads to uncertainty about how they should be. On the other hand, the fact that they can no longer be taken for granted might eventually encourage negotiation of more satisfying, committed, and stable relationships that work well for the individuals involved.

This leads to the third conclusion, that family diversity is not in itself a problem; people have always found innovative ways of forming families and households that work for them. The instability of neighborhoods, households, and relationships that accompanies multiple family change is the greatest threat to children's well-being. For those who care about their future, the challenge is to identify ways of enhancing quality and stability of relationships in families, regardless of their structure.

9

Overview and Future Directions

The increase in marital instability has not brought society to the brink of chaos, but neither has it led to a golden age of freedom and self-actualization.

Amato, 2000

As we have seen throughout this book, the causes and consequences of family change are as complex as families themselves, and mustering the individual components of what we know into a manageable whole is rather like trying to herd cats that persist in producing kittens. Paradoxically, as we find more sophisticated ways of studying family change, so our appreciation of the complexities increases. Children, though, cannot wait while we search for conclusive answers. They and their families continue to change, and to need support for what is happening to them now. We are faced, then, with the challenges of better understanding, and the more immediate task of applying what we know presently to policy and practice. In this final chapter we will address some of the specific areas of research that we see as important and add our suggestions to those of other writers for policy and practice.

Future Research: What We Know and What We Need to Know

The risks for children that accompany family change are by now very obvious. It is apparent that to talk of the "effects" of divorce is mistaken. There is an extended process of instability and change in families spanning some years, of which parental separation is but one, albeit tangible, transition. The challenge of identifying key factors associated with this process, that increase or lessen risks for children, has also been taken up and met to a considerable extent. We know with a fair degree of certainty that conflict, economic and social stress, and parental mental health are key factors and that, in the main, their impact on children's well-being is channeled via parent–child relationships. Although our knowledge is still imprecise, in themselves these understandings provide sufficient knowledge to inform policy and practice. There are, though, several significant questions that have not yet been answered satisfactorily.

Stepfamily outcomes

Although the amount of research that describes processes and outcomes in stepfamilies is steadily increasing, so far the key explanatory factors for children's well-being are elusive. The impact of obvious factors such as conflict and parenting is not so clear as in original families, although their patterns of influence seem to be similar to those in other family structures. In seeking to explain academic outcomes, for example, McLanahan and Sandefur were able to identify only residential mobility as a predictor in stepfamilies (McLanahan & Sandefur, 1994). Because there is so much variation in the composition of stepfamilies, studies that are able to compare processes in different stepfamily forms and to investigate possibly specific patterns of influence may help to identify key processes that explain the risks faced by children. One possibility is that the higher risks for children in stepfamilies compared with those in original families are associated with conflict and other adversity that accompanies the first transition when their parents separated, rather than the subsequent transition into stepfamily living (Anderson et al., 1999). If that is the case, then a focus on stepfamily factors that confer resilience and enhance children's lives is a priority. More generally, the study of stepfamilies that succeed and the identification of protective factors would go some way in addressing the current unfortunate emphasis on the pathology of stepfamilies.

Multiple transitions

Living in a stepfamily does not increase risks appreciably for children compared with living in a lone-parent family; however, further transitions out of a stepfamily and into another confer risks beyond those associated with separation and stepfamily formation. Our understanding of the processes associated with multiple transitions for children is rudimentary. Studies indicate that children are at particularly high risk when they experience several changes in family structure, and that the mental health of adults who have several marriages or partnerships is relatively poor.

One explanation for risks in these families is that adults with personality disorders, for example, or whose relationship skills are inadequate are those most likely to have several relationships and to end up in multiple-transition households. In these situations, low psychological well-being and suboptimal relationship skills will have an impact on children's well-being through poor parenting, and may be transmitted directly as aspects of personality that reduce children's abilities to cope. Alternatively or as well, the experiences of making and breaking relationships through several household transitions may themselves be risk factors for children. Longitudinal studies that track the trajectories of family members through several transitions are needed in order to understand better the mechanisms of risk.

Cohabitation

In the US, adults who cohabit are known to differ in some important ways from those who marry (Nock, 1995). They are less satisfied with their relationships, have lower levels of commitment, and their relationships are more vulnerable to breakdown than marriages are. These are potential risk factors for children, yet little is known about children's well-being, experiences, and perceptions according to whether or not their parents are married. We know little about family dynamics and children's well-being in cohabiting families, and whether or not they differ from those where parents are legally married. Apart from the obvious risks arising from unhappy parental relationships and the comparative instability of cohabiting relationships, it is possible that having unmarried parents is of no consequence to children. The level and nature of commitment to relationships and family might be far more crucial for children than the legal status of their parents' partnership. Given the increasing numbers living in cohabiting households, these questions should be addressed.

We know little about family dynamics and children's well-being in co-habiting families, and whether or not they differ from those where parents are legally married. Apart from the obvious risks arising from unhappy parental relationships and the comparative instability of cohabiting relationships, it is possible that having unmarried parents is of no consequence to children. The level and nature of commitment to relationships and family might be far more crucial for children than the legal status of their parents' partnership.

Individual differences in children

The contribution that children make to their own experiences is widely acknowledged, but less often measured in studies of family transitions. Some children may, for example, increase the likelihood of their parents separating if they place a high burden on parents through disability or difficult behavior. A lone parent may, too, choose to partner if she feels that her son needs a father figure. There may also be aspects of individual children that contribute to the way they appraise and cope with transitions.

Those who have included child measures report varying degrees of contribution to outcomes (Hetherington, 1991; Kim et al., 1997; Deater-Deckard & Dunn, 1999). It is difficult to identify stable factors in children that might be of consequence, for two reasons. First, it is often hard to measure the factors before transitions occur, unless the children are part of longitudinal studies. Second, there is always the possibility that family distress preceding separation has an impact on, for example, temperament or locus of control. Nonetheless, the contribution of children both to the likelihood of transitions themselves and to their own outcomes needs to be better understood, and again longitudinal studies offer a useful methodology for overcoming many of the measurement difficulties. Inclusion of more than one child from a family is also an important strategy for understanding individual differences in children and, in particular, the contribution of genetic relatedness in stepfamilies, and has been implemented in studies in the UK (Dunn et al., 1999) and in the US (Hetherington et al., 1999).

Change in levels of stresses and resources

Although there is a wide understanding of what particular factors constitute risks for children, we are far less clear about the processes by which they work. It is possible that *changes* in, for example, household income and levels of conflict across transitions will be as informative as actual levels at a particular time. The notion of process becomes somewhat different when viewed this way, since it suggests a focus on an increase or decrease in the levels of risk factors during transitions rather than on the transitions themselves. Figure 9.1 shows the major risk factors that might change with transitions.

All these factors, and others, are susceptible to either increase or decrease across family transitions. An examination of the processes by which

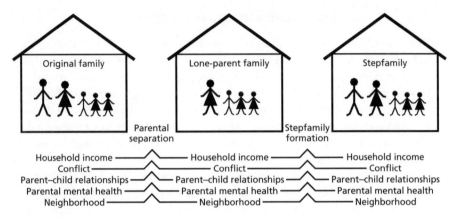

Figure 9.1 Major risk factors that are liable to change with family transitions

these changes occur and interact with each other might be particularly informative. The persistence of changes may also be important, although again there are gaps in our knowledge. Living in a lone-parent household with low income over a long period, for example, does not seem to exacerbate outcomes (McLanahan & Sandefur, 1994). On the other hand, continuing interparental acrimony and poor parenting does appear to heighten risks for children (Johnston et al., 1989; Hetherington, 1999). The *configuration* of changes might, too, be important. For instance, the potential risks of a reduction in household income might be offset by the reduction in conflict experienced by the child. The transitions from lone-parent households to stepfamily households can also be viewed this way. Household income usually increases, but parenting declines when stepfamilies are formed (DeGarmo & Forgatch, 1999). Changes in parental mental health, conflict, and neighborhoods are not well understood in stepfamilies. The combination of changes and the interplay of individual factors may be important for children in stepfamilies who also face the formation of new relationships with stepkin. Multiple transitions, in turn, expose children and their parents to successive changes in these family and environmental factors. Studies that examine changes in risks and resources with various transitions might help our understanding of the significance of the dynamics as well as their absolute levels.

The importance of short-term outcomes

In the aftermath of separation, children are typically distressed and their behavior and well-being are affected by the reduced quality of parenting they receive. After about two years, though, distress diminishes and behavior problems usually return to preseparation levels. How important are the nature and levels of immediate distress? Clearly they are outcomes in their own right, but are they predictive of future well-being? High levels may lead to medium- and long-term emotional or psychological disadvantage; on the other hand, the expression of distress at the time may be beneficial in helping children to cope constructively with the changes. Levels of distress may interact with factors such as support and communication from parents or other adults, ongoing levels of conflict, and children's own coping strategies in predicting outcomes; but more research, preferably longitudinal, is needed to unravel these factors and their interactions.

Qualitative studies

There is a striking lack of qualitative studies, especially in the US, that either elaborate on findings from quantitative research or illuminate new research questions to be examined in larger populations. An example of the usefulness of this approach is in the interview studies of children that reveal their feelings and perspectives on parental separation and stepfamily living. As we mentioned in an earlier chapter, these studies' insights into family change are remarkably accurate and sophisticated. The use of qualitative methodologies alongside analyses based on large databases can only enrich our understanding of the experiences of children and adults in families.

Longitudinal studies

Several of the aspects of research mentioned above would be addressed most effectively by the use of longitudinal studies. Many of the studies we have referred to in this book have used data from longitudinal databases in the US and in the UK, although most do no have a specific focus on family transitions. We believe that there is a need for more longitudinal studies with family processes as their major focus, which can draw on the knowledge and experience gained from work on cohort studies but can focus more specifically on family change and test hypotheses in a more

Table 9.1 Areas of policy and practice for original, lone-parent, and stepfamilies

Level of support	Original families	Separated families	Stepfamilies
Individual/family	Parenting education	Parenting education	Parenting education
	Mental healthcare (children & adults)	Mental healthcare (children & adults)	Mental healthcare (children & adults)
	Physical healthcare (children & adults)	Physical healthcare (children & adults)	Physical healthcare (children & adults)
	Adequate household income	Adequate household income	Adequate household income
	Support for partnership	Living & visiting arrangements for children	Support for partnership
		Extended family relations	Extended family relations
		Education for professionals working with families	Education for professionals working with families
		Access to counseling, information for children & parents	Access to counseling, information for children & parents
		Children's rights & involvement	Children's rights & involvement
Community/neighborhood	Childcare	Childcare	Childcare
	Involvement with schools	Involvement with schools (both parents)	Involvement with schools (both parents)
	Workplace factors (flexible hours, family-	Workplace factors (flexible hours, family-	Workplace factors (flexible hours, family-

Law and policy	friendly practices)	friendly practices)	friendly practices)
	Identification of families at risk	Referral services	Referral services
	Child protection	Child protection	Child protection
	Family-friendly political policies (recognition of diversity)	Family-friendly political policies (recognition of diversity)	Family-friendly political policies (recognition of diversity)
	Economic support	Economic support	Economic support
		Guardianship, residence issues	Legal, adoption issues for stepparents

direct manner. Measurement of factors that are known to be sources of risk for children and, in particular, of their changes across transitions and their interplay with each other, would help to address questions about multiple transitions, the importance of individual differences in children, and the persistence or attenuation of outcomes into adulthood.

Policy and Practice

The translation of research findings into concrete recommendations for policy and practice is complicated by the difficulties that are posed by the fact that families continue to change and diversify. The complicated mosaic presented by research findings makes it a challenge to identify conclusions that are easily applied to practice. In this section we offer our suggestions about the implications of research. In table 9.1 we have summarized areas of practice and policy that are relevant to original, lone-parent, and stepfamilies at three levels: the individual and family level, the community and neighborhood level, and in areas of policy and law.

Several aspects of policy and practice deserve particular discussion. Here we focus on the identification of families at risk; support for families who are breaking down; education for professionals working with families; relationships with parents after separation; economic support; children's involvement; and support for stepfamilies.

1   Identification of families at risk for transitions

Children stand the best chance of developing optimally and thriving when they live in stable, happy, well-functioning families. Policies and practices that optimize families' chances of nurturing children in these ways are, then, paramount, and these include economic support, affordable access to childcare, and flexible workplace practices. Employers, for example, need to develop policies that enable parents to combine work and parenting, and that acknowledge different family structures. Although women are increasingly supported in some quarters in this regard, it is harder for fathers and in particular lone fathers to gain support for their parenting.

Identification of families at risk or already in distress, and support for them, will go some way in reducing rates of family breakdown. An example of this is a screening program at postnatal checkups for new mothers in the UK, where those who indicate that their relationships are vulnerable are offered help (personal communication, John Simons, consultant head of research, One Plus One Marriage & Partnership Research). Positive interventions like this have a better chance of reducing family dissolution than, for example, introducing legal barriers to divorce, and should be offered regardless of family structure or marital status.

2   Education, counseling, and support for families

Separation and its aftermath are characterized by confusion about how to rearrange households, disagreement and often conflict between parents, and reduced parenting practices as adults flounder to come to terms with the changes. Information and help at this time is very much needed, and not always available. However, provision of programs that give parents information and help with making decisions about living arrangements is increasingly common. In the US there was a 180 percent increase in the number of programs provided between 1994 and 1998 (Geasler & Blaisure, 1999). How well do they work? In general, evaluations of programs indicate high levels of satisfaction in participants, but few other benefits. A problem with many of the courses provided is that they are not based on research findings about factors surrounding separation, but are very general in nature. An exception to this is "kids in divorce and separation" (kids), developed specifically to prevent and intervene in family conflict and intended to increase parents' knowledge about the impact of conflict on their children (Shifflett & Cummings, 1999). Parents who took part in this program reported increases in knowledge and decreases in conflicted behavior both in themselves and in their spouses. Another, which focused on reducing loyalty conflicts in children, found better conflict resolution skills and greater likelihood of protecting children from conflict in the group that took the course in comparison with a control group of parents (Arbuthnot & Gordon, 1996). Development of programs that are more clearly focused and grounded in good research and practice, and are evaluated, is needed, but in the meantime they should continue to be provided since, at the least, participants feel as if they are helpful.

Who should provide programs for separating families? In some cases they are available through family courts, although in countries like the UK and New Zealand, where only a small proportion of separating couples approach the court, this is not effective in reaching a majority of separating families. Programs need to be widely and easily available in community settings where the possibly negative association with courts is avoided. Cost should not be a prohibitive factor; free or subsidized programs need to be available to low-income families, paid for by the state which, in turn, will want to see evidence of their effectiveness in tangible ways such as reducing the need to use court services. In some US states programs are mandatory, and parents who have been compelled to attend rate them positively. If programs are to be mandated, however, they need to take place early in the process of separation, before conflict and negativity have become entrenched.

Of particular significance to children is the way in which parents talk to them about the separation. Children often do not get explanations about why parents separate and many have no idea that their parents were considering separation before it happened. When it is unexpected it is especially stressful for children; when they do not know the reasons for disruptive events, they cope less well. Talking to children at the time they are parting is probably one of the most painful tasks faced by parents; they need advice and possibly even professional help in doing so, for their children's sake.

The cumulative nature of life-course trajectories alerts us to the fact that young people would benefit, too, from support beyond the time of separation. In particular, early transitions to adult roles, which are more likely for children who experience separation and stepfamily living, are both outcomes in themselves and risk factors for adult adversity including effects on mental health and their own relationship dissolution. Active interventions that help adolescents to stay in education and to avoid early partnership and parenting are, then, ways of helping to reduce the intergenerational continuity of disadvantage.

3 Education for professionals

A major public health issue in regard to providing education and support for families is how to reach them when help is needed. As we mentioned above, courts are not necessarily effective in providing resources for the majority of distressed and separating families. Furthermore, there is sometimes a need for specialized intervention programs where high-risk families need focused support and attention. At the time of family transitions, families turn to a range of professionals for advice, including family doctors, teachers, health visitors, lawyers, counselors, and psychologists. Many of these have a dearth of information or knowledge that is based on research, because the dissemination of research-based information is often sporadic or inadequate. Yet they are in unique positions to identify families who need help, both general and specialized. In one initiative in the UK, One Plus One Marriage and Partnership Research is using contemporary reviews of research findings as a basis for working with educators associated with professional organizations, such as teachers, lawyers, and doctors, to provide those working with families with up-to-date, research-based information. Similar endeavors that provide systematic and widespread education for professionals who are helping families are to be encouraged since they are potentially able to provide general help and to refer families to more specialized services where needed.

> At the time of family transitions families turn to a range of professionals for advice, including family doctors, teachers, health visitors, lawyers, counselors, and psychologists. Many of these have a dearth of information or knowledge that is based on research, because the dissemination of research-based information is often sporadic or inadequate. Yet they are in unique positions to identify families who need help, both general and specialized.

4   Relationships with parents after separation

Legal structures in most countries encourage the continuing involvement of both parents in children's lives after separation by (in the UK, for example) emphasizing parental responsibilities or (in the US in several states) having a presumption of joint legal custody. Two other aspects of recent legislation are also important. One is the removal of parental gender as a basis for decisions about custody and living arrangements. The second is a move away from state intervention in the affairs of families, toward the private ordering of living arrangements. Despite the emphasis on the roles of both parents in the lives of their children, however, in most cases families make arrangements that reflect normative levels of preseparation involvement with parents. So children usually live with their mothers and have varying degrees of contact with their fathers.

> Much of the debate about living arrangements is adult-centered. Men's groups argue from a perspective of fathers' rights, and feminist lobbies are often based on arguments about the abilities and rights of women to raise their children. A less partisan perspective on living and visiting arrangements comes from considering the perspectives and needs of children. Children are measurably advantaged if they have a close relationship with a nonresidential parent that encompasses support and monitoring, *and* they want ongoing relationships with that parent. The advantages are measured in both economic and psychological terms.

Much of the debate about living arrangements is adult-centered. Men's groups argue from a perspective of fathers' rights, and feminist lobbies are often based on arguments about the abilities and rights of women to raise their children. A less partisan perspective on living and visiting arrangements comes from considering the perspectives and needs of children. Children are measurably advantaged if they have a close relationship with a nonresidential parent that encompasses support and monitoring, *and* they want ongoing relationships with that parent. The advantages are measured in both economic and psychological terms: regular contact with nonresidential parents, for example, is associated with economic support by those parents and in turn with academic outcomes. An important point too is that preseparation involvement does not predict the quality of fathering involvement postseparation (Lamb, 1999). Furthermore, for resident parents the active involvement in their children's lives of their ex-partners is potentially beneficial since the responsibilities of parenting are shared and they have child-free time. What makes this difficult, however, is the possibility that ongoing contact between children and nonresidential parents increases the likelihood of conflict between parents.

Of particular concern is the situation where domestic violence has occurred. Is it worse for children to have contact with a parent who has abused the other, or to have no contact whatsoever with that parent? In chapter 4 the conflicting feelings of children about contact with an abusing parent were discussed; there is little research available that compares the advantages and disadvantages for children of contact with a parent who has demonstrated violence toward a partner but not to the children.

Especially worrying in many countries is that in cases where domestic violence has occurred or has been alleged, there is no intervention until a court makes final orders. This can take up to two years, during which time children may continue to witness or even to experience abuse. In Australia, the family court is identifying cases of abuse that were previously unknown to child protection services, and the Magellan Project has been set up in order that such cases are put on a fast track toward being settled (Brown et al., 1998). In New Zealand, the Domestic Violence Act prohibits contact where abuse is alleged, until it is determined whether or not a child is safe. Often, orders for supervised access will be made; the challenge is, then, to determine whether and when unsupervised access will be safe. This depends on the characteristics of the violence that has occurred, and on the willingness and ability of the abusive parent to accept responsibility and benefit from programs to address violent behavior (Pryor, 2000). The possibility of violence coming from a resident parent's new partner is also an issue that must be addressed by those working with children in these families.

> We believe that unless there are factors such as violence or abuse that militate against contact, then ongoing parenting relationships between children and their nonresidential parents should be facilitated and nurtured. This does not necessarily mean joint physical custody, and in practice many families find that arrangement difficult to manage. It does mean active involvement by the nonresident parent in their children's lives, including providing a second home base, and communication and involvement with school and community activities with their children.

Nonetheless, we believe that unless there are factors such as violence or abuse that militate against contact, then ongoing parenting relationships between children and their nonresidential parents should be facilitated and nurtured. This does not necessarily mean equal time with both parents, and in practice many families find that arrangement difficult to manage. It does mean active involvement by the nonresident parent in their children's lives, including providing a second home base, and communication and involvement with school and community activities with their children. There are strategies for avoiding face-to-face contact between parents where this is difficult by, for example, children making the transitions from one parent's care to the other at school or in a supervised access facility for younger children. Mediation as a means of reaching decisions about living arrangements has been shown recently to have demonstrable benefits in the long term in facilitating involvement of nonresidential parents in their children's lives without increasing co-parental conflict (Emery et al., in press). Another tool for helping parents to make decisions about children is a parenting plan, which consists of a series of questions and issues commonly faced by separating families that can be addressed systematically either by parents themselves or with the help of a third person (Richards, 1999). Parenting plans are also used in Australia, and parts of the US. In sum, then, where possible the fostering of relationships between children and nonresidential parents should be seen as an important priority for parents and professionals who are working with families.

5   Economic support

Reduction in household income for children is a well-recognized outcome of parental separation. In turn, it is linked in particular with poor educational outcomes (McLanahan & Sandefur, 1994), and, not surprisingly, payment of child support by fathers is positively related to academic achievement in children (King, 1994a; Argys et al., 1998). Moreover, economic resources from child support have a more positive impact on well-being for children than money from other sources (Seltzer, 1998b), especially if fathers pay cooperatively (Argys et al., 1998). Although compliance with child support orders is often low, its payment appears to have advantages above and beyond the increased level of household income, yet men who do not pay are often poor or unemployed. What should be done about these fathers? The extra benefit of child support beyond dollars is probably associated with increased involvement by fathers in their children's lives; to punish men who cannot pay is unlikely to increase involvement with their children. An evaluation of a father's ability to pay is obviously needed, and since economic provision is important in its own right, payment where possible should be enforced through taxes and other means. Where payment is difficult or impossible, then children's well-being and wider social benefits are enhanced by adequate state support for lone-parent families. Growing up in poverty has ongoing cumulative disadvantages for both individuals and societies.

6　Children's involvement and children's rights

The concept of the best interests of the child does not in itself imply that children have rights, or even perspectives, in regard to family change and decisions made; rather, children's interests may be equally well determined by adults. The United Nations Charter on the Rights of the Child has given some legal weight to children's rights, however, and there is uneven recognition internationally of the implications of this. The extent and the limitations of children's feelings and wishes about participation in decisions associated with family transitions are becoming better understood (Brannen et al., 1999b; Lyon et al., 1999; Gollop et al., 2000) and they parallel the wider changes in power balances between children and adults in families discussed in chapter 1. As a result of these several influences, children are increasingly included in situations where court processes are involved. Children's wishes and feelings are ascertained by guardians *ad litem* in the UK and in some US states, and in New Zealand by lawyers who are counsel for children or by psychologists appointed by the court, although this happens only in cases where parents cannot agree. There are some attempts, too, to involve children in mediation processes, although there is disagreement about the ways in which this might be done.

Where public processes such as court-based intervention are not involved, the situation is not so clear. In the UK under the Family Law Act, information is provided through parents attending information sessions for children. However, in many cases parents do not pass the information leaflets on to their children, saying that they feel they are not appropriate, or that their children are not ready for them (Richards, 1999). Since all but a small proportion of separation arrangements are made by families without state or court intervention, children's participation is mediated by parents who may be reluctant to involve them in decisions or to listen to their views. There is, then, a need to provide children with information and support that is accessible to them, and to educate parents and professionals involved with them about ways of listening and taking their views into account. Ways of informing children that might be used include public provision of material in libraries and on the internet; education and support courses for children whose parents separate; and sending material directly to children instead of providing it through their parents. In all situations where children are involved, however, there is a need for a balance between their rights to be informed and heard, and burdening them with undue responsibility for decisions made.

7   Support for stepfamilies

The visibility of stepfamilies in the media and in policy debates is surprisingly low, despite the transition to stepfamily living being a common experience for children. The fact that this transition is often outside the ambit of family courts and other institutions means, too, that it is difficult to identify points where intervention and help might be offered. The complexity and variety of stepfamilies also makes the provision of support and information a considerable challenge, and there is a particular danger of taking a "one size fits all" approach. Nevertheless it is important to find ways to provide effective support and intervention for stepfamilies in order to help members of this vulnerable family structure to stabilize and establish functional relationships.

The development of appropriate programs for stepfamilies is relatively new, and evaluations suggest that they are difficult to get right (Nicholson & Sanders, 1999). The comparative difficulties involved in making stepfamilies work need to be acknowledged, including the challenges of establishing workable relationships with family members to whom children are not related, and with whom they have not grown up. Stepfamilies should not be endeavoring to become just like other families, but need to find ways of relating that suit family members. Success is more likely if difficulties are faced realistically, and expectations adjusted toward what is possible and workable rather than what might be envisaged as ideal.

Children whose parents are repartnering need particular support, since their feelings about the new family may be opposed to those of their parents. Schools provide one possible avenue for identifying children and adolescents who are not coping with stepfamily formation, and who could benefit from support from outside the family.

Another issue for stepfamilies is the legal status of the relationships between stepchildren and stepparents. At present they are legal strangers, and although formalization of their relationship might not be appropriate in every situation (especially with older children), children feel closer to their parents in stepfamilies where the parents are legally married, so structures that enable them to make legal commitments to each other might serve to enhance and strengthen a relationship that is otherwise often diffuse and ambiguous, both legally and psychologically. As with the marriage of their parent and stepparent, legal underpinning of the relationship could signal a degree of commitment to stepchildren that might not otherwise be apparent to them.

Finale

The diversity of families has been a major theme in this book. It is sometimes said that there are few blueprints for stepfamilies on how to function; we suggest that, despite the persistence of the ideal of the nuclear family, many other family groups are having to find ways of adapting and functioning that fit no socially sanctioned prescriptions. The historic and concurrent upheavals for families have not just changed their nature; they present fundamental questions about the meaning of family. Two paradoxical aspects are clear, however. First, change is not going to go away: our energies are better used in supporting children and their parents in diverse family structures than yearning for a somewhat mythical bygone golden age of nuclear families. Second, families are not going to stop mattering. Their salience for adults and children, and their primary roles as environments for rearing children and providing emotional and psychological nurturance for their members, will continue.

The historic and concurrent upheavals for families have not just changed their nature; they present fundamental questions about the meaning of family. Two paradoxical aspects are clear, however. First, change is not going to go away: our energies are better used in supporting children and their parents in diverse family structures than yearning for a somewhat mythical bygone golden age of nuclear families. Second, families are not going to stop mattering. Their salience for adults and children, and their primary roles as environments for rearing children and providing emotional and psychological nurturance for their members, will continue.

Families and the well-being of their members remain of overwhelming importance at every level, from the individual concerned with surviving and thriving within a unique network of relationships through to politicians and policy-makers facing the responsibilities of making decisions for their communities and societies. At the beginning of this book we noted the polarization of perspectives on family change, based often in personal experience; the topic is, then, inevitably emotionally charged, and it is imperative that those who make families their professional concern step back as far as possible from personal positions and approach their subject dispassionately. It is particularly important that researchers, educators, and those who work with families examine their biases even if they cannot entirely eliminate them. It is hoped that ours are apparent; the most compelling is the focus on the well-being and rights of children.

The fact that family change and diversity is as dynamic as ever makes the task of being definitive particularly elusive. A challenge for researchers, then, is to be reflexive, and to respond to change with appropriate methodologies and frameworks that reflect the dynamism of family change. In this regard, longitudinal studies offer a powerful tool for understanding. In turn, the communication of what is known to professionals, politicians, and policy-makers needs to be both accurate and efficient.

The twentieth century was declared the Century of the Child by a Swedish feminist in 1900 (Cunningham, 1995). In ways unimagined then, childhood has changed. We may now be embarking on the Century of the Family, in which the worlds of children and adults transform each other in ways that are impossible to predict. Alongside the survival of the environment, the task of nurturing the survival of families in all their diversity might be the challenge with the greatest implications for us all.

References

Abraham, K. (1927). Notes on the psycho-analytical investigations and treatment of manic-depressive insanity and allied conditions. In *Selected Papers on Psycho-analysis*. Hogarth Press, London.

Ainsworth, M. D. S., Blehar, M., Waters, E., and Wall, S. (1978). *Patterns of Attachment: A Psychological Study of the Strange Situation*. Lawrence Erlbaum Associates, Hillsdale, NJ.

Allatt, P. (1996). Conceptualizing parenting from the standpoint of children: relationship and transition in the life course. In J. Brannen and M. O'Brien (eds.), *Children in Families: Research and Policy*. The Falmer Press, London.

Allison, P. D. and Furstenberg, F. F. (1989). How marital dissolution affects children: variations by age and sex. *Developmental Psychology* 25, 540–9.

Amato, P. (1987a). Children's reactions to parental separation and divorce: the views of children and custodial mothers. *Australian Journal of Social Issues* 22, 610–23.

Amato, P. (1989). Family processes and the competence of primary school children and adolescents. *Journal of Youth and Adolescence* 18, 39–53.

Amato, P. (1990). Dimensions of the family environment as perceived by children: a multidimensional scaling analysis. *Journal of Marriage and the Family* 52, 613–20.

Amato, P. (1998). More than money? Men's contributions to their children's lives. In A. Booth and A. C. Crouter (eds.), *Men in Families: When Do They Get Involved? What Difference Does it Make?* Lawrence Erlbaum Associates, Mahwah, NJ.

Amato, P. and Booth, A. (1997). *A Generation at Risk: Growing Up in an Era of Family Upheaval*. Harvard University Press, Cambridge, Mass.

Amato, P. and Gilbreth, J. G. (1999). Nonresident fathers and children's well-being: a meta-analysis. *Journal of Marriage and the Family* 61, 557–73.

Amato, P. and Rezac, S. J. (1994). Contact with nonresident parents, interparental conflict, and children's behavior. *Journal of Family Issues* 15, 191–207.

Amato, P. and Rivera, F. (1999). Paternal involvement and children's behavior problems. *Journal of Marriage and the Family* 61, 375–84.

Amato, P. and Rogers, S. (1997). A longitudinal study of marital problems and subsequent divorce. *Journal of Marriage and the Family* 59, 612–24.

Amato, P. R. (1987b). *Children in Australian Families: The Growth of Competence*. Prentice-Hall, Sydney.

Amato, P. R. (1987c). Family processes in one-parent, stepparent, and intact families: the child's point of view. *Journal of Marriage and the Family* 49, 327–37.

Amato, P. R. (1991). Parental absence during childhood and depression in later life. *Sociological Quarterly* 32, 543–56.

Amato, P. R. (1993). Children's adjustment to divorce: theories, hypotheses, and empirical support. *Journal of Marriage and the Family* 55, 23–8.

Amato, P. R. (1996). Explaining the intergenerational transmission of divorce. *Journal of Marriage and the Family* 58, 628–40.

Amato, P. R. (1999). Children of divorced parents as young adults. In E. M. Hetherington (ed.), *Coping with Divorce, Single Parenting, and Remarriage: A Risk and Resiliency Perspective*. Lawrence Erlbaum Associates, Mahwah, NJ.

Amato, P. R. (2000). The consequences of divorce for adults and children. *Journal of Marriage and the Family* 62, 1269–87.

Amato, P. R. and Booth, A. (1991). Consequences of parental divorce and marital unhappiness for adult well-being. *Social Forces* 69, 895–914.

Amato, P. R. and Booth, A. (1996). A prospective study of divorce and parent-child relationships. *Journal of Marriage and the Family* 58, 356–65.

Amato, P. R. and Keith, B. (1991a). Parental divorce and adult well-being: a meta-analysis. *Journal of Marriage and the Family* 53, 43–58.

Amato, P. R. and Keith, B. (1991b). Parental divorce and the well-being of children: a meta-analysis. *Psychological Bulletin* 110, 26–46.

Ambrose, P., Harper, J., and Pemberton, R. (1983). *Surviving Divorce: Men Beyond Marriage*. Wheatsheaf Books, Brighton.

Anderson, E. R., Greene, S. M., Hetherington, E. M., and Clingempeel, W. G. (1999). The dynamics of parental remarriage: adolescent, parent, and sibling influences. In E. M. Hetherington (ed.), *Coping With Divorce, Single Parenting, and Remarriage*. Lawrence Erlbaum Associates, Mahwah, NJ.

Anderson, E. R., Lindner, M. S., and Bennion, L. D. (1992). The effect of family relationships on adolescent development during family reorganization. In E. M. Hetherington and W. G. Clingempeel (eds.), *Coping with Marital Transitions*, Serial No. 227. *Monographs of the Society for Research in Child Development* 57, 177-99.

Anyan, S. (1998). Adolescents' Perceptions of Family. Master's thesis, Department of Psychology, University of Auckland, Auckland.

Aquilino, W. (1996). The life course of children born to unmarried mothers: childhood living arrangements and young adult outcomes. *Journal of Marriage and the Family* 58, 293–310.

Arbuthnot, J. and Gordon, D. A. (1996). Does mandatory divorce education for parents work? *Family and Conciliation Courts Review* 34, 60–81.

Archard, D. (1993). *Children, Rights and Childhood*. Routledge, London.

Arditti, J. (1999). Rethinking relationships between divorced mothers and their children: capitalising on family strengths. *Family Relations* 48, 109–19.

Arditti, J. and Bickley, P. (1996). Fathers' involvement and mothers' parenting stress postdivorce. *Journal of Divorce and Remarriage* 26, 1–23.

Arditti, J. A. (1992). Factors related to custody, visitation, and child support for divorced fathers: an exploratory analysis. *Journal of Divorce and Remarriage* 17, 23–41.

Arditti, J. A. (1994). Noncustodial parents: emergent themes of diversity and process. *Marriage and Family Review* 20, 229–48.

Arditti, J. A. and Keith, T. Z. (1993). Visitation frequency, child support payment, and the father-child relationships postdivorce. *Journal of Marriage and the Family* 55, 699–712.

Argys, L. M., Peters, E., Brooks-Gunn, J., and Smith, J. (1998). The impact of child support on cognitive outcomes of young children. *Demography* 35, 159–73.

Ariès, P. (1970). *Centuries of Childhood*. Penguin, London.

Armistead, L., McCombs, A., Forehand, R., and Wierson, M. (1990). Coping with divorce: a study of young adolescents. *Journal of Clinical Child Psychology* 19, 79–84.

Arndt, B. (1999). Divide and ruin. *Sydney Morning Herald*, Oct. 9, Spectrum, pp. 1s–6s.

Aseltine, R. H., Jr. (1996). Pathways linking parental divorce with adolescent depression. *Journal of Health and Social Behavior* 37, 133–48.

Aseltine, R. H. and Kessler, R. C. (1993). Marital disruption and depression in a community sample. *Journal of Health and Social Behavior* 34, 237–51.

Atkinson, M. P. and Blackwelder, S. P. (1993). Fathering in the 20th Century. *Journal of Marriage and the Family* 55, 975–86.

Australian Bureau of Statistics (1991). *Australia's One Parent Families*. Cat. No. 1385.0. ABS, Canberra.

Australian Bureau of Statistics (1992). *1989-90 National Health Survey. Children's Immunisation, Australia*. Cat. No. 4379.0. ABS, Canberra.

Australian Bureau of Statistics (1993). *Australia's Families: Selected Findings from the Survey of Families in Australia 1992*. Cat. No. 4418.0. ABS, Canberra.

Australian Bureau of Statistics (1998). *Family Characteristics Australia 1997*. Cat. No. 3310.0. ABS, Canberra.

Australian Bureau of Statistics (1999). *Mental Health and Wellbeing: Profile of Adults, Australia*. Cat. No. 4326.0. ABS, Canberra.

Avenevoli, S., Sessa, F. M. and Steinberg, L. (1999). Family structure, parenting practices, and adolescent adjustment: an ecological examination. In E. M. Hetherington (ed.), *Coping With Divorce, Single Parenting, and Remarriage: A Risk and Resiliency Perspective*. Lawrence Erlbaum Associates, Mahwah, NJ.

Bachrach, L. L. (1975). *Marital Status and Mental Disorder: An Analytical Review*. DHEW Pub. No. (ADM) 75–217. US Government Printing Office, Washington, DC.

Bagley, C. and Ramsey, R. (1985). Sexual abuse in childhood: psychosocial outcomes and implications for social work practice. *Journal of Social Work and Human Sexuality* 4, 33–48.

Banister, H. and Ravden, M. (1944). The problem child and his environment. *British Journal of Psychology, General Section* 34, 60–5.

Banister, H. and Ravden, M. (1945). The environment and the child. *British Journal of Psychology, General Section* 35, 82–7.

Barber, B. L. and Lyons, J. M. (1994). Family processes and adolescent adjustment in intact and remarried families. *Journal of Youth and Adolescence* 23, 421–36.

Barnes, G. M. (1984). Adolescent alcohol abuse and other problem behaviors: their relationships and common parental influences. *Journal of Youth and Adolescence* 13, 329–48.

Baron, R. M. and Kenny, D. A. (1986). The moderator-mediator variable distinction in social psychological research: conceptual, strategic and statistical considerations. *Journal of Personality and Social Psychology* 51, 1173–82.

Baumrind, D. (1971). Current patterns of parental authority. *Developmental Psychology Monograph* 4 (pt. 2), 1–103.

Baumrind, D. (1991). Effective parenting during the early adolescent transition. In P. A. Cowan and E. M. Hetherington (eds.), *Family Transitions*. Lawrence Erlbaum Associates, Hillsdale, NJ.

Beautrais, A. L., Joyce, P. R., and Mulder, R. T. (1996). Risk factors for serious suicide attempts among youths aged 13 through 24 years. *Journal of the American Academy of Child and Adolescent Psychiatry* 35, 1174–82.

Bebbington, P. (1996). The origins of sex differences in depressive disorder: bridging the gap. *International Review of Psychiatry* 8, 295–332.

Beck, U. and Beck-Gernsheim, E. (1995). *The Normal Chaos of Love*. Polity Press, Cambridge, UK.

Bell, D. S. and Champion, R. A. (1979). Deviancy, delinquency and drug use. *British Journal of Psychiatry* 134, 269–76.

Belsky, J. (1984). The determinants of parenting: a process model. *Child Development* 55, 83-96.

Benzeval, M. (1998). The self-reported health status of lone parents. *Social Science and Medicine* 46, 1337–53.

Bernstein, B. (1970). A socio-linguistic approach to socialization. In J. Gumperz and D. Hymes (eds.), *Directions in Sociolinguistics*. Holt, Rinehart and Winston, New York.

Biblarz, T. J. and Gottainer, G. (2000). Family structure and children's success: a comparison of widowed and divorced single-mother families. *Journal of Marriage and the Family* 62, 533–48.

Biller, H. (1993). *Fathers and Families*. Auburn House, Westport, Conn.

Blankenhorn, D. (1995). *Fatherless America: Confronting Our Most Urgent Social Problem*. Basic Books, New York.

Block, J. H., Block, J., and Gjerde, P. F. (1986). The personality of children prior to divorce: a prospective study. *Child Development* 57, 827–40.

Bloom, B. L., Asher, S. J., and White, S. W. (1978). Marital disruption as a stressor: a review and analysis. *Psychological Bulletin* 85, 867–94.

Bohannen, P. (1970). Divorce chains, households of remarriage, and multiple divorcers. In P. Bohannen (ed.), *Divorce and After*. Doubleday, New York.

Bolger, N., DeLongis, A., Kessler, R. C., and Wethington, E. (1989). The contagion of stress across multiple roles. *Journal of Marriage and the Family* 51, 175–83.

Booth, A. (1999). Causes and consequences of divorce: reflections on recent research. In R. A. Thompson and P. A. Amato (eds.), *The Postdivorce Family: Children, Parenting, and Society*. Sage, Thousand Oaks.

Booth, A. and Amato, P. R. (1991). Divorce and psychological stress. *Journal of Health and Social Behavior* 32, 396–407.

Booth, A. and Amato, P. R. (2001). Parental pre-divorce relations and offspring post-divorce well-being. *Journal of Marriage and the Family* 65, 197–212.

Bowlby, J. (1969). *Attachment and Loss, vol. I: Attachment*. Hogarth, London.

Bowlby, J. (1988). Developmental psychiatry comes of age. *American Journal of Psychiatry* 145, 1–10.

Boyum, L. A. and Parke, R. D. (1995). The role of family emotional expressiveness in the development of children's social competence. *Journal of Marriage and the Family* 57, 593–608.

Bracher, M., Santow, G., Morgan, S. P., and Trussell, J. (1993). Marriage dissolution in Australia: models and explanations. *Population Studies* 47, 403–25.

Bradburn, N. (1967). *The Structure of Psychological Well-Being*. Aldine, Chicago.

Bradshaw, J. (1998). International comparisons of support for lone parents. In R. Ford and J. Millar (eds.), *Private Lives and Public Responses: Lone Parenthood and Future Policy in the UK*. Policy Studies Institute, London.

Brannen, J., Hantrais, L., O'Brien, M., and Wilson, G., eds. (1989). *Cross-National Studies of Household Resources After Divorce*. Aston University, Birmingham, UK.

Brannen, J., Heptinstall, E., and Bhopal, K. (1999a). *Children's Views and Experiences of FamilyLlife*. Thomas Coram Institute, London.

Brannen, J., Heptinstall, E. and Bhopal, K. (1999b). *Connecting Children: Care and Family Life in Later Childhood*. Routledge, Andover, Hants.

Bray, J. (1999). From marriage to remarriage and beyond: findings from the Developmental Issues in Stepfamilies Research Project. In E. M. Hetherington (ed.), *Coping with Divorce, Single Parenting, and Remarriage: A Risk and Resiliency Perspective*. Lawrence Erlbaum Associates, Mahwah, NJ.

Bray, J. H. (1988). Children's development during early remarriage. In E. M. Hetherington and J. D. Arasteh (eds.), *Impact of Divorce, Single Parenting, and*

Stepparenting on Children. Lawrence Erlbaum Associates, Hillsdale, NJ.

Bray, J. H. and Berger, S. H. (1993a). Developmental Issues in Stepfamilies Research Project: family relationships and parent-child interactions. *Journal of Family Psychology* 7, 76–90.

Bray, J. H. and Berger, S. H. (1993b). Nonresidential parent-child relationships following divorce and remarriage. In C. E. Depner and J. Bray (eds.), *Nonresidential Parenting: New Vistas in Family Living*. Sage, Newbury Park, Calif.

Bruce, M. L. and Kim, K. M. (1992). Differences in the effects of divorce on major depression in men and women. *American Journal of Psychiatry* 149, 914–17.

Bryson, A., Ford, R., and White, M. (1997). *Making Work Pay: Lone Mothers, Employment and Well-Being*. Joseph Rowntree Foundation, York, UK.

Buchanan, C. M. and Maccoby, E. E. (1996). *Adolescents After Divorce*. Harvard University Press, Cambridge, Mass.

Buchanan, C. M., Maccoby, E. E., and Dornbusch, S. N. (1991). Caught between parents: adolescents' experience in divorced homes. *Child Development* 62, 1008–29.

Bumpass, L. L. (1995). *The Declining Significance of Marriage: Changing Family Life in the United States*. National Survey of Families and Households Working Paper 66. Center for Demography and Ecology, Madison, Wis.

Bumpass, L. L. and Lu, H.-H. (2000). Trends in cohabitation and implications for children's family contexts in the United States. *Population Studies* 54, 29–41.

Bumpass, L. L., Martin, T. C., and Sweet, J. A. (1991). The impact of family background and early marital factors on marital disruption. *Journal of Family Issues* 12, 22–42.

Bumpass, L. L. and Sweet, J. A. (1989). National estimates of cohabitation. *Demography* 26, 615–25.

Bumpass, L. L., Sweet, J. A., and Castro-Martin, T. C. (1990). Changing pattern of remarriage. *Journal of Marriage and the Family* 52, 747–56.

Burghes, L. L. (1994). What happens to the children of single parent families? *British Medical Journal* 308, 1114–15.

Burns, A. (1980). *Breaking Up: Separation and Divorce in Australia*. Nelson, Melbourne.

Burns, A. (1984). Perceived causes of marriage breakdown and conditions of life. *Journal of Marriage and the Family* 46, 551–62.

Burns, A. and Dunlop, R. (1999). "How did you feel about it?" Children's feelings about their parents' divorce at the time and three and ten years later. *Journal of Divorce and Remarriage* 31, 19–36.

Burström, B., Diderichsen, F., Shouls, S., and Whitehead, M. (1999). Lone mothers in Sweden: trends in health and socioeconomic circumstances, 1979–1995. *Journal of Epidemiology and Community Health* 53, 750–6.

Camara, K. A. and Resnick, G. (1988). Interparental conflict and co-operation: factors moderating chidlen's post-divorce adjustment. In E. M. Hetherington and J. D. Arasteh (eds.), *Impact of Divorce, Single Parenting, and Stepparenting on Children*. Lawrence Erlbaum Associates, Hillsdale, NJ.

Cancian, M. and Meyer, D. (1998). Who gets custody? *Demography* 35, 147–57.

Capaldi, D. M. and Patterson, G. R. (1991). Relation of parental transitions to boys' adjustment problems, I: A linear hypothesis. II: Mothers at risk for transitions and unskilled parenting. *Developmental Psychology* 27, 489–504.

Carlson, M. and Danziger, S. (1999). Conabitation and the measurement of child poverty. *Review of Income and Wealth* 2, 179–91.

Casper, L. M. and Cohen, P. N. (2000). How does POSSLQ measure up? Historical estimates of cohabitation. *Demography* 37, 237–45.

Caya, M. L. and Liem, J. H. (1998). The role of sibling support in high-conflict families. *American Journal of Orthopsychiatry* 68, 327–33.

Cherlin, A. (1978). Remarriage as an incomplete institution. *American Journal of Sociology* 84, 634–50.

Cherlin, A. J. (1992). *Marriage, Divorce, Remarriage.* Revised and enlarged edn. Harvard University Press, Cambridge, Mass.

Cherlin, A. J., Chase-Lansdale, P. L., and McRae, C. (1998). Effects of parental divorce on mental health throughout the life course. *American Sociological Review* 63, 239–49.

Cherlin, A. J. and Furstenberg, F. F. (1986). *The New American Grandparent: A Place in the Family, a Life Apart.* Basic Books, New York.

Cherlin, A. J. and Furstenberg, F. F. (1994). Stepfamilies in the United States: a reconsideration. *Annual Review of Sociology* 20, 359–81.

Cherlin, A. J., Furstenberg, F. F., Chase-Lansdale, P. L., Kiernan, K. E., Robins, P. K., Morrison, D. R., and Teitler, J. O. (1991). Longitudinal studies of effects of divorce on children in Great Britain and the United States. *Science* 252, 1386–9.

Chetwin, A., Knaggs, T. and Young, P. T. W. A. (1998). *The Domestic Violence Legislation and Child Access in New Zealand.* Ministry of Justice, Wellington.

Clarke, A. D. B. and Clarke, A. M. (1976). The formative years? In A. M. Clarke and A. D. B. Clarke (eds.), *Early Experience: Myth and Evidence.* Open Books, London.

Clarke, L. and Berrington, A. (1999). Socio-demographic predictors of divorce. In J. Simons (ed.), *High Divorce Rates: the State of the Evidence on Reasons and Remedies.* Lord Chancellor's Department, London.

Clarke-Stewart, K. A., Vandell, D. L., McCartney, K., Owen, M. T., and Booth, C. (2000). Effects of parental separation and divorce on very young children. *Journal of Family Psychology* 14, 304–26.

Cleek, M. and Pearson, T. (1985). Perceived causes of divorce: an analysis of interrelationships. *Journal of Marriage and the Family* 47, 179–83.

Clingempeel, W. G., Colyar, J. J., Brand, E., and Hetherington, E. M. (1992). Children's relationships with maternal grandparents: a longitudinal study of family structure and pubertal status effects. *Child Development* 63, 1404–22.

Cockett, M. and Tripp, J. (1994). *The Exeter Family Study.* University of Exeter, Exeter, UK.

Cogswell, C. and Henry, C. S. (1995). Grandchildren's perceptions of grandparental support in divorced and intact families. *Journal of Divorce and Remarriage* 23, 127–50.

Cohen, O. (1995). Divorced fathers raise their children by themselves. *Journal of Divorce and Remarriage* 23, 55–73.

Coleman, J. S. (1988). Social capital in the creation of human capital. *American Journal of Sociology* 94, S95–S120.

Coleman, M. (1994). Stepfamilies in the United States: challenging biased assumptions. In A. Booth and J. Dunn (eds.), *Stepfamilies: Who Benefits? Who Does Not?*. Lawrence Erlbaum Associates, Hillsdale, NJ.

Coleman, M. and Ganong, L. (1984). Effect of family structure on family attitudes and expectations. *Family Relations* 33, 425–532.

Coleman, M. and Ganong, L. (1994). *Remarried Family Relationships*. Sage, Thousand Oaks, Calif.

Coleman, M. and Ganong, L. H. (1997). Stepfamilies from the stepfamily's perspective. *Marriage and Family Review* 26, 107–21.

Conger, R. D. and Elder, G. H. (1994). *Families in Troubled Times*. De Gruyter, New York.

Connell, J. P. (1985). A new multidimensional measure of children's perceptions of control. *Child Development* 56, 1018–41.

Cooksey, E. C. and Craig, P. H. (1998). Parenting from a distance: the effects of paternal characteristics on contact between nonresidential fathers and their children. *Demography* 35, 187–200.

Cooksey, E. C. and Fondell, M. M. (1996). Spending time with his kids: effects of family structure on fathers' and children's lives. *Journal of Marriage and the Family* 58, 693–707.

Cowan, R. and Roth, R. (1972). The turned on generation: where will they turn to? *Journal of Drug Education* 2, 39–47.

Cramer, D. (1993). Living alone, marital status, gender and health. *Journal of Community and Applied Social Psychology* 3, 1–15.

Creasey, G. L. (1993). The association between divorce and late adolescent grandchildren's relations with grandparents. *Journal of Youth and Adolescence* 22, 513–29.

Crook, T. and Eliot, J. (1980). Parental death during childhood and adult depression: a critical review of the literature. *Psychological Bulletin* 87, 252–9.

Crosbie-Burnett, M. and Giles-Sims, J. (1994). Adolescent adjustment and stepparenting styles. *Family Relations* 43, 394–9.

Cummings, E. M. and Davies, P. (1994). *Children and Marital Conflict: The Impact of Family Dispute and Resolution*. The Guildford Press, New York.

Cunningham, H. (1995). *Children and Childhood in Western Society since 1500*. Longman, Harlow, Essex.

Cunningham, J. M., Westerman, H. H., and Fischhoff, J. (1956). A follow-up study of patients seen in a psychiatric clinic for children. *American Journal of Orthopsychology* 26, 602–11.

Daly, M. and Wilson, M. (1998). *The Truth About Cinderella: A Darwinian View of Parental Love*. Weidenfeld and Nicolson, London.

D'Andrea, A. (1983). Joint custody as related to paternal involvement and paternal self-esteem. *Conciliation Courts Review* 21, 81–7.

Davies, L., Avison, W. R., and McAlpine, D. D. (1997). Significant life experiences and depression among single and married mothers. *Journal of Marriage and the Family* 59, 294–308.

Dawson, D. A. (1991). Family structure and children's health and well-being: data from the 1988 National Health Interview Study on Child Health. *Journal of Marriage and the Family* 53, 573–84.

De Mause, L. (1974). *The History of Childhood*. Psychohistory Press, New York.

de Singly, F. (1993). The social construction of a new paternal identity. In *Fathers of Tomorrow*. Denmark Ministry of Social Affairs, Copenhagen.

De Vaus, D. (1997). Family values in the nineties: gap or generation gap? *Family Matters* 48, 4–10.

Deater-Deckard, K. and Dunn, J. (1999). Multiple risks and adjustment in young children growing up in different family settings. In E. M. Hetherington (ed.), *Coping With Divorce, Single Parenting, and Remarriage: A Risk and Resiliency Perspective*. Lawrence Erlbaum Associates, Mahwah, NJ.

Deater-Deckard, K., Pickering, K., Dunn, J., and Golding, J. (1998). Family structure and depressive symptoms in men preceding and following the birth of a child. *American Journal of Psychiatry* 155, 818–23.

De'Ath, E. (1992). Stepfamilies in the context of contemporary family life. In E. De'Ath (ed.), *Stepfamilies: What Do We Know and What Do We Need to Know*. Significant Publications, Croydon.

DeGarmo, D. S. and Forgatch, M. S. (1999). Contexts as predictors of changing parenting practices in diverse family structures: a social interactional perspective of risk and resilience. In E. M. Hetherington (ed.), *Coping With Divorce, Single Parenting, and Remarriage: A Risk and Resiliency Perspective*. Lawrence Erlbaum Associates, Mahwah, NJ.

DeMaris, A. and Greif, G. L. (1997). Single custodial fathers and their children. In A. J. Hawkins and D. C. Dollahite (eds.), *Generative Fathering: Beyond Deficit Perspectives*. Sage, Thousand Oaks, Calif.

Demo, D. H. and Acock, A. C. (1996). Family structure, family process, and adolescent well-being. *Journal of Research on Adolescence* 6, 457–88.

Derevensky, J. L. and Deschamps, L. (1997). Young adults from divorced and intact families: perceptions about preferred custodial arrangements. *Journal of Divorce and Remarriage* 27, 105–22.

Doherty, W. J. and Needle, R. (1991). Psychological adjustment and substance use among adolescents before and after a parental divorce. *Child Development* 62, 328–37.

Doherty, W. J., Su, S., and Needle, R. (1989). Marital disruption and psychological well-being. *Journal of Family Issues* 10, 72–85.

Dornbusch, S. M., Ritter, P. L., Leiderman, P. H., Roberts, D. F., and Fraleigh, M. J. (1985). Single parents, extended households, and the control of adolescents. *Child Development* 56, 326–41.

Dornbusch, S. M., Ritter, P. L., Leiderman, P. H., Roberts, D. F., and Fraleigh, M. J. (1987). The relation of parenting style to adolescent school performance. *Child Development* 58, 1244–57.

Douglas, J. W. B. (1970). Broken families and child behaviour. *Journal of the Royal College of Physicians London* 4, 203–10.

Douglas, J. W. B. (1973). Early disturbing events and later enuresis. In I. Kolvin, R. C. MacKeith, and S. R. Meadow (eds.), *Bladder Control and Enuresis*. William Heinemann Books, London.

Downey, D. (1994). The school performance of children from single-mother and single-father families: economic or interpersonal deprivation? *Journal of Family Issues* 15, 129–47.

Downey, D. B., Ainsworth-Darnell, J. W., and Dufur, M. J. (1998). Sex of parent and children's well-being in single parent households. *Journal of Marriage and the Family* 60, 878–93.

Drapeau, S., Samson, C., and Saint-Jacques, M. (1999). The coping process among children of separated parents. *Journal of Divorce and Remarriage* 31, 15–37.

Dudley, J. R. (1991). The consequences of divorce proceedings for divorced fathers. *Journal of Divorce and Remarriage* 16, 17193.

Dunlop, R. and Burns, A. (1995). The sleeper effect myth or reality? *Journal of Marriage and the Family* 57, 37586.

Dunlop, R. and Burns, A. (1998). How did you feel about it? Children's reactions to their parents' divorce, at the time and three and ten years later. In *6th Australian Institute of Family Studies Conference*. AIFS, Melbourne.

Dunn, J. (1992). Sisters and brothers: current issues in developmental research. In F. Boer and J. Dunn (eds.), *Children's Sibling Relationships: Developmental and Clinical Issues*. Lawrence Erlbaum Associates, Hillsdale, NJ.

Dunn, J., Davies, L. C., O'Connor, T. G., and Sturgess, W. (in press a). Family lives and friendships: the perspectives of children in step-, single-parent and nonstep families. *Journal of Family Psychology*.

Dunn, J., Davies, L. C., O'Connor, T. G., and Sturgess, W. (in press b). Parents' and partners' life course and family experiences: links with parent–child relationships in different family settings. *Journal of Child Psychology and Psychiatry*.

Dunn, J., Deater-Deckard, K., Pickering, K., and Golding, J. (1999). Siblings, parents, and partners: family relationships within a longitudinal community study. *Journal of Child Psychology and Psychiatry* 40, 102537.

Dunn, J., Deater-Deckard, K., Pickering, K., O'Connor, T. G., Golding, J., and the ALSPAC Study Team (1998). Children's adjustment and prosocial behaviour in step-, single- and nonstep-family settings: findings from a community study. *Journal of Child Psychology and Psychiatry* 39, 108395.

Economic and Policy Analysis Division (1993). *A Profile of Early School Leavers*. Youth Profile No. 1. Dept. of Employment, Education and Training, Canberra, Australia.

Edgar, D. (1997). Developing the New Links Workplace: the future of family, work, and community relationships. In S. Dreman (ed.), *The Family on the*

Threshold of the 21st Century. Lawrence Erlbaum Associates, Mahwah, NJ.

Elder, G. H. (1994). Time, human agency, and social change: perspectives on the life course. *Social Psychology Quarterly* 57, 4–15.

Elder, G. H. (1998). The life course as developmental theory. *Child Development* 69, 1–12.

Elliott, B. J. and Richards, M. P. M. (1991a). Children and divorce: educational performance and behaviour before and after parental separation. *International Journal of Law and the Family* 5, 258–76.

Elliott, J. and Richards, M. (1991b). Parental divorce and the life chances of children. *Family Law* , 481–4.

Elliott, J., Richards, M., and Warwick, H. (1993). *The Consequences of Divorce for the Health and Well-Being of Adults and Children.* Final Report for Health Promotion Research Trust No. 2. Centre for Family Research, Cambridge.

Ellis, D. and Stuckless, N. (1996). *Mediating and Negotiating Marital Conflicts.* Sage, Thousand Oaks, Calif.

Ely, M., Richards, M. P. M., Wadsworth, M. E. J., and Elliott, B. J. (1999). Secular changes in the association of parental divorce and children's educational attainment – evidence from three British cohorts. *Journal of Social Policy* 28, 437–55.

Ely, M., West, P., Sweeting, H., and Richards, M. (2000). Teenage family life, life chances, lifestyles and health: a comparison of two contemporary cohorts. *International Journal of Law, Policy and the Family* 14, 1–30.

Emery, R. (1994). Psychological research on children, parents, and divorce. In R. Emery (ed.), *Renegotiating Family Relationships: Divorce, Child Custody, and Mediation.* Guildford Press, New York.

Emery, R. (1999). *Marriage, Divorce, and Children's Adjustment,* 2nd edn. Sage, Thousand Oaks, Calif.

Emery, R., Waldron, M., Kitzmann, K. M., and Aaron, J. (1999). Delinquent behavior, future divorce or nonmarital childbearing, and externalizing behavior among offspring: a 14-year prospective study. *Journal of Family Psychology* 13, 568–79.

Emery, R. E. (1982). Interparental conflict and the children of discord and divorce. *Psychological Bulletin* 92, 310–30.

Emery, R. E., Laumann-Billings, L., Waldron, M., Sbarra, D. A., and Dillon, P. (in press). Child custody mediation and litigation: Custody, contact, and co-parenting 12 years after initial dispute resolution. *Journal of Consulting and Clinical Psychology.*

Emery, R. E., Matthews, S. G., and Kitzmann, K. M. (1994). Child custody mediation and litigation: parents' satisfaction and functioning one year after settlement. *Journal of Consulting and Clinical Psychology* 62, 124–9.

Essen, J. (1978). Living in one-parent families: income and expenditure study. *Poverty* 40, 23–8.

Estaugh, V. and Power, C. (1991). Family disruption in early life and drinking in young adulthood. *Alcohol and Alcoholism* 26, 639–44.

Fergusson, D., Horwood, J., and Shannon, F. (1984). A proportional hazards model of family breakdown. *Journal of Marriage and the Family* 46, 539–49.

Fergusson, D. and Woodward, L. (2000). Teenage pregnancy and female educational underachievement: a prospective study of a New Zealand birth cohort. *Journal of Marriage and the Family* 62, 147–61.

Fergusson, D. M., Dimond, M. E., and Horwood, L. J. (1986). Childhood family placement history and behaviour problems in 6-year-old children. *Journal of Child Psychology and Psychiatry* 27, 213–26.

Fergusson, D. M., Horwood, L. J., and Lynskey, M. T. (1992). Family change, parental discord and early offending. *Journal of Child Psychology and Psychiatry* 33, 1059-75.

Fergusson, D. M., Lynskey, M. T., and Horwood, L. J. (1994). The effects of parental separation, the timing of separation and gender on children's performance on cognitive tests. *Journal of Child Psychology and Psychiatry* 35, 1077–92.

Ferri, E. (1976). *Growing Up in a One-Parent Family*. NFER Publishing Co., Windsor.

Ferri, E. (1984). *Step Children: A National Study*. NFER-Nelson, Windsor.

Ferri, E. and Smith, K. (1998). *Step-parenting in the 1990s*. Family Policy Studies Centre, London.

Finch, J. and Mason, J. (1993). *Negotiating Family Responsibilities*. Tavistock/Routledge, London.

Fine, M. A. and Demo, D. H. (2000). Divorce: societal ill or normative transition? In R. Milardo and S. Duck (eds.), *Families as Relationships*. John Wiley and Sons Ltd., Chichester, NY.

Fine, M. A. and Kurdek, L. A. (1995). Relation between marital quality and (step) parent-child relationship quality for parents and stepparents in stepfamilies. *Journal of Family Psychology* 9, 216–23.

Fine, M. A., Voydanoff, P., and Donnelly, B. W. (1993). Relations between parental control and warmth and well-being in stepfamilies. *Journal of Family Psychology* 7, 222–32.

Finlay-Jones, R. A. and Burvill, P. W. (1977). The prevalence of minor psychiatric morbidity in the community. *Psychological Medicine* 7, 475–89.

Fleming, R. (1999). *Families of a Different Kind*. Families of Remarriage Project: Wellington, New Zealand.

Flewelling, R. L. and Bauman, K. E. (1990). Family structure as a predictor of initial substance use and sexual intercourse in early adolescence. *Journal of Marriage and the Family* 52, 171–81.

Fogas, B. S., Wolchik, S., Braver, S. L., Freedom, D. S., and Bay, C. (1992). Locus of control as a mediator of negative divorce-related events and adjustment problems in children. *American Journal of Orthopsychiatry* 62, 589–98.

Ford, R. and Millar, J. (eds.) (1998). *Private Lives and Public Responses: Lone Parenthood and Future Policy in the UK*. Policy Studies Institute, London.

Forehand, R., Long, N., Brody, G. H., and Fauber, R. (1986). Home predictors of young adolescents' school behavior and academic performance. *Child Development* 57, 1528–33.

Forehand, R., Thomas, A. M., Wierson, M., Brody, G., and Fauber, R. (1990). Role of maternal functioning and parenting skills in adolescent functioning following parental divorce. *Journal of Abnormal Psychology* 99, 278–83.

Forgatch, M. S., Patterson, G. R., and Ray, J. A. (1996). Divorce and boys' adjustment problems: two paths with a single model. In E. M. Hetherington and E. A. Blechman (eds.), *Stress, Coping, and Resilience in Children and Families.* Lawrence Erlbaum Associates, Mahwah, NJ.

Forgatch, M. S., Patterson, G. R., and Skinner, M. L. (1988). A mediation model for the effect of divorce on antisocial behaviour in boys. In E. M. Hetherington and J. D. Arasteh (eds.), *Impact of Divorce, Single Parenting and Stepparenting on Children.* Lawrence Erlbaum Associates, Hillsdale, NJ.

Forthofer, M. S., Kessler, R. C., Story, A. L., and Gotlib, I. H. (1996). The effects of psychiatric disorders on the probability and timing of first marriage. *Journal of Health and Social Behavior* 37, 121–32.

Fox, G. L. and Kelly, R. F. (1995). Determinants of child custody arrangements at divorce. *Journal of Marriage and the Family* 57, 693–708.

Free, M. D. (1991). Clarifying the relationship between the broken home and juvenile delinquency: a critique of the current literature. *Deviant Behavior* 12, 109–67.

Freud, S. (1913). The claims of psycho-analysis to scientific interest: the interest of psycho-analysis from a developmental point of view. In J. Strachey (ed.), *The Standard Edition of the Complete Psychological Works of Sigmund Freud.* Hogarth Press, London.

Freud, S. (1940). An outline of psychoanalysis. In J. Strachey (ed.), *The Standard Edition of the Complete Psychological Works of Sigmund Freud.* Hogarth Press, London.

Freud, S. (1955). The psychogenesis of a case of homosexuality in a woman. In J. Strachey (ed.), *The Standard Edition of the Complete Psychological Works of Sigmund Freud.* Hogarth Press, London.

Fryer, D. (1990). The mental health costs of unemployment: towards a social psychological concept of poverty? *British Journal of Clinical and Social Psychiatry* 7, 164–75.

Funder, K. (1996). *Remaking Families: Adaptation of Parents and Children to Divorce.* Australian Institute of Family Studies, Melbourne.

Funder, K., Harrison, M., and Weston, R. (1993). *Settling Down: Pathways of Parents after Divorce.* Australian Institute of Family Studies, Melbourne.

Funder, K. and Smyth, B. (1996). Family law reforms and attitudes to parental responsibility. *Family Matters* 45, 10–15.

Furstenberg, F. F. (1988). Child care after divorce and remarriage. In E. M. Hetherington and J. D. Arasteh (eds.), *Impact of Divorce, Single Parenting, and Stepparenting on Children.* Lawrence Erlbaum Associates, Hillsdale, NJ.

Furstenberg, F. F. (1990). Divorce and the American family. *Annual Review of Sociology* 16, 379–403.

Furstenberg, F. F. and Hughes, M. E. (1995). Social capital and successful development among at-risk youth. *Journal of Marriage and the Family* 57, 580–92.

Furstenberg, F. F. and Kiernan, K. E. (in press). Delayed parental divorce: how much do children benefit? *Journal of Marriage and the Family*.

Furstenberg, F. F., Morgan, S., and Allison, P. (1987). Paternal participation and children's well-being after marital dissolution. *American Sociological Review* 52, 695–701.

Furstenberg, F. F. and Nord, C. W. (1985). Parenting apart: patterns of childrearing after marital dissolution. *Journal of Marriage and the Family* 47, 893–904.

Furstenberg, F. F., Nord, C. W., Peterson, J. L., and Zill, N. (1983). The life course of children of divorce: marital disruption and parental contact. *American Sociological Review* 48, 656–68.

Furstenberg, F. F. and Teitler, J. O. (1994). Reconsidering the effects of marital disruption: What happens to children of divorce in early adulthood? *Journal of Family Issues* 15, 173–90.

Gabardi, L. and Rosen, L. A. (1992). Intimate relationships: college students from divorced and intact families. *Journal of Divorce and Remarriage* 18 (3/4), 25–56.

Galligan, R. J. and Bahr, S. J. (1978). Economic well-being and marital stability: implications for income maintenance programs. *Journal of Marriage and the Family* 40, 283–90.

Ganong, L. H. and Coleman, M. (1994). Adolescent stepchild–stepparent relationships: changes over time. In K. Pasley and M. Ihinger-Tallman (eds.), *Stepparenting: Issues in Theory, Research, and Practice*. Greenwood Press, Westport, Conn.

Garfinkel, I. and McLanahan, S. (1986). *Single Mothers and Their Children: A New American Dilemma*. Urban Institute, Washington, DC.

Garmezy, N. (1985). Stress resistent children: the search for protective factors. In J. Stevenson (ed.), *Recent Research in Developmental Psychopathology*. Pergamon Press, Oxford.

Geasler, M. J. and Blaisure, K. R. (1999). 1998 nationwide survey of court-connected divorce education programs. *Family and Conciliation Courts Review* 37, 36-63.

Gerstel, N., Riessman, C. K., and Rosenfield, S. (1985). Explaining the symptomatology of separated and divorced women and men: the role of material conditions and social networks. *Social Forces* 64, 84–101.

Gibson, H. B. (1969). Early delinquency in relation to broken homes. *Journal of Child Psychology and Psychiatry* 10, 195–204.

Gibson, J. (1992). *Custodial Fathers and Access Patterns*. Family Court Research Report No. 10. Family Court of Australia, Office of the Chief Executive, Sydney.

Giddens, A. (1992). *The Transformation of Intimacy: Sexuality, Love and Eroticism in Modern Societies*. Polity Press, Cambridge, UK.

Gigy, L. and Kelly, J. (1992). Reasons for divorce: perspectives of divorcing men and women. *Journal of Divorce and Remarriage* 18, 169–87.

Gilby, R. L. and Pederson, D. R. (1982). The development of the child's concept of family. *Canadian Journal of Behavioral Sciences* 14, 111–21.

Gladstone, G., Parker, G., Wilhelm, K., Mitchell, P., and Austin, M.-P. (1999). Characteristics of depressed patients who report childhood sexual abuse. *American Journal of Psychiatry* 156, 431–7.

Glenn, N. D. (1997). A reconsideration of the effect of no-fault divorce on divorce rates. *Journal of Marriage and the Family* 59, 1023–5.

Glenn, N. D. (1999). Further discussion of the effects of no-fault divorce on divorce rates. *Journal of Marriage and the Family* 61, 800–2.

Glenn, N. D. and Kramer, K. B. (1985). The psychological well-being of adult children of divorce. *Journal of Marriage and the Family* 47, 905–12.

Glenn, N. D. and Kramer, K. B. (1987). The marriages and divorces of the children of divorce. *Journal of Marriage and the Family* 49, 811–25.

Glick, P. C. (1989). Remarried families, stepfamilies, and stepchildren: A brief demographic profile. *Family Relations* 38, 24–7.

Gollop, M. M., Taylor, N., and Smith, A. (2000). Children's perspectives on their parents' separation. In A. Smith, N. Taylor and M. M. Gollop (eds.), *Childen's Voices*. Pearson Education, Auckland.

Goode, W. J. (1993). *World Changes in Divorce Patterns*. Yale University Press, New Haven.

Gorrell Barnes, G., Thompson, P., Daniel, G., and Burchardt, N. (1998). *Growing Up in Stefamilies*. Clarendon Press, Oxford.

Gotlib, I. H. and McCabe, S. B. (1990). Marriage and psychopathology. In F. D. Fincham and T. N. Bradbury (eds.), *The Psychology of Marriage: Basic Issues and Applications*. Guilford Press, New York.

Gottman, J. M. (1998). Toward a process model of men in marriages and families. In A. Booth and A. C. Crouter (eds.), *Men in Families: When Do They Get Involved? What Difference Does It Make?* Lawrence Erlbaum Associates, Mahwah, NJ.

Granville-Grossman, K. L. (1968). The early environment in affective disorders. In A. Coppen and A. Walk (eds.), *Recent Developments in Affective Disorders*. Royal Medico-Psychological Association, London.

Gregg, P., Harkness, S., and Machin, S. (1999). *Child Development and Family Income*. Joseph Rowntree Foundation, York.

Grief, G. L. (1995). When divorced fathers want no contact with their children: a preliminary analysis. *Journal of Divorce and Remarriage* 23, 75–84.

Gross, P. (1987). Defining post-divorce remarriage families: a typology based on the subjective perceptions of children. *Journal of Divorce* 10, 205–17.

Grossman, F. K., Pollack, W. S., and Golding, E. (1988). Fathers and children: predicting the quality and quantity of fathering. *Developmental Psychology* 24, 82–91.

Grych, J. H. (1998). Children's appraisals of interparental conflict: situational and contextual influences. *Journal of Family Psychology* 12, 437–53.

Grych, J. H. and Fincham, F. D. (1990). Marital conflict and children's adjustment: a cognitive contextual framework. *Psychological Bulletin* 108, 267–90.

Gunnoe, M. L. (1993). Noncustodial mothers' and fathers' contribution to the adjustment of adolescent stepchildren. Unpublished doctoral dissertation, University of Virginia, Charlottesville .

Gunnoe, M. L. and Hetherington, E. M. (1995). *Custodial Parents, Noncustodial Parents, Stepparents, and Adolescent Adjustment in Enduring Stepfamily Systems*. Child Trends Inc., Washington, DC.

Guttman, J. (1993). *Divorce in Psycho-social Perspective: Theory and Research*. Lawrence Erlbaum Associates, Hillsdale, NJ.

Häfner, H. (1992). Epidemiology of schizophrenia. In F. P. Ferrero, A. E. Haynal, and N. Sartorius (eds.), *Schizophrenia and Affective Psychoses: Nosology in Contemporary Psychiatry*. John Libbey, London.

Hajema, K.-J. and Knibbe, R. A. (1998). Changes in social roles as predictors of changes in drinking behaviour. *Addiction* 93, 1717–27.

Halford, W. K. and Osgarby, S. M. (1993). Alcohol abuse in clients presenting with marital problems. *Journal of Family Psychology* 6, 1–11.

Hall, W., Teesson, M., Lynskey, M., and Degenhardt, L. (1999). The 12-month prevalence of substance use and ICD-10 substance use disorders in Australian adults: findings from the National Survey of Mental Health and Well-Being. *Addiction* 94, 1541–50.

Hanson, T. L. (1999). Does parental conflict explain why divorce is negatively associated with child welfare? *Social Forces* 77, 1283–1315.

Hanson, T. L., McLanahan, S. S., and Thomson, E. (1996). Double jeopardy: parental conflict and stepfamily outcomes for children. *Journal of Marriage and the Family* 58, 141–54.

Hanson, T. L., McLanahan, S. S., and Thomson, E. (1998). Windows on divorce: before and after. *Social Science Research* 27, 329–49.

Harris, T., Brown, G. W., and Bifulco, A. (1986). Loss of parent in childhood and adult psychiatric disorder: the role of lack of adequate parental care. *Psychological Medicine* 16, 641–59.

Haskey, J. (1992). Patterns of marriage, divorce, and cohabitation in the different countries of Europe. *Population Trends* 69, 27–36.

Haskey, J. (1993). Lone parents and married parents with dependent children in Great Britain: a comparison of their occupation and social class profiles. *Population Trends* 72, 34–44.

Haskey, J. (1994a). Estimated numbers of one-parent families and their prevalence in Great Britain in 1991. *Population Trends* 78, 5–19.

Haskey, J. (1994b). Stepfamilies and stepchildren in Great Britain. *Population Trends* 76, 17–28.

Helgason, T. (1964). Epidemiology of mental disorders in Iceland. *Acta Psychiatrica Scandinavica* 173, 11–258.

Helzer, J. E., Burnham, A., and McEvoy, L. T. (1991). Alcohol abuse and dependence. In L. N. Robins and D. A. Regier (eds.), *Psychiatric Disorders in America*. Free Press, New York.

Henderson, S., Byrne, D. G., and Duncan-Jones, P. (1981). *Neurosis and the Social Environment*. Academic Press, Sydney.

Henry, C. S. and Lovelace, S. G. (1995). Family resources and adolescent family life satisfaction in remarried family households. *Journal of Family Issues* 16, 765–86.

Herrerias, C. (1995). Noncustodial mothers following divorce. *Marriage and Family Review* 20, 233–55.

Hetherington, E. M. (1972). Effects of father absence on personality development in adolescent daughters. *Developmental Psychology* 7, 313–26.

Hetherington, E. M. (1989). Coping with family transitions: Winners, losers, and survivors. *Child Development* 60, 1–14.

Hetherington, E. M. (1991). The role of individual differences and family relationships in children's coping with divorce and remarriage. In P. A. Cowan and E. M. Hetherington (eds.), *Family Transitions*. Lawrence Erlbaum Associates, Hillsdale, NJ.

Hetherington, E. M. (1993). An overview of the Virginia Longitudinal Study of Divorce and Remarriage with a focus on early adolescence. *Journal of Family Psychology* 7, 39–56.

Hetherington, E. M. (1999). Should we stay together for the sake of the children? In E. M. Hetherington (ed.), *Coping with Divorce, Single Parenting, and Remarriage: A Risk and Resiliency Perspective*. Lawrence Erlbaum Associates, Mahwah, NJ.

Hetherington, E. M. and Clingempeel, W. G. (1992). Coping with marital transitions. *Monographs of the Society for Research in Child Development* 57, 1-242.

Hetherington, E. M. and Henderson, S. H. (1997). Fathers in stepfamilies. In M. E. Lamb (ed.), *The Role of the Father in Child Development*, 3rd edn. John Wiley and Sons, New York.

Hetherington, E. M., Henderson, S. H., and Reiss, D. (1999). Adolescent functioning in stepfamilies: family functioning and adolescent adjustment. *Child Development Monograph* 64, 1–222.

Hetherington, E. M. and Jodl, K. M. (1994). Stepfamilies as settings for child development. In A. Booth and J. Dunn (eds.), *Stepfamilies: Who Benefits? Who Does Not?* Lawrence Erlbaum Associates, Hillsdale, NJ.

Hetherington, E. M. and Stanley-Hagan, M. (1999). The adjustment of children with divorced parents: a risk and resiliency perspective. *Journal of Child Psychology and Psychiatry* 40, 129–40.

Hilton, J. M. and Macari, D. P. (1997). Grandparent involvement following divorce: a comparison of single-mother and single-father families. *Journal of Divorce and Remarriage* 28, 203–24.

Holden, G. W., Geffner, R., and Jouriles, E. N. (1998). *Children Exposed to Marital Violence: Theory, Research, and Applied Issues*. American Psychological Association, Washington, DC.

Holden, K. C. and Smock, P. J. (1991). The economic costs of marital dissolution: why do women bear a disproportionate cost? *Annual Review of Sociology* 17, 51–78.

Hope, S., Power, C., and Rodgers, B. (1998). The relationship between parental separation in childhood and problem drinking in adulthood. *Addiction* 93, 505–14.

Hope, S., Power, C., and Rodgers, B. (1999). Does financial hardship account for elevated psychological distress in lone mothers? *Social Science and Medicine* 49, 1637–49.

Hope, S., Rodgers, B., and Power, C. (1999). Marital status transitions and psychological distress: Longitudinal evidence from a national population sample. *Psychological Medicine* 29, 381–9.

Illsley, R. and Thompson, B. (1961). Women from broken homes. *Sociological Review* 43, 27–54.

James, A. (1999). Parents: a children's perspective. In A. Bainham, S. D. Sclater, and M. Richards (eds.), *What is a Parent? A Socio-Legal Analysis*. Hart Publishing, Oxford.

James, A., Jenks, C. and Prout, A. (1991). *Theorizing Childhood*. Polity Press, Cambridge, UK.

Jarvis, S. and Jenkins, S. P. (1998). Marital dissolution and income change: evidence for Britain. In R. Ford and J. Millar (eds.), *Private Lives and Public Responses: Lone Parenthood and Future Policy in the UK*. Policy Studies Institute, London.

Jarvis, T. J., Copeland, J., and Walton, L. (1998). Exploring the nature of the relationship between child sexual abuse and substance use among women. *Addiction* 93, 865–75.

Jekielek, S. M. (1998). Parental conflict, marital disruption and children's emotional well-being. *Social Forces* 76, 905–36.

Jenkins, J. (1992). Sibling relationships in disharmonious homes: Potential difficulties and protective factors. In F. Boer and J. Dunn (eds.), *Children's Sibling Relationships: Developmental and Clinical Issues*. Lawrence Erlbaum Associates, Hillsdale, NJ.

Johnston, J. (1999). Response to Clare Dalton's "When paradigms collide: protecting battered parents and their children in the family court system." *Family and Conciliation Courts Review* 37, 422–8.

Johnston, J., Kline, M., and Tschann, J. (1989). Ongoing postdivorce conflict: effects on children of joint custody and frequent access. *American Journal of Orthopsychiatry* 59, 576–92.

Jordan, P. (1985). *The Effects of Marital Separation on Men*. Family Court Research Report No. 5. Family Court of Australia, Office of the Chief Executive, Sydney.

Joung, I. M. A., Stronks, K., van de Mheen, H., and Mackenbach, J. P. (1995). Health behaviours explain part of the differences in self-reported health associated with partner/marital status in The Netherlands. *Journal of Epidemiology and Community Health* 49, 482–8.

Juby, H. and Farrington, D. P. (2001). Disentangling the link between disrupted families and delinquency. *British Journal of Criminology* 41, 22–40.

Kalter, N. (1987). Long-term effects of divorce on children: a developmental vulnerability model. *American Journal of Orthopsychiatry* 57, 587–600.

Kalter, N. and Plunkett, J. W. (1984). Children's perceptions of the causes and consequences of divorce. *Journal of the American Academy of Child and Adolescent Psychiatry* 23, 326–34.

Kalter, N., Riemer, B., Brickman, A., and Chen, J. W. (1985). Implications of parental divorce for female development. *Journal of the American Academy of Child Psychiatry* 24, 538–44.

Karney, B. R. and Bradbury, T. N. (1995). The longitudinal course of marital quality and stability: a review of theory, method, and research. *Psychological Bulletin* 118, 3–34.

Kelly, J. (1991). Parent interaction after divorce: comparison of mediated and adversarial divorce processes. *Behavioral Sciences and the Law* 9, 387–98.

Kempton, T., Armistead, L., Wierson, M., and Forehand, R. (1991). Presence of a sibling as a potential buffer following parent divorce: an examination of young adolescents. *Journal of Clinical Child Psychology* 20, 434–8.

Kendler, K. S., Walters, E. E., Neale, M. C., Kessler, R. C., Heath, A. C., and Eaves, L. J. (1995). The structure of the genetic and environmental risk factors for six major psychiatric disorders in women: phobia, generalized anxiety disorder, panic disorder, bulimia, major depression and alcoholism. *Archives of General Psychiatry* 52, 374–83.

Kennedy, G. E. and Kennedy, C. E. (1993). Grandparents: A special resource for children in stepfamilies. *Journal of Divorce and Remarriage* 19, 45–68.

Kessler, R., Davis, C. G., and Kendler, K. S. (1997). Childhood adversity and adult psychiatric disorder in the US National Comorbidity Survey. *Psychological Medicine* 27, 1101–19.

Kessler, R. C. and Magee, W. J. (1993). Childhood adversities and adult depression: basic patterns of association in a US national survey. *Psychological Medicine* 23, 679–90.

Kessler, R. C. and Magee, W. J. (1994). Childhood family violence and adult recurrent depression. *Journal of Health and Social Behavior* 35, 13–27.

Kessler, R. C., McGonagle, K. A., Zhao, S., Nelson, C. B., Hughes, M., Eshleman, S., Wittchen, H.-U., and Kendler, K. S. (1994). Lifetime and 12-month prevalence of DSM-III-R psychiatric disorders in the United States. *Archives of General Psychiatry* 51, 8–19.

Kessler, R. C., Walters, E. E., and Forthofer, M. S. (1998). The social consequences of psychiatric disorders, III: probability of marital stability. *American Journal of Psychiatry* 155, 1092–6.

Kiernan, K. (1997). *The Legacy of Parental Divorce: Social, Economic and Demographic Experiences in Adulthood*. CASE paper 1. Centre for Analysis of

Social Exclusion, London.

Kiernan, K. (1999a). Cohabitation in western Europe. *Population Trends* 96, 25–32.

Kiernan, K. (1999b). European perspectives on non-marital childbearing. *Population Trends* 98, 11–20.

Kiernan, K. and Hobcraft, J. (1997). Parental divorce during childhood: age at first intercourse, partnership and parenthood. *Population Studies* 51, 41–55.

Kiernan, K. E. (1992). The impact of family disruption in childhood and transitions made in young adult life. *Population Studies* 46, 213–34.

Kiernan, K. E. and Mueller, G. (1999). Who divorces? In S. MacRae (ed.), *Population Change in Britain*. Oxford University Press, Oxford.

Kim, L. S., Sandler, I. N., and Tein, J.-Y. (1997). Locus of control as a stress moderator and mediator in children of divorce. *Journal of Abnormal Child Psychology* 25, 145–55.

King, V. (1994a). Nonresident father involvement and child well-being: can dads make a difference? *Journal of Family Issues* 15, 78–96.

King, V. (1994b). Variation in the consequences of nonresident father involvement for children's well-being. *Journal of Marriage and the Family* 56, 963–72.

Kinnaird, K. L. and Gerrard, M. (1986). Premarital sexual behavior and attitudes toward marriage and divorce among young women as a function of their mothers' marital status. *Journal of Marriage and the Family* 48, 757–65.

Kitson, G., Babri, K., and Raschke, B. (1985). Who divorces and why? A review. *Journal of Family Issues* 6, 255–93.

Kitson, G. and Sussman, M. (1982). Marital complaints, demographic characteristics and symptoms of mental distress in divorce. *Journal of Marriage and the Family* 44, 87-101.

Koestner, R., Franz, C. E., and Weinberger, J. (1990). The family origins of empathetic concern: a 26-year longitudinal study. *Journal of Personality and Social Psychology* 58, 709–11.

Koller, K. M. (1971). Parental deprivation, family background and female delinquency. *British Journal of Psychiatry* 118, 319–27.

Koller, K. M. and Castanos, J. N. (1968). The influence of childhood parental deprivation in attempted suicide. *Medical Journal of Australia* 1, 396–9.

Koller, K. M. and Castanos, J. N. (1969). Family background and life situation in alcoholics: a comparative study of parental deprivation and other features in Australians. *Archives of General Psychiatry* 21, 602–10.

Koller, K. M. and Castanos, J. N. (1970). Family background in prison groups. *British Journal of Psychiatry* 117, 371–80.

Koller, K. M. and Williams, W. T. (1974). Early parental deprivation and later behavioural outcomes: cluster analysis study of normal and abnormal groups. *Australian and New Zealand Journal of Psychiatry* 8, 89–96.

Kolvin, I., Miller, F. J. W., Fleeting, M., and Kolvin, P. A. (1988). Social and parenting factors affecting criminal offence rates: findings from the Newcastle Thousand Family Study (1947–1980). *British Journal of Psychiatry* 152, 80–90.

Kruk, E. (1991). Discontinuity between pre- and post-divorce father–child relationships: new evidence regarding paternal disengagement. *Journal of Divorce and Remarriage* 16, 195–227.

Kruk, E. and Hall, B. L. (1995). The disengagement of paternal grandparents subsequent to divorce. *Journal of Divorce and Remarriage* 23, 131–47.

Kuh, D. and Maclean, M. (1990). Women's childhood experience of parental separation and their subsequent health and socioeconomic status in adulthood. *Journal of Biosocial Science* 22, 121–35.

Kulka, R. A. and Weingarten, H. (1979). The long-term effects of parental divorce in childhood on adult adjustment. *Journal of Social Issues* 35, 50–78.

Kurdek, C. A., Blisk, D., and Siesky, A. E. (1981). Correlates of children's long term adjustment to their parents' divorce. *Developmental Psychology* 17, 565–79.

Kurdek, L. and Berg, B. (1987). Children's beliefs about parental divorce scale: psychometric characteristics and concurrent validity. *Journal of Consulting and Clinical Psychology* 55, 712–18.

Kurdek, L. and Sinclair, R. J. (1986). Adolescents' views on issues related to divorce. *Journal of Adolescent Research* 1, 373–87.

Kurdek, L. A. (1994). Remarriages and stepfamilies are not inherently problematic. In A. Booth and J. Dunn (eds.), *Stepfamilies: Who Benefits? Who Does Not?* Lawrence Erlbaum Associates, Hillsdale, NJ.

Kurdek, L. A. and Fine, M. A. (1995). Mothers, fathers, stepfathers, and siblings as providers of supervision, acceptance, and autonomy to young adolescents. *Journal of Family Psychology* 9, 95–9.

Kurdek, L. A., Fine, M. A., and Sinclair, R. J. (1995). School adjustment in sixth graders: Parenting transitions, family climate, and peer norm effects. *Child Development* 66, 430–45.

Kurdek, L. A. and Siesky, A. E. (1980). Children's perceptions of their parents' divorce. *Journal of Divorce* 3, 339–78.

Lahey, B. B., Hartdagen, S. E., Frick, P. J., McBurnett, K., Connor, R., and Hynd, G. W. (1988). Conduct disorder: Parsing the confounded relation to parental divorce and antisocial personality. *Journal of Abnormal Psychology* 97, 334–7.

Lamb, M. (1995). Paternal influences on child development. In M. C. P. van Dongen, G. A. B. Frinking, and M. J. G. Jacobs (eds.), *Changing Fatherhood: An Interdisciplinary Perspective*. Thesis Publishers, Amsterdam.

Lamb, M. E. (1999). Noncustodial fathers and their impact on children of divorce. In R. A. Thompson and P. R. Amato (eds.), *The Postdivorce Family: Children, Parenting, and Society*. Sage, Thousand Oaks, Calif.

Lamborn, S. D., Mounts, N. S., Steinberg, L., and Dornbusch, S. M. (1991). Patterns of competence and adjustment among adolescents from authoritative, authoritarian, indulgent, and neglectful families. *Child Development* 62, 1049–65.

Laumann-Billings, L. and Emery, R. (2000). Distress among young adults from divorced families. *Journal of Abnormal Psychology* 14, 671–87.

Lavers, C. A. and Sonuga-Barke, E. J. S. (1997). On the grandmothers' role in the adjustment and maladjustment of grandchildren. *Journal of Child Psychology and Psychiatry* 38, 747–53.

Lee, V. E. and Burkham, D. T. (1994). Family structure and its effect on behavioral and emotional problems in young adolescents. *Journal of Research on Adolescence* 4, 405–37.

Lefcourt, H. M. (1976). *Locus of Control: Current Trends in Theory and Research*, 2nd edn. Lawrence Erlbaum Associates, Hillsdale, NJ.

Lindelow, M., Hardy, R. and Rodgers, B. (1997). Development of a scale to measure symptoms of anxiety and depression in the general population: the Psychiatric Symptom Frequency (PSF) scale in the UK general population. *Journal of Epidemiology and Community Health* 51, 549–57.

Lipman, E. L., Boyle, M. H., Dooley, M. D., and Offord, D. R. (1998). *Children and Lone-mother Families: An Investigation of Factors Influencing Child Well-being*. Report No. WP-98-11E. Human Resources Development Canada, Ottawa.

Lloyd, C. (1980). Life events and depressive disorder reviewed, I: Events as predisposing factors. *Archives of General Psychiatry* 37, 529–35.

Lorenz, F. O., Simons, R. L., Conger, R. D., Elder, G. H., Johnson, C., and Chao, W. (1997). Married and recently divorced mothers' stressful events and distress: tracing change across time. *Journal of Marriage and the Family* 59, 219–32.

Lussier, G., Deater-Deckard, K., Dunn, J., and Davies, L. (submitted). Support across two generations: Children's closeness to grandparents following parental divorce and remarriage. *Journal of Family Psychology*.

Lyon, C. M., Surrey, E., and Timms, J. E. (1999). *Effective Support Services for Children and Young People When Parental Relationships Break Down*. Gulbenkian Foundation. Centre for the Study of the Child, the Family, and the Law, Liverpool.

Maccoby, E. and Martin, J. (1983). Socialisation in the context of the family. In E. Hetherington (ed.), *Handbook of Child Psychology: Socialisation, Personality, and Social Development*. Wiley, New York.

Maccoby, E. E. and Mnookin, R. H. (1992). *Dividing the Child: Social and Legal Dilemmas of Custody*. Harvard University Press, Cambridge, Mass.

MacKinnon, A., Henderson, S., and Andrews, G. (1993). Parental "affectionless control" as an antecedent to adult depression: a risk factor refined. *Psychological Medicine* 23, 135–41.

Maclean, M. and Eekelaar, J. (1983). *Children and Divorce: Economic Factors*. Centre for Socio-Legal Studies, Oxford.

Maclean, M. and Eekelaar, J. (1997). *The Parental Obligation: A Study of Parenthood Across Households*. Hart Publishing, Oxford.

Maclean, M. and Kuh, D. (1991). The long term effects for girls of parental divorce. In M. Maclean and D. Groves (eds.), *Women's Issues in Social Policy*. Routledge, London.

MacLean, M. and Richards, M. (1999). Parents and divorce: changing patterns of public intervention. In A. Bainham, S. D. Sclater and M. Richards (eds.), *What is a Parent? A Socio-Legal Analysis*. Hart Publishing, Oxford.

Maclean, M. and Wadsworth, M. E. J. (1988). The interests of children after parental divorce: A long-term perspective. *International Journal of Law and the Family* 2, 155–66.

Manning, W. D. and Lichter, D. T. (1996). Parental cohabitation and children's economic well-being. *Journal of Marriage and the Family* 58, 998–1010.

Marris, P. (1958). *Widows and Their Families*. Routledge, London.

Marsiglio, W. (1991). Paternal engagement activities with minor children. *Journal of Marriage and the Family* 53, 973–86.

Martin, T. C. and Bumpass, L. L. (1989). Recent trends in marital disruption. *Demography* 26, 37-51.

Mastekaasa, A. (1994). Psychological well-being and marital dissolution: selection effects? *Journal of Family Issues* 15, 208–28.

Mazur, E. (1993). Developmental differences in children's understanding of marriage, divorce, and remarriage. *Journal of Applied Developmental Psychology* 14, 191–212.

McDonald, M. (1990). *Children's Perceptions of Access and Their Adjustment in the Post-Separation Period*. Family Court Research Report No 9. Family Court of Australia, Office of the Chief Executive, Sydney.

McDonald, W. L. and DeMaris, A. (1995). Remarriage, stepchildren, and marital conflict: challenges to the incomplete institutionalisation hypothesis. *Journal of Marriage and the Family* 57, 387–98.

McFarlane, A. H., Bellissimo, A., and Norman, G. R. (1995). Family structure, family functioning and adolescent well-being, the transcendent influence of parental style. *Journal of Child Psychology and Psychiatry* 36, 847–64.

McGee, R., Williams, S., Kashani, J. H., and Silva, P. A. (1983). Prevalence of self-reported depressive symptoms and associated social factors in mothers in Dunedin. *British Journal of Psychiatry* 143, 473–9.

McGurk, H. and Glachan, M. (1987). Children's conception of the continuity of parenthood following divorce. *Journal of Child Psychology and Psychiatry* 28, 427–35.

McHenry, P. C., McKelvey, M. W., Leigh, D., and Wark, L. (1996). Nonresidential father involvement: a comparison of divorced, separated, never married, and remarried fathers. *Journal of Divorce and Remarriage* 25, 1–13.

McLanahan, S. (1983). Family structure and stress: a longitudinal comparison of two-parent and female-headed families. *Journal of Marriage and the Family* 45, 347–57.

McLanahan, S. (1999). Father absence and the welfare of children. In E. M. Hetherington (ed.), *Coping With Divorce, Single Parenting, and Remarriage: A Risk and Resiliency Perspective*. Lawrence Erlbaum Associates, Mahwah, NJ.

McLanahan, S., Astone, N. M., and Marks, N. F. (1991). The role of mother-only families in reducing poverty. In C. A. Huston (ed.), *Children in Poverty: Child*

Development and Public Policy. Cambridge University Press, Cambridge.

McLanahan, S. and Sandefur, G. (1994). *Growing Up with a Single Parent: What Helps, What Hurts*. Harvard University Press, Cambridge, Mass.

McLeod, J. D. (1991). Childhood parental loss and adult depression. *Journal of Health and Social Behavior* 32, 205–20.

McLeod, J. D. and Shanahan, M. J. (1996). Trajectories of poverty and children's mental health. *Journal of Health and Social Behavior* 37, 207–20.

Menaghan, E. G. (1985). Depressive affect and subsequent divorce: a panel analysis. *Journal of Family Issues* 6, 295–306.

Menaghan, E. G. and Lieberman, M. A. (1986). Changes in depression following divorce: a panel study. *Journal of Marriage and the Family* 48, 319–28.

Merikangas, K. R. (1984). Divorce and assortative mating among depressed patients. *American Journal of Psychiatry* 141, 74–6.

Meyer, D. R. and Garasky, S. (1993). Custodial fathers: myths, realities and child support policy. *Journal of Marriage and the Family* 55, 73–90.

Mintz, S. (1998). From patriachy to androgyny and other myths: placing men's family roles in historical perspective. In A. Booth and A. C. Crouter (eds.), *Men in Families When do They Get Involved: What Difference Does it Make?* Lawrence Erlbaum Associates, Mahwah, NJ.

Minuchin, S. (1974). *Families and Family Therapy*. Harvard University Press, Cambridge, Mass.

Mitchell, A. (1985). *Children in the Middle: Living Through Divorce*. Tavistock Publications, London.

Moore, N. V. (1976). Cognitive level, intactness of family, and sex in relation to the child's development of the concept of family. *Dissertations Abstracts International* 37, 4117B–118B.

Morris, D. P., Soroker, E., and Burruss, G. (1954). Follow-up studies of shy, withdrawn children, I: Evaluation of later adjustment. *American Journal of Orthopsychiatry* , 743–54.

Morrison, D. A. and Coiro, M. J. (1999). Parental conflict and marital disruption: do children benefit when high-conflict marriages are dissolved? *Journal of Marriage and the Family* 61, 626–37.

Morrison, D. R. (1995). The divorce process and young children's well-being: a prospective analysis. *Journal of Marriage and the Family* 57, 800–12.

Morrison, K. and Thompson-Guppy, A. (1985). Cinderella's stepmother syndrome. *Canadian Journal of Psychiatry* 30, 521–9.

Morrow, V. (1998). *Understanding Families: Children's Perspectives*. National Children's Bureau, London.

Morrow, V. (1999). Conceptualising social capital in relation to the well-being of children and young people: a critical review. *The Sociological Review* 47, 744–65.

Mott, F. L., Kowaleski-Jones, L., and Menaghan, E. G. (1997). Parental absence and child behavior: does a child's gender make a difference? *Journal of Marriage and the Family* 59, 103–18.

Mueller, C. W. and Pope, H. (1977). Marital instability: A study of its transmission between generations. *Journal of Marriage and the Family* 39, 83–93.

Mullen, P. E., Martin, J. L., Anderson, J. C., Romans, S. E., and Herbison, G. (1996). The long-term impact of the physical, emotional, and sexual abuse of children: a community study. *Child Abuse and Neglect* 20, 7–21.

Munsch, J., Woodward, J., and Darling, N. (1995). Children's perceptions of their relationships with coresiding and non-coresiding fathers. *Journal of Divorce and Remarriage* 23, 39–54.

Najman, J. M., Behrens, B. C., Anderson, M., Bor, W., O'Callaghan, M., and Williams, G. M. (1997). Impact of family type and family quality on child behavior problems: a longitudinal study. *Journal of the American Academy of Child and Adolescent Psychiatry* 36, 1357–65.

Nakonezny, P. A., Shull, R. D., and Rodgers, J. L. (1995). The effect of no-fault divorce law on the divorce rate across the 50 states and its relation to income, education, and religiosity. *Journal of Marriage and the Family* 57, 477–88.

Neugebauer, R. (1989). Divorce, custody and visitation: the child's point of view. *Journal of Divorce* 12, 153–68.

Newcomb, M. (1996). Pseudomaturity among adolescents: construct validation, sex differences, and associations in adulthood. *Journal of Drug Issues* 26, 477–504.

Newcomb, M. D. (1986). Cohabitation, marriage and divorce among adolescents and young adults. *Journal of Social and Personal Relationships* 3, 473–94.

Nicholson, J. M. (1999). Effect on later adjustment of living in a stepfamily during childhood and adolescence. *Journal of Child Psychology and Psychiatry* 40, 405–16.

Nicholson, J. M. and Sanders, M. R. (1999). Randomized controlled trial of behavioral family intervention for the treatment of child behavior problems in stepfamilies. *Journal of Divorce and Remarriage* 30, 1–23.

Nielsen, L. (1999). Stepmothers: why so much stress? A review of the research. *Journal of Divorce and Remarriage* 30, 115–48.

Nieto, D. S. (1990). The custodial single father: who does he think he is? *Journal of Divorce* 13, 27–43.

Nock, S. L. (1995). A comparison of marriages and cohabiting relationships. *Journal of Family Issues* 16, 53–76.

Nolo (2001). Determining custody and visitation FAQ. Retrieved April 20, 2001: www.nolo.com/enclyclopedia/articles/div/pc22.html

Nye, F. I. (1957). Child adjustment in broken and in unhappy unbroken homes. *Marriage and Family Living* 1957, 356–61.

O'Brien, M., Alldred, P., and Jones, P. (1996). Children's constructions of family and kinship. In J. Brannen and M. O'Brien (eds.), *Children in Families: Research and Policy*. Falmer Press, Brighton.

O'Connor, T. G., Caspi, A., DeFries, J. C., and Plomin, R. (2000). Are associations between parental divorce and children's adjustment genetically mediated? An adoption study. *Developmental Psychology* 36, 429–37.

O'Connor, T. G., Hetherington, E. M., and Clingempeel, W. G. (1997). Systems and bidirectional influences in families. *Journal of Social and Personal Relationships* 14, 491–504.

O'Connor, T. G., Pickering, K., Dunn, J., and Golding, J. (1999a). Frequency and predictors of relationship dissolution in a community sample in England. *Journal of Family Psychology* 13, 436–49.

O'Connor, T. G., Thorpe, K., Dunn, J., and Golding, J. (1999b). Parental divorce and adjustment in adulthood: findings from a community sample. *Journal of Child Psychology and Psychiatry* 40, 777–89.

Office for National Statistics (1998). *Marriage and Divorce Statistics: Review of the Registrar General on Marriages and Divorces in England and Wales, 1994.* Series FM2 No. 22. The Stationery Office, London.

Olson, D., Russell, C., and Sprenkle, D. (1983). Circumplex model of marital and family systems, VI: Theoretical update. *Family Process* 22, 69–84.

Oltman, J. E., McGarry, J. J., and Friedman, S. (1952). Parental deprivation and the "broken home" in dementia praecox and other mental disorders. *American Journal of Psychiatry* 109, 685–94.

Ono, H. (1998). Husbands' and wives' resources and marital dissolution. *Journal of Marriage and the Family* 60, 674–89.

Ornduff, S. R. and Monahan, K. (1999). Children's understanding of parental violence. *Child and Youth Care Forum* 28, 351–64.

Parker, G. (1979). Parental deprivation and depression in a non-clinical group. *Australian and New Zealand Journal of Psychiatry* 13, 51–6.

Parker, G. (1992). Early environment. In E. S. Paykel (ed.), *Handbook of Affective Disorders*, 2nd edn. Guilford Press, New York.

Parry, M. (1994). Children's welfare and the law: the Children Act 1989 and recent developments. *Panel News* 7, 19–27, 4–11.

Patterson, C. J., Vaden, N. A., and Kupersmidt, J. B. (1992). Family background, recent life events and peer rejection. *Journal of Social and Personal Relationships* 8, 347–61.

Pearlin, L. I. and Johnson, J. S. (1977). Marital status, life-strains and depression. *American Sociological Review* 42, 704–15.

Pearson, J. and Thoennes, N. (1985). A preliminary portrait of clients' reactions to three court mediation programmes. *Conciliation Courts Review* 23, 1–14.

Perese, S. (1999). Dealing with Samoan children and their families. In *Challenging patterns of Practice: Workshop for Advanced Counsel for the Child*. New Zealand Law Society, Wellington, New Zealand.

Perris, C., Arrindell, W. A., Perris, H., Eisemann, M., Van Der Ende, J., and Von Knorring, L. (1986). Perceived depriving parental rearing and depression. *British Journal of Psychiatry* 148, 170–5.

Perris, C., Jacobsson, L., Lindstrom, H., Von Knorring, L., and Perris, H. (1980). Development of a new inventory for assessing memories of parental rearing behaviour. *Acta Psychiatrica Scandinavia* 61, 265–74.

Peterson, J. L. and Zill, N. (1986). Marital disruption, parent-child relationships, and behavior problems in children. *Journal of Marriage and the Family* 48, 295–307.

Peterson, R. R. (1996). A re-evaluation of the economic consequences of divorce. *American Sociological Review* 61, 528–36.

Pettit, E. and Bloom, B. (1984). Whose decision was it? The effects of initiator status on adjustment to marital disruption. *Journal of Marriage and the Family* 46, 587–95.

Phares, V. (1996). *Fathers and Developmental Psychology*. John Wiley and Sons, New York.

Phillips, M. (1998a). "Let's hear it for adultery folks! Give selfishness a big hand! No need to worry about the kids – they'll positively thrive!" *The Observer*, June 28, p. 27.

Phillips, M. (1998b). "Top of the Morning" interview with Brian Edwards. *National Radio*, Sept. 5.

Phillips, R. (1981). *Divorce in New Zealand: A Social History*. Oxford University Press, Auckland.

Phillips, R. (1988). *Putting Asunder: A History of Divorce in Western Society*. Cambridge University Press, Cambridge.

Pleck, J. H. (1985). *Working Wives, Working Husbands*. Sage, Beverley Hills, Calif.

Pleck, J. H. (1997). Paternal involvement: levels, sources, and consequences. In M. E. Lamb (ed.), *The Role of the Father in Child Development*, 3rd edn. John Wiley and Sons, New York.

Plomin, R. and Bergeman, C. S. (1991). The nature of nurture: genetic influence on "environmental" measures. *Behavioural and Brain Sciences* 14, 373–427.

Plunkett, J. W. and Kalter, N. (1984). Children's beliefs about reactions to parental divorce. *Journal of the American Academy of Child and Adolescent Psychiatry* 23, 616–21.

Pong, S. and Ju, D. (2000). The effects of change in family structure and income on dropping out of middle and high school. *Journal of Family Issues* 21, 147-69.

Popenoe, D. (1993). American family decline 1960–1990: a review and appraisal. *Journal of Marriage and the Family* 55, 527–55.

Popenoe, D. (1994). The evolution of marriage and the problem of stepfamilies: a biosocial perspective. In A. Booth and J. Dunn (eds.), *Stepfamilies: Who Benefits? Who Does Not?* Lawrence Erlbaum Associates, Hillsdale, NJ.

Popenoe, D. (1996). *Life Without Father*. Free Press, New York.

Power, C., Rodgers, B., and Hope, S. (1999). Heavy alcohol consumption and marital status: disentangling the relationship in a national study of young adults. *Addiction* 94, 1477–87.

Pritchard, R. (1998). *When Parents Part: How Children Adapt*. Penguin, Auckland.

Pruett, C. L., Caslyn, R. J. and Jensen, F. M. (1993). Social support received by children in stepmother, stepfather, and intact families. *Journal of Divorce and Remarriage* 19, 165–79.

Pryor, J. (1998). Adolescents' attitudes to living arrangements after parental separation. In *International Society for the Study of Behavioral Development XVth Biennial Conference*. ISSBD, Berne, Switzerland.

Pryor, J. (1999). Waiting until they leave home: the experiences of young adults whose parents separate. *Journal of Divorce and Remarriage* 32, 47–61.

Pryor, J. (2000). Abusive adults and their children: dogmas and dilemmas. Given paper, Institute for Judicial Studies, Wellington.

Radin, N. and Sagi, A. (1992). Childrearing fathers in intact families in Israel and the USA. *Merrill-Palmer Quarterly* 28, 111–36.

Rankin, J. H. (1983). The family context of delinquency. *Social Problems* 30, 466–79.

Raphael, B., Cubis, J., Dunne, M., Lewin, T., and Kelly, B. (1990). The impact of parental loss on adolescents' psychosocial characteristics. *Adolescence* 25, 689–700.

Rawlings, S. and Saluter, A. (1996). *Houshold and Family Characteristics: March 1994*. Current Population Reports P20-483. US Department of Commerce, Washington, DC.

Reeves, J., Kendrick, D., Denman, S., and Roberts, H. (1994). Lone mothers: their health and lifestyle. *Health Education Journal* 53, 291–9.

Rhoades, H., Graycar, R., and Harrison, M. (1999). *The Family Law Reform Act 1995: Can Changing Legislation Change Legal Culture, Legal Practice, and Community Expectations?* Interim Report. Family Court of Australia, Sydney.

Richards, M. (1999). The Family Law Act 1996 of England and Wales – pilot research on information meetings. *Butterworths Family Law Journal* 3, 43–6.

Richards, M. (2000). Children's understanding of inheritance and family. *Child Psychology and Psychiatry Review* 5, 2–8.

Richards, M., Hardy, R., and Wadsworth (1997). The effects of divorce and separation on mental health in a national UK birth cohort. *Psychological Medicine* 27, 1121–8.

Richards, M. P. M. and Dyson, M. (1982). *Separation, Divorce and the Development of Children: A Review*. Child Care and Development Group, Cambridge, UK.

Robertson, J. and Bowlby, J. (1952). A two-year-old goes to hospital: a scientific film. *Proceedings of the Royal Society of Medicine* 46, 425–7.

Robertson, N. C. (1974). The relationship between marital status and the risk of psychiatric referral. *British Journal of Psychiatry* 124, 191–202.

Robins, L. N. (1966). *Deviant Children Grown Up*. Williams and Wilkins, Baltimore.

Robins, L. N. (1979). Follow-up studies. In H. C. Quay and J. S. Werry (eds.), *Psychopathological Disorders of Childhood*, 2nd edn. John Wiley, New York.

Robins, L. N. and Regier, D. A. (eds.) (1991). *Psychiatric Disorders in America: The Epidemiologic Catchment Area Study*. Free Press, New York.

Robins, L. N., Tipp, J., and Przybeck, T. (1991). Antisocial personality. In L. N. Robins and D. A. Regier (eds.), *Psychiatric Disorders in America: The Epidemiologic Catchment Area Study*. Free Press, New York.

Roche, J. (1996). The politics of children's rights. In J. Brannen and M. O'Brien (eds.), *Children in Families: Research and Policy*. Falmer Press, London.

Roche, J. (1999). Children and divorce: a private affair? In S. Day Sclater and C. Piper (eds.), *Undercurrents of Divorce*. Ashgate Publishing, Aldershot, UK.

Rodgers, B. (1990a). Adult affective disorder and early environment. *British Journal of Psychiatry* 157, 539–50.

Rodgers, B. (1990b). Behaviour and personality in childhood as predictors of adult psychiatric disorder. *Journal of Child Psychology and Psychiatry* 31, 393–414.

Rodgers, B. (1991). Socio-economic status, employment and neurosis. *Social Psychiatry and Psychiatric Epidemiology* 26, 104–14.

Rodgers, B. (1994). Pathways between parental divorce and adult depression. *Journal of Child Psychology and Psychiatry* 35, 1289–1308.

Rodgers, B. (1995). Separation, divorce and mental health. In A. F. Jorm (ed.), *Men and Mental Health*. National Health and Medical Research Council, Canberra.

Rodgers, B. (1996a). Reported parental behaviour and adult affective symptoms, 1: Associations and moderating factors. *Psychological Medicine* 26, 51–61.

Rodgers, B. (1996b). Social and psychological wellbeing of children from divorced families: Australian research findings. *Australian Psychologist* 31, 174–82.

Rodgers, B. (1998). Social and psychological outcomes for children from divorced families: Australian research findings. In N. J. Taylor and A. B. Smith (eds.), *Enhancing Children's Potential: Minimising Risk and Maximising Resiliency*. Children's Issues Centre, Dunedin, New Zealand.

Rodgers, B. and Mann, S. A. (1986). The reliability and validity of PSE assessments by lay interviewers: A national population survey. *Psychological Medicine* 16, 689–700.

Rodgers, B., Pickles, A., Power, C., Collishaw, S. and Maughan, B. (1999). Validity of the Malaise Inventory in general population samples. *Social Psychiatry and Psychiatric Epidemiology*.

Rodgers, B., Power, C., and Hope, S. (1997). Parental divorce and adult psychological distress: evidence from a national birth cohort. *Journal of Child Psychology and Psychiatry* 38, 867–72.

Rodgers, B. and Pryor, J. (1998). *Divorce and Separation: The Outcomes for Children*. Joseph Rowntree Foundation, York.

Romelsjo, A., Lazarus, N. B., Kaplan, G. A., and Cohen, R. D. (1991). The relationship between stressful life situations and changes in alcohol consumption in a general population sample. *British Journal of Addiction* 86, 157–69.

Roy, A. (1978). Vulnerability factors and depression in women. *British Journal of Psychiatry* 133, 106–10.

Roy, A. (1985). Early parental separation and adult depression. *Archives of General Psychiatry* 42, 987–91.

Russell, G. (1986). Primary caretakers and role sharing fathers. In M. E. Lamb (ed.), *The Father's Role: Applied Perspectives*. John Wiley, New York.

Rutter, M. (1987). Psychosocial resilience and protective mechanisms. *American Journal of Orthopsychiatry* 57, 316–31.

Rutter, M. (1990). Psychosocial resilience and protective mechanisms. In J. Rolf, A. S. Masten, D. Cicchetti, D. H. Neichterlein, and S. Weintraub (eds.), *Risk and Protective Factors in the Development of Psychopathology*. Cambridge University Press, New York.

Rutter, M. L. (1972). Relationships between child and adult psychiatric disorders. *Acta Psychiatrica Scandinavica* 48, 3–21.

Salem, D. A., Zimmerman, M. A., and Notaro, P. C. (1998). Effects of family structure, family process, and father involvement on psychosocial outcomes among African American adolescents. *Family Relations* 47, 331–41.

Saluter, A. (1996). *Marital Status and Living Arrangements: March 1994*. Current Population Reports, Population Characteristics P20–483. US Department of Commerce, Washington, DC.

Sandefur, G. D., McLanahan, S. S., and Wojtkiewicz, R. A. (1992). The effects of parental marital status during adolescence on high school graduation. *Social Forces* 71, 103–21.

Santamaria, J. N. (1972). The social implications of alcoholism. *Medical Journal of Australia* 2, 523–8.

Scott, J. (1997). Changing households in Britain: do families still matter? *The Sociological Review*, 591–620.

Seltzer, J. (2000). Families formed outside marriage. *Journal of Marriage and the Family* 62, 1247–68.

Seltzer, J. A. (1991). Relationships between fathers and children who live apart: the father's role after separation. *Journal of Marriage and the Family* 53, 79–101.

Seltzer, J. A. (1994). Consequences of marital dissolution for children. *Annual Review of Sociology* 20, 235–66.

Seltzer, J. A. (1998a). Fathers by law: effects of joint legal custody on nonresident fathers' involvement with children. *Demography* 35, 135–46.

Seltzer, J. A. (1998b). Men's contributions to children and social policy. In A. Booth and A. C. Crouter (eds.), *Men in Families: When do They Get Involved? What Difference Does it Make?*. Lawrence Erlbaum Associates, Mahwah, NJ.

Shaw, D. S., Emery, R. E., and Tuer, M. D. (1993). Parental functioning and children's adjustment in families of divorce: a prospective study. *Journal of Abnormal Child Psychology* 21, 119–34.

Shifflett, K. and Cummings, E. M. (1999). A program for educating parents about the effects of divorce and conflict on children: an initial evaluation. *Family Relations* 48, 79–89.

Simons, R., Whitbeck, L. B., Beaman, J., and Conger, R. D. (1994). The impact of mothers' parenting, involvement by nonresidential fathers, and parental conflict on the adjustment of adolescent children. *Journal of Marriage and the Family* 56, 356–74.

Simons, R. L. and Associates (1996). *Understanding Differences Between Divorced and Intact Families: Stress, Interaction, and Child Outcome.* Sage Publications, Thousand Oaks, Calif.

Simons, R. L., Johnson, C., and Lorenz, F. O. (1996). Family structure differences in stress and behavioral disposition. In *Understanding Differences Between Divorced and Intact Families: Stress, Interaction, and Child Outcome.* Sage Publications, Thousand Oaks, Calif.

Simons, R. L., Lorenz, F. O., Wu, C., and Conger, R. D. (1993). Social network and marital support as mediators and moderators of the impact of stress and depression on parental behavior. *Developmental Psychology* 29, 368–81.

Simpson, B., McCarthy, P. and Walker, J. (1995). *Being there: Fathers After Divorce.* Relate Centre for Family Studies, Newcastle, UK.

Skolnick, A. (1997). The triple revolution : social sources of family change. In S. Dreman (ed.), *The Family on the Threshold of the 21st Century.* Lawrence Erlbaum Associates, Mahwah, NJ.

Smart, C. and Neale, B. (1999). *Family Fragments?* Polity Press, Cambridge, UK.

Smart, C., Wade, A., and Neale, B. (2000). *New childhoods: Children and Co-parenting after Divorce.* Research Briefing. Children 5–16 Research Programme, Stirling, UK.

Smith, A. B., Taylor, N. J., Gollop, M., Gaffney, M., Gold, M., and Heneghan, M. (1997). *Access and Other Post-separation Issues.* Children's Issues Centre, Dunedin, New Zealand.

Smith, T. A. (1992). Family cohesion in remarried families. *Journal of Divorce and Remarriage* 17, 49–66.

Sourindhrin, I. and Baird, J. A. (1984). Management of solvent misuse: a Glasgow community approach. *British Journal of Addiction* 79, 227–32.

South, S. J., Crowder, K. D., and Trent, K. (1998). Children's residential mobility and neighborhood environment following parental divorce and remarriage. *Social Forces* 77, 667–93.

South, S. J. and Spitze, G. (1986). Determinants of divorce over the marital life course. *American Sociological Review* 51, 583–90.

Speare, A., Jr. and Goldscheider, F. K. (1987). Effects of marital status change on residential mobility. *Journal of Marriage and the Family* 49, 455–64.

Stacey, J. (1993). Good riddance to "the family": a response to David Popenoe. *Journal of Marriage and the Family* 55, 545–7.

Stacey, J. (1996). *In the Name of the Family: Rethinking Family Values in the Postmodern Age.* Beacon Press, Boston.

Stack, S. and Eshleman, R. (1998). Marital status and happiness: a 17-nation study. *Journal of Marriage and the Family* 60, 527–36.

Statistics Canada (1999a). *Annual Demographic Statistics 1998.* Cat. No. 91-213. Statistics Canada, Ottawa.

Statistics Canada (1999b). 1996 Census: nation tables. Marital status. Retrieved 13 Dec. 2000: www.statcan.ca/english/census96/oct14/law.htm

Statistics New Zealand (1998). *New Zealand Now: Families and Households.* Statistics New Zealand, Wellington.

Steinberg, L. (1987). Single parents, stepparents, and the susceptibility of adolescents to antisocial peer pressure. *Child Development* 58, 269–75.

Steinberg, L., Elmen, J. D., and Mounts, N. S. (1989). Authoritative parenting, psychosocial maturity, and academic success among adolescents. *Child Development* 60, 1424–36.

Steinberg, L., Mounts, N. S., Lamborn, S. D., and Dornbusch, S. M. (1991). Authoritative parenting and adolescent adjustment across varied ecological niches. *Journal of Research on Adolescence* 1, 19–36.

Sternberg, K. J., Lamb, M. E., Greenbaum, C., and Dawud, S. (1995). The effects of domestic violence on children's perceptions of their perpetrating and nonperpetrating parents. *International Journal of Behavioral Development* 17, 779–95.

Stewart, J. R., Schwebel, A. I., and Fine, M. A. (1986). The impact of custody arrangement on the adjustment of recently divorced fathers. *Journal of Divorce* 9, 55–65.

Stewart, S. D. (1999). Nonresident mothers' and fathers' social contact with children. *Journal of Marriage and the Family* 61, 894–907.

Stone, L. (1990). *Road to Divorce: England 1530–1987.* Oxford University Press, Oxford.

Svanum, S., Bringle, R. G., and McLaughlin, J. E. (1982). Father absence and cognitive performance in a large sample of six- to eleven-year-old children. *Child Development* 53, 136–43.

Sweeting, H. and West, P. (1994). The patterning of life events in mid- to late adolescence: markers for the future? *Journal of Adolescence* 17, 283–304.

Sweeting, H. and West, P. (1995a). Family life and health in adolescence: a role for culture in the health inequalities debate? *Social Science and Medicine* 40, 163–75.

Sweeting, H. and West, P. (1995b). *Young People and their Families: Analyses of Data from the Twenty-07 Study Youth Cohort.* Working Paper No. 49. MRC Medical Sociology Unit: Glasgow.

Sweeting, H., West, P., and Richards, M. P. M. (1998). Teenage family life, lifestyles and life chances: associations with family structure, conflict with parents, and joint family activity. *International Journal of Law, Policy and the Family* 12, 15–46.

Tasker, F. (1992). Anti-marriage attitudes and motivations to marry amongst adolescents with divorced parents. *Journal of Divorce and Remarriage* 18, 105–19.

Temple, M. T., Fillmore, K. M., Hartke, E., Johnstone, B., Leino, E. V., and Motoyoshi, M. (1991). A meta-analysis of change in marital and employment status as predictors of alcohol consumption on a typical occasion. *British Journal of Addiction* 86, 1269–81.

Tennant, C. (1988). Parental loss in childhood. *Archives of General Psychiatry* 45, 1045–50.

Tennant, C., Bebbington, P. and Hurry, J. (1980). Parental death in childhood and risk of adult depressive disorders: a review. *Psychological Medicine* 10, 289–99.

Tennant, C. and Bernardi, E. (1988). Childhood loss in alcoholics and narcotic addicts. *British Journal of Addiction* 83, 695–03.

Tennant, C., Hurry, J., and Bebbington, P. (1982). The relation of childhood separation experiences to adult depressive and anxiety states. *British Journal of Psychiatry* 141, 475–82.

Tennant, F. S., Detels, R., and Clark, V. (1975). Some childhood antecedents of drug and alcohol abuse. *American Journal of Epidemiology* 102, 377–85.

Thomas, A. and Chess, S. (1977). *Temperament and Development*. Brunner/Mazel, New York.

Thomas, A., Chess, S., Birch, H., Hertzig, M., and Korn, S. (1963). *Behavioral Individuality in Early Childhood*. New York University Press, New York.

Thompson, R. A. (1986). Fathers and the child's "best interests': judicial decision making in custody disputes. In M. E. Lamb (ed.), *The Father's Role: Applied Perspectives*. John Wiley and Sons, New York.

Thompson, R. A. and Amato, P., eds. (1999). *The Postdivorce Family: Children, Parenting, and Society*. Sage, Thousand Oaks, Calif.

Thomson, E. (1994). "Settings" and "development" from a demographic point of view. In A. Booth and J. Dunn (eds.), *Stepfamilies: Who Benefits? Who Does Not?*. Lawrence Erlbaum Associates, Hillsdale, NJ.

Thomson, E., Hanson, T. L., and McLanahan, S. S. (1994). Family structure and child well-being: Economic resources vs. parental behaviors. *Social Forces* 73, 221–42.

Thomson, E., McLanahan, S. S., and Curtin, R. B. (1992). Family structure, gender, and parental socialization. *Journal of Marriage and the Family* 54, 368–78.

Thornton, A. (1985). Changing attitudes towards separation and divorce: causes and consequences. *American Journal of Sociology* 90, 856–72.

Thornton, A. (1989). Changing attitudes toward family issues in the United States. *Journal of Marriage and the Family* 51, 873–93.

Thornton, A. (1991). Influence of marital history of parents on the marital and cohabitational experiences of children. *American Journal of Sociology* 96, 868–94.

Trinder, L. (1997). Competing constructions of childhood: Children's rights and children's wishes in divorce. *Journal of Social Welfare and Family Law* 19, 291–305.

Tucker, J. S., Friedman, H. S., Schwartz, J. E., Criqui, M. H., Tomlinson-Keasey, C., Wingard, D. L., and Martin, L. R. (1997). Parental divorce: effects on individual behavior and longevity. *Journal of Personality and Social Psychology* 73, 381–91.

Vemer, E., Coleman, M., Ganong, L. H., and Cooper, H. (1989). Marital satisfaction in remarriage: a meta-analysis. *Journal of Marriage and the Family* 51, 713–25.

Visher, E. B. and Visher, J. S. (1990). Dynamics of successful stepfamilies. *Journal of Divorce and Remarriage* 14, 3–12.

Voydanoff, P., Fine, M., and Donnelly, B. W. (1994). Family structure, family organisation, and quality of family life. *Journal of Family and Economic Issues* 15, 175–200.

Vuchinich, S., Hetheringtoh, E. M., Vuchinich, R. A., and Clingempeel, W. G. (1991). Parent-child interaction and gender differences in early adolescents' adaptation to stepfamilies. *Developmental Psychology* 27, 618–26.

Wadsworth, J., Burnell, I., Taylor, B., and Butler, N. (1983). Family type and accidents in preschool children. *Journal of Epidemiology and Community Health* 37, 100–4.

Wadsworth, J., Burnell, I., Taylor, B., and Butler, N. (1985). The influence of family type on children's behaviour and development at five years. *Journal of Child Psychology and Psychiatry* 26, 245–54.

Wadsworth, M. (1979). *Roots of Delinquency: Infancy, Adolescence and Crime.* Martin Robertson, Oxford.

Wadsworth, M. E. J. and Maclean, M. (1986). Parents' divorce and children's life chances. *Children and Youth Services Review* 8, 145–59.

Walczak, Y. and Burns, S. (1984). *Divorce: The Child's Point of View.* Harper and Row, London.

Wallerstein, J. S. (1985). Children of divorce: Preliminary report of a ten-year follow-up of older children and adolescents. *Journal of the American Academy of Child Psychiatry* 24, 545–53.

Wallerstein, J. S. and Blakeslee, S. (1989). *Second Chances: Men, Women, and Children a Decade after Divorce.* Ticknor and Fields, New York.

Wallerstein, J. S. and Corbin, S. B. (1989). Daughters of divorce: Report from a ten-year follow-up. *American Journal of Orthopsychiatry* 59, 593–604.

Wallerstein, J. S. and Kelly, J. B. (1980). *Surviving the Breakup: How Children and Parents Cope with Divorce.* Basic Books, New York.

Webb, G. R., Redman, S., Hennrikus, D., Rostas, J. A., and Sanson-Fisher, R. W. (1990). The prevalence and sociodemographic correlates of high-risk and problem drinking at an industrial worksite. *British Journal of Addiction* 85, 495–507.

Weingarten, H. R. (1985). Marital status and well-being: a national study comparing first-married, currently divorced, and remarried adults. *Journal of Marriage and the Family* 47, 653–62.

Weissman, M. M., Bland, R., Joyce, P. R., Newman, S., Wells, J. E., and Wittchen, H.-U. (1993). Sex differences in rates of depression: cross-national perspectives. *Journal of Affective Disorders* 29, 77–84.

Weitzman, L. J. (1985). *The Divorce Revolution: The Unexpected Social and Economic Consequences for Women and Children in America.* The Free Press, New York.

Wells, L. E. and Rankin, J. H. (1991). Families and delinquency: a meta-analysis of the impact of broken homes. *Social Problems* 38, 71–93.

West, D. J. and Farrington, D. P. (1973). *Who Becomes Delinquent?* Heinemann, London.

West, D. J. and Farrington, D. P. (1977). *The Delinquent Way of Life.* Heinemann, London.

Weston, R. (1986). Changes in household income circumstances. In P. McDonald (ed.), *Settling Up: Property and Income Distribution on Divorce in Australia.* Prentice-Hall, Sydney.

Weston, R. and Hughes, J. (1999). Family forms – family wellbeing. *Family Matters* 53, 14–20.

Whelan, C. T., Hannan, D. F., and Creighton, S. (1991). *Unemployment, Poverty and Psychological Distress.* Economic and Social Research Institute, Dublin.

White, L. (1990). Determinants of divorce: a review of research in the eighties. *Journal of Marriage and the Family* 52, 904–12.

Whitehead, L. (1979). Sex differences in children's responses to family stress: a re-evaluation. *Journal of Child Psychology and Psychiatry* 20, 247–54.

Whiteside, M. F. and Becker, B. J. (2000). Parental factors and the young child's postdivorce adjustment: a meta-analysis with implications for parenting arrangements. *Journal of Family Psychology* 14, 5–26.

Willetts-Bloom, M. C. and Nock, S. L. (1992). The effects of childhood family structure and perceptions of parents' marital happiness on familial aspirations. *Journal of Divorce and Remarriage* 18, 3–23.

Wilsnack, R. W., Wilsnack, S. C., and Klassen, A. D. (1984). Women's drinking and drinking problems: patterns from a 1981 national survey. *American Journal of Public Health* 74, 1231–8.

Winkler, A. E. (1997). Economic decision-making by cohabitors: findings regarding income pooling. *Applied Economics* 29, 1079–90.

Wolcott, H. and Hughes, J. (1999). *Towards Understanding the Reasons for Divorce.* Working Paper No. 20. Australian Institute of Family Studies, Melbourne.

Woodward, L., Fergusson, D. and Belsky, J. (2000). Timing of parental separation and attachment to parents in adolescence: results of a prospective study from birth to age 16. *Journal of Marriage and the Family* 62, 162–74.

Wu, L. and Martinson, B. (1993). Family structure and the risk of a premarital birth. *American Sociological Review* 58, 210–32.

Wu, Z. and Balakrishnan, T. R. (1995). Dissolution of premarital cohabitation in Canada. *Demography* 32, 521–32.

Young, M. H., Miller, B. C., Norton, M. C., and Hill, E. J. (1995). The effect of parental supportive behaviors on life satisfaction of adolescent offspring. *Journal of Marriage and the Family* 57, 813–22.

Zaslow, M. J. (1988). Sex differences in children's response to parental divorce, 1: Research methodology and postdivorce family forms. *American Journal of Orthopsychiatry* 58, 355–78.

Zaslow, M. J. (1989). Sex differences in children's response to parental divorce, 2: Samples, variables, ages, and sources. *American Journal of Orthopsychiatry* 59, 118–41.

Zill, N. (1988). Behavior, achievement, and health problems among children in stepfamilies: findings from a national survey of child health. In E. M.

Hetherington and J. Arasteh (eds.), *The Impact of Divorce, Single Parenting, and Stepparenting on Children*. Lawrence Erlbaum Associates, Hillsdale.

Zill, N., Morrison, D. R., and Coiro, M. J. (1993). Long-term effects of parental divorce on parent-child relationships, adjustment, and achievement in young adulthood. *Journal of Family Psychology* 7, 91–103.

Zimilies, H. and Lee, V. E. (1991). Adolescent family structure and educational progress. *Developmental Psychology* 27, 314–20.

Zubrick, S. R., Silburn, S. R., Garton, A., Burton, P., Dalby, R., Carlton, J., Shepherd, C., and Lawrence, D. (1995). *Western Australian Child Health Survey: Developing Health and Well-Being in the Nineties*. Cat. no. 4303.5. Australian Bureau of Statistics and the Institute for Child Health Research, Perth.

Zubrick, S. R., Silburn, S. R., Gurrin, L., Teoh, H., Shepherd, C., and Lawrence, D. (1997). *Western Australian Child Health Survey: Education, Health and Competence*. Cat. no. 4305.5. Australian Bureau of Statistics and the TVW Telethon Institute for Child Health Research, Perth.

Index